W9-AGG-205

Practicing Christian Doctrine

Practicing Christian Doctrine

An INTRODUCTION *to* THINKING *and* LIVING THEOLOGICALLY

BETH FELKER JONES

Baker Academic
a division of Baker Publishing Group
Grand Rapids, Michigan

© 2014 by Beth Felker Jones

Published by Baker Academic
a division of Baker Publishing Group
P.O. Box 6287, Grand Rapids, MI 49516-6287
www.bakeracademic.com

Printed in the United States of America

All rights reserved. No part of this publication may be reproduced, stored in a retrieval system, or transmitted in any form or by any means—for example, electronic, photocopy, recording—without the prior written permission of the publisher. The only exception is brief quotations in printed reviews.

Library of Congress Cataloging-in-Publication Data is on file at the Library of Congress, Washington, DC.

ISBN 978-0-8010-4933-0 (pbk.)

Unless otherwise indicated, Scripture quotations are from the New Revised Standard Version of the Bible, copyright © 1989, by the Division of Christian Education of the National Council of the Churches of Christ in the United States of America. Used by permission. All rights reserved.

Scripture quotations labeled ESV are from The Holy Bible, English Standard Version® (ESV®), copyright © 2001 by Crossway, a publishing ministry of Good News Publishers. Used by permission. All rights reserved. Text Edition: 2011.

16   17   18   19   20   7   6   5   4   3

In keeping with biblical principles of creation stewardship, Baker Publishing Group advocates the responsible use of our natural resources. As a member of the Green Press Initiative, our company uses recycled paper when possible. The text paper of this book is composed in part of post-consumer waste.

For my students—
"May the mind of Christ our Savior
live in us from day to day"

Contents

Acknowledgments

This project was born of teaching, and I am grateful to my students at Huntington University and Wheaton College, to whom this book is dedicated. It is my privilege to be in conversation with you. Thanks for the good questions, the thoughtful conversations, and the desire to put faith into practice. You have helped make doctrine come alive for me.

I am grateful to many friends and colleagues who helped make this book possible: for the wonderful team at Baker and Brazos; for the support of my dean, Jill Baumgaertner, and associate dean, Jeff Greenman; for the remarkable work of my research assistant, Ella Myer; for my colleague Keith Johnson, with whom I developed some of the early ideas for this text. Thanks to those who gifted me with time and talent, reading and commenting on portions of the text: Aimee Barbeau, Jeff Barbeau, Gary Burge, Lynn Cohick, Holly Taylor Coolman, Michael Graves, Gene Green, George Kalantzis, Tiffany Kriner, Christina Bieber Lake, Tim Larsen, David Lauber, Steve Long, Miho Nonaka, Amy Peeler, Nick Perrin, Noah Toly, and Dan Treier. The book is better because of you all.

Thanks piled on thanks to my husband, Brian, whose support of my work is one of the most tender gifts in my life, and to our children, Gwen, Sam, Tess, and Zeke, for hanging in there with me and enduring my speeches about things like the Trinity.

Chapter 8 and a small portion of chapter 2 appear in slightly different form in my *God the Spirit: Introducing Pneumatology in Wesleyan and Ecumenical Perspective*. Copyright Cascade Books, 2014. Used by permission of Wipf and Stock Publishers.

Beth Felker Jones
Lent 2013

Introduction

To Practice Doctrine

Times were troubled when Josiah assumed the throne. A brutal invasion and the faithless leadership of several apostate kings had left Israel in chaos. The people of Israel were living desperate and uncertain lives. In the midst of their struggles, they still worshiped the Lord, the God of their ancestors, but they turned to other gods as well, hoping those other gods could help them meet the challenges they faced. God, however, had not forgotten his people or his promises to them. He worked in the heart of the young king, and Josiah began to "seek the God of his ancestor David" (2 Chron. 34:3). The temple in Jerusalem, the center of worship, had suffered years of neglect and misuse, and Josiah funded carpenters, builders, and masons to begin to restore it. In the midst of the dust flying, the high priest made a discovery, a "book of the covenant"—Scripture.

When Josiah heard the ancient words read aloud, he recognized the depth of Israel's unfaithfulness. Tearing his robes in grief, he repented, and he took action. After consulting with the prophetess Huldah, Josiah gathered together "all the people both great and small" and read the book aloud to them. Then, in front of his people, Josiah "made a covenant before the LORD, to follow the LORD, keeping his commandments, his decrees, and his statutes, with all his heart and all his soul, to perform the words of the covenant that were written in this book" (2 Chron. 34:30–31). He led his people to join in the same commitment. The entire nation promised to *perform the book*, to return to faithful relationship with God. Josiah spent the following months purifying Israel. He purged the temple of idols,

1

destroyed altars to idols, and scattered their remains over the graves of false priests. Josiah's reforms culminated in a celebration of Passover, where the people remembered what God had done for them. The discovery of the lost book and the acceptance of its teaching changed the lives of God's people.

This story may seem like an odd beginning to a book meant to introduce theology, but Josiah's story provides a wonderful window into the relationship between Scripture, doctrine, and practice. Christian theology is a conversation about Scripture, about how to read and interpret it better, how to understand the Bible as a whole and imagine a way of life that is faithful to the God whose Word this is. This conversation about Scripture produces distinct Christian teachings, called **doctrine**, but the work of theology does not stop there. Notice the key to Josiah's story. He moved directly from the teaching he found in the rediscovered book to action. He immediately connected belief with practice, the Word of God with reform, and he led the people to follow in his footsteps, bringing his community along with him as he sought faithfulness to the true God.

I open with the story of Josiah's reforms in Israel because it displays the core premise of this book: our beliefs must be put into practice, and faithful practice matters for what we believe. When we, like Josiah and his people, perform the book of Scripture, when we connect truth with action and doctrine with discipleship, God does marvelous things.

This book's title reflects my confidence that Christian doctrine is intimately interconnected with faithful practice in the Christian life. This book will introduce the basics of Christian doctrine, but without our practicing that doctrine, that introduction will be meaningless. Christian doctrine informs Christian identity and action. Certainly, the idea of doctrine implies belief, but doctrine is about so much more than just believing certain things. The word *doctrine* has taken on cold, hard connotations. Many assume that it is about rigidity and control or that it points to an inaccessible arena of knowledge outside the realm of ordinary Christians. I hope that this book does some work to rehabilitate the word *doctrine*, to show ways that good Christian teaching can help us to grow in faith, reach out in love, and look to the future in hope.

The study of doctrine belongs right in the middle of the Christian life. It is part of our worship of God and service to God's people. Jesus commanded us to love God with our mind as well as our heart, soul, and strength (Luke 10:27). All four are connected: the heart's passion, the soul's yearning, the strength God grants us, and the intellectual task of seeking the truth of God. This means that the study of doctrine is an act of love for God: in studying the things of God, we are formed as worshipers and as God's servants in the world. To practice doctrine is to yearn for a deeper understanding of the Christian faith, to seek the logic and the beauty of that faith, and to live out what we have learned in the everyday realities of the Christian life.

All of that becomes richer as we gain familiarity with Christian teaching. Practicing doctrine is not unlike practicing the piano or going to basketball practice. New pianists begin by becoming familiar with the instrument. Before they can play sonatas, they must spend a lot of time on basic exercises like running scales. New basketball players do not start with shooting three-pointers; first they have to learn how to dribble and how to run a play. Before playing a game, they must master rules and repeat basic drills until these things become second nature. Only after much practice are they ready to play. Newcomers to the study of doctrine are in a similar position and need to spend time becoming familiar with the discipline of theology. It takes time and patience to learn how to practice doctrine well. Learning Christian doctrine is something like learning a new language: it takes time to learn the vocabulary and concepts used in Christian thought in order to understand what other people are saying. Along with this basic study, students of doctrine have to immerse themselves in the teachings of Scripture, listen to the wisdom of other practitioners of doctrine throughout history, and pray for the insight and guidance of the Holy Spirit.

But there is an important difference between a beginning student of doctrine and a new pianist or basketball player. Many students new to the formal or academic study of doctrine will *not* be new to the Christian faith, and many basic habits and skills may be familiar. There is continuity between the faith embraced by the littlest child or the newest believer and the faith embraced by the most competent Bible scholar or articulate theologian. Readers should expect continuity between the living faith they bring to the practice of doctrine and the knowledge and challenges that practice will bring to them. Some doctrines will be easy to learn, and application will be immediately apparent. Some concepts may lead to "aha!" moments when studying doctrine brings clarity to some familiar belief or practice. At other times, the study of doctrine challenges our assumptions and preconceptions. Some of God's greatest gifts can come when we face disconnect between our assumptions and what we learn through study. None of us has our doctrine exactly right, and as we search eagerly for the truth that comes from God, we must also search for the humility to see where we may be wrong. The best practitioners of doctrine are open to correction, and like Josiah we must be willing to change. The practice of doctrine will be more fruitful if we are open to change and reform. Humility and repentance are keys to the faithful practice of doctrine.

> ### Key Scripture
>
> I appeal to you therefore, brothers and sisters, by the mercies of God, to present your bodies as a living sacrifice, holy and acceptable to God, which is your spiritual worship. Do not be conformed to this world, but be transformed by the renewing of your minds, so that you may discern what is the will of God—what is good and acceptable and perfect. For by the grace given to me I say to everyone among you not to think of yourself more highly than you ought to think, but to think with sober judgment, each according to the measure of faith that God has assigned. For as in one body we have many members, and not all the members have the same function, so we, who are many, are one body in Christ, and individually we are members one of another. (Rom. 12:1–5)

John Calvin claimed, "All right knowledge of God is born of obedience."[1] Doctrine and discipleship always go together. Our job as we study doctrine is not to get all our answers right. The point of our study is to grow in our knowledge of and faithfulness to God. God can use our study of doctrine to form us. As you read, I encourage you to think of yourself as a doctrinal theologian, a disciple of Jesus Christ who practices doctrine by seeking knowledge of God and of the things of God, reading Scripture faithfully and regularly, rejoicing in the continuity between saving faith as you have already known it and doctrine as you are coming to know it, welcoming the disruption that God may bring into your life in challenging you to more faithful and truthful practice of the Christian faith, and embracing the practice of doctrine as part of Christian identity.

Evangelical *and* Ecumenical

While no two theologians will ever introduce doctrine in precisely the same way, Christians share a great deal in common, and this introduction

---

1. John Calvin, *Institutes of the Christian Religion*, ed. John T. McNeill (Philadelphia: Westminster, 1960), 1.6.2.

is focused on that common ground as surveyed in evangelical and ecumenical perspective. The word *evangelical* comes from the Greek *euangelion*, meaning "the gospel," the good news of Jesus Christ. All Christians belong to that good news. The term is also used to indicate a particular context, one in which evangelical Christianity—especially in Great Britain, North America, and global churches with roots in the movement—takes more specific historical form. Still, this evangelicalism is diverse. It includes Christians from several centuries and many cultures, and so it cannot simply be identified with one confession of faith, denomination, institution, or cultural form. Historians have offered different ways of understanding evangelical Christianity.

David Bebbington identifies evangelicalism by pointing to four characteristics shared across denominational or cultural lines: biblicism, conversionism, activism, and crucicentrism.[2] *Biblicism* is a focus on Scripture as the ultimate authority for faith and practice; *conversionism* is an emphasis on life-altering religious experience; *activism* is a concern for sharing the faith and doing good works; and *crucicentrism* names a focus on Jesus's saving work on the cross. This description provides an account of evangelicalism that is not limited by culture or denomination. Evangelicals are a varied lot, and you can find them in many groups, including Baptists in the United States, Anglicans in Africa, Presbyterians in Scotland, and Pentecostals in Latin America. Bebbington shows how these diverse Christians have certain beliefs and characteristics in common. His definition also balances doctrinal affirmations (biblicism and crucicentrism) with experiential aspects of evangelicalism (conversionism and activism), indicating a broad spectrum of emphases within evangelical life.

The breadth of Bebbington's description is also a potential drawback, a lack of specificity. Historian Timothy Larsen points out that St. Francis of Assisi, a medieval monk, could fit within Bebbington's definition. This is a problem, Larsen reasons, because the term "evangelical" then loses "its utility for identifying a specific Christian community."[3] Larsen adds a particular historical context to the doctrinal and experiential aspects of Bebbington's definition: "An evangelical is an orthodox Protestant

2. David Bebbington, *Evangelicalism in Modern Britain: A History from the 1730s to the 1980s* (London: Unwin Hyman, 1989), 2–17.
3. Timothy Larsen, "Defining and Locating Evangelicalism," in *The Cambridge Companion to Evangelical Theology*, ed. Timothy Larsen and Daniel Treier (New York: Cambridge University Press, 2007), 2.

who stands in the tradition of global Christian networks arising from the eighteenth-century revival movements associated with John Wesley and George Whitefield."[4] This definition locates evangelical Christianity within the larger story of the church. Evangelical Christianity is orthodox because it shares the doctrinal commitments of the early church's creedal tradition, such as a belief in a Triune God. This orthodoxy is a point of connection between evangelicals and the bigger Christian story, beginning with the early church. The evangelical movement is Protestant, which identifies it as belonging to a theological tradition in continuity with the Reformation of the sixteenth century. Larsen's definition accounts for the distinctive claims of Protestant theology. The definition grows yet more specific: not all Protestants are evangelicals, not least because Protestant Christianity existed for nearly two centuries before evangelicalism became a distinct movement. Larsen recognizes that eighteenth-century revival movements brought about a distinct community within Christian history, and that most evangelical Christians today can trace their spiritual roots back to those movements. Even though evangelicalism shares much in common with other Christian groups, it also has a particular history within the Christian tradition.

A third historian, George Marsden, helps us understand evangelicalism in light of twentieth-century conversations about the relationship between the church and the wider culture.[5] In the 1920s, liberal theology emerged as a powerful voice in Protestant churches, privileging human experience and feelings as the best authorities for Christian faith and maintaining that Christianity was about ethics and not doctrine. The term "liberal" here does not refer to American politics. Instead, it names a theological tradition that reinterprets much of orthodox doctrine in light of modern life. In opposition to liberalism, a broad coalition of doctrinally conservative Protestants identified themselves as "fundamentalist," seeing liberal interpretations of doctrine as a rejection of fundamental scriptural teaching. Between the 1950s and the 1970s, a split occurred in this coalition. Billy Graham's "new evangelicalism" remained doctrinally conservative while cooperating with other Christian traditions and insisting on active engagement in and with the culture. Separatist Christians, rejecting any association with a world

4. Ibid., 1.
5. George Marsden, *Fundamentalism and American Culture* (New York: Oxford University Press, 2006).

seen as sinful or with other Christians seen as accommodating that sinful world, kept the "fundamentalist" label. For Marsden, evangelical Christianity takes a self-consciously mediating position between liberalism on the one side and separatist fundamentalism on the other.

The evangelical perspective in this book lives within the complexities of these historical definitions. As the author, I identify with the practical and doctrinal tendencies that Bebbington sees among evangelicals, and as the title of the book makes clear, I do not see those tendencies as opposed to one another. I am part of the particular history that Larsen and Marsden identify with evangelicalism: I am "evangelical" because the evangelical story that began with those eighteenth-century revivals is *my* story. I came to Christ in, and remain committed to, a church descended from the Wesleyan revivals, and I teach in the same evangelical Christian college that sent Billy Graham into the world. My faith is lived in the North American context in which evangelical Christians felt the need to distinguish themselves first from liberal modernism and later from separatist fundamentalism, and I continue to see good reason for both distinctions. I, with all three historians, resonate with the idea that orthodox Protestant doctrine and activism in the world are strengths of evangelical Christianity. All of this gives you, the reader, a better sense of the context and commitments from which I, the author, practice doctrine. Doctrine is indispensable to evangelical Christianity, but most evangelical doctrine is not unique to evangelicalism.

> ### Evangelical Theology
>
> - Seeks faithfulness to the *euangelion*, the gospel of salvation in Jesus Christ.
> - Connects to a historical Christian community that emerged from eighteenth-century revivalism.
> - Holds practices in the evangelical tradition—emphasizing conversion and activism—together with key doctrinal claims about the authority of Scripture and the centrality of Christ's work on the cross.
> - Is committed to active cultural engagement "in" the world while maintaining the distinctive commitments that identify Christians as not "of" the world "so that the world may know" the good news (John 17:23).

This is where the **ecumenical** perspective of the book is important. The word comes from the Greek *oikoumene*, which means "the entire inhabited earth." This term reminds Christians that God's salvific love applies to the whole world—every nation, every tribe, and every person. Ecumenical

Christian teaching is the teaching of the whole church, the faith of the whole body of Christ spread across the centuries and around the globe, and Christian efforts at ecumenism are efforts to converse across lines that divide us, to find common ground, to recognize that diverse groups of Christians have a great deal in common, and to work toward unity in the body of Christ. Timothy Tennent notes the importance of ecumenical theology in his acknowledgment that "it would be arrogant to believe that one or more of the theologies our culture has produced have somehow managed to raise and systematically answer all questions, for all Christians, for all time. Every culture in every age has blind spots and biases that we are often oblivious to, but which are evident to those outside of our culture or time."[6]

> ### Ecumenical Theology
>
> IIIIIIIIIIIIIIIIIIIIIIIIIIIIIIIIIIIIIIIIIIIIIIIIIIIII
>
> - Recognizes that no one part of the church is the whole body of Christ.
> - Rejoices in the shared doctrine and practice that belong to the whole of that body.
> - Allows difference to flourish, without seeing it as a threat to unity.
> - Humbly listens to other parts of the body.
> - Looks for God's active work in the whole world.

My perspective in this book is ecumenical in several senses. First, in introducing the various Christian doctrines, my main focus is not on questions that divide the church. Christians hold much doctrine in common, an ecumenical consensus about important truths of the faith. This agreement is often underplayed, and I try to highlight areas of Christian unity. Second, I want to introduce you to an ecumenical gathering of Christian voices—men and women, North American and European and African and Latin American and Asian, contemporary, medieval, ancient, old, young, black, white, and brown. Space is limited, and this attempt is woefully inadequate, but I try to give you a glimpse of the beautiful diversity of the church as a global reality. Finally, I do all my work as a theologian with a strong sense that the gospel is truly for the whole world. Jesus told his disciples to be "witnesses in Jerusalem, in all Judea and Samaria, and to the ends of the earth" (Acts 1:8). The gospel is global because it is for everyone, in all times and all places. Athanasius (c. 296–373), an early church leader, appreciates the ecumenical nature of the gospel when he

---

6. Timothy Tennent, *Theology in the Context of World Christianity* (Grand Rapids: Zondervan, 2007), 12.

reminds us that God "is working mightily among humans, every day invisibly persuading numbers of people all over the world."[7]

This takes us back to the word *evangelical*. Most simply, evangelical Christians are people of the gospel, called to be witnesses to Jesus in the world. The gospel has not been entrusted to *any* single group of Christians in history, as if it were their sole possession. The gospel is God's good news to the world, and God has raised witnesses for the gospel across generations and cultures. Evangelical theology has to be ecumenical theology. We simply cannot tell the story of theology—nor can we practice discipleship faithfully—without accounting for the wide variety of ways that God has used Christians throughout history to spread the gospel to the world. So, while I stand as part of the tradition of evangelicalism—and while I think that this tradition has much to offer the wider Christian tradition—I also believe in the need for conversation between Christians from across centuries and backgrounds whose lives have been shaped by the gospel of salvation in Jesus Christ. These conversations can be difficult and challenging. New perspectives can expose our assumptions and reveal areas where we have wrongly identified contextual elements of our time and place as essential to the gospel. In engaging with others, we are held accountable for mistakes we might make because of our limited perspectives, and we gain insights about God that we would be unable to see on our own. As we talk with one another, we are forced to do the hard work of articulating what we believe and why we believe it. This hard work becomes a gift to us, because, through it, we are strengthened to be the people God has called us to be and to fulfill the task that God has set out for us in our own time and place. As we live in this way, we stand in a long line of Christians who together make up the great "cloud of witnesses" (Heb. 12:1) called by God to put doctrine into practice as we share the good news of salvation.

7. St. Athanasius, *On the Incarnation* (Crestwood, NY: St. Vladimir's Seminary Press, 1993), 61.

1

|||||||||||||||||||||||||||||||||||||||||||||||||||||||||||

Speaking of God

Theology and the Christian Life

The word *theology* can be a conversation stopper. When people ask what I teach, and I answer "theology," the most common response is a short "Oh," followed by uncertain silence. That "Oh" seems to cover several reactions, both from Christians and from those who are not of the faith. First, many people do not know what theology is. The word implies something obscure, even pretentious. Other people, again both Christian and not, have strong negative ideas about theology. Perhaps they have heard stories about the study of theology causing people to lose their faith. Perhaps they associate theology with self-righteousness or, worse, with violence against people who disagree with a certain theology. Still other people simply cannot imagine why anyone would care about such a thing. It sounds far removed from what really matters in life. While I understand these reactions, the ideas about theology they represent could not be further from my own experience in the discipline. It goes against the nature of theology for it to suffer elitism, sanctimoniousness, or uselessness. **Theology**, as the study of the things of God, a God who loves the world, is a discipline for all Christians. It is to be practiced with love, and, by God's grace, it can make the practitioner more loving.

What Is Theology?

The word *theology* brings the Greek term *logos*—translated "word," "speech," or "reason"—together with the term *theos*, the word for "God." In the Gospel of John, *logos* is identified with Jesus, who was "in the beginning . . . with God" and then "became flesh" (John 1:1, 14). Paul encourages Christians to "let the word [*logos*] of Christ dwell in you" when teaching one another (Col. 3:16). He uses the same root word when he talks about worship of God being "rational" (*logike*), an idea he connects to presenting our "bodies as a living sacrifice" and being "transformed by the renewing of your minds" (Rom. 12:1–2). Knowledge of the *logos* (Jesus) is reflected in true worship of him, which is manifested in the ways we act and think. It is also reflected in the ways we speak about God to others. When we, as Christians, bear witness to the gospel, we are doing theology. Early Christians called preaching about Jesus the "word [*logos*] of God" (Acts 8:14), and we are called to be ready to make a "defense to anyone who demands from you a reason [*logos*] for the hope that is in you" (1 Pet. 3:15 ESV). All of these moments in Scripture point to the fact that words about God matter. Those words are right at the heart of Christian faith and life.

Theology begins with God's revelatory word to us. It continues as we respond with words: words to God and to each other. So prayer, praise, testimony, preaching, and teaching are all parts of the daily theological work of the people of God. We also respond in the academic practice of theology, when theology is taught and written in the context of formal education and publication. Such academic theology can never proceed rightly if it is separated from the Christian life. The early church articulated this connection with the phrase *lex orandi, lex credendi*, "the law of prayer is the law of belief." Theologian Geoffrey Wainwright points out that this expression contains a double suggestion; it "makes the rule of prayer a norm for belief," but it also implies that "what must be believed governs what may and should be prayed."[1] The "law of prayer" suggests the whole of an active life of discipleship, a life in which individuals and churches are in personal relationship with God. That living relationship informs orthodox or correct belief even while belief informs the life of faith. So, the connection between academic theology and theology that happens in the life of the church runs both ways.

1. Geoffrey Wainwright, *Doxology: The Praise of God in Worship, Doctrine, and Life* (New York: Oxford University Press, 1984), 218.

While shaping our words, theology also shapes our reason, our lives as disciples, our worship as the church, and our mission to the world. As theology affects the way we talk about God, it also affects the way we think. We are to love God with our minds, and so part of our task is to think well about God. This is not easy, because as sinners we are "estranged and hostile in mind" (Col. 1:21). Before we can hope to reason correctly, we need God's grace to transform our minds. This transformation takes place, in part, through the process of learning how to speak rightly about God. The study of theology affects the way we live. As our thoughts about God draw near the truth of God, our lives reflect this transformation. Paul points to this reality when he talks about Christians as people who "take every thought captive to obey Christ" (2 Cor. 10:5). The discipline of theology is not first about gaining information or building a system of knowledge. It is about discipleship: we learn to speak and think well about God so that we can be more faithful followers of Jesus. By helping the church think about God, theology helps the church

> ### Key Scripture
>
> Now this I affirm and insist on in the Lord: you must no longer live as the Gentiles live, in the futility of their minds. They are darkened in their understanding, alienated from the life of God because of their ignorance and hardness of heart. They have lost all sensitivity and have abandoned themselves to licentiousness, greedy to practice every kind of impurity. That is not the way you learned Christ! For surely you have heard about him and were taught in him, as truth is in Jesus. You were taught to put away your former way of life, your old self, corrupt and deluded by its lusts, and to be renewed in the spirit of your minds, and to clothe yourselves with the new self, created according to the likeness of God in true righteousness and holiness. So then, putting away falsehood, let all of us speak the truth to our neighbors, for we are members of one another. (Eph. 4:17–25)

worship rightly. It also helps the church measure its words, so that it can pray, praise, preach, and perform in ways that reflect the truth about God and the gospel. Finally, as theology forms worship, it also provides training for our mission in the world. As we witness to the good news of Jesus Christ, we want to speak truthfully as we talk about God and the gift of salvation. The study of theology gives us words to say—and ways to say them—that we did not have before and helps us better recognize when our words or actions fail to reflect the truth about God. Theology prepares our minds for the challenges we will encounter, helping us to think about

the questions people have about God. Theology is the discipline of learning from the Word of God and learning to use words faithfully when we
speak about God.

Doctrine

If theology is the discipline of speaking faithfully about God, then, in
the big picture, theology speaks about almost everything. Everything, all
of creation, belongs to God and therefore is subject matter for theology.
For this reason, medieval Christians knew theology as the "queen of the
sciences." Theology is a queen, not because it is a trump card over other
disciplines, not because other disciplines are unimportant, but because
the topics studied in other disciplines—biology, psychology, economics,
chemistry, and all the rest—are topics about God's creation. Theology takes
a bird's-eye view of the other disciplines, seeing them all in light of God's
Word. On a smaller scale, though, theology speaks about an organized
set of Christian teachings, doctrines about important themes in Scripture
and Christian life. Christian doctrine, viewed as a whole, gives us a picture
of the Christian faith.

There is a fairly standard list of doctrines, and this book introduces
those major doctrines by giving a chapter to each: revelation and Scripture, God, creation, human beings, Jesus, salvation, the Holy Spirit, the
church, and final Christian hope. Beginning with the doctrine of Scripture
is a traditional Protestant move, one based on the belief that Scripture
has a special status in the practice of theology. After the chapter on Scripture, the other doctrinal chapters in this book are ordered loosely in line
with the biblical narrative, which begins with creation and ends with the
kingdom of God. This is not the only possible list of doctrines, nor is this
the only order in which we could consider them. The doctrines also have
possible subcategories. Theologians have interesting conversations about
what belongs on the list and what should come first.

Theologians also pay attention to the connections between these doctrines. The teachings of Christian faith are interrelated. For example, if
we were to make major revisions to our beliefs about Jesus—Christology—those revisions would have repercussions for the other doctrines.
What we believe about Jesus is intertwined with what we believe about
salvation, humanity, and the church. Theological training helps us to see

Theologians on Dogma and Doctrine

Theologians describe the concept of doctrine and dogma in different ways.

For Karl Barth, "dogma is the agreement of Church proclamation with the revelation attested in Holy Scripture. Into this agreement, and therefore into dogma, dogmatics inquires."[a] Barth argues that, as sinners, we never get this agreement right, and so our attempts at practicing doctrine are always only proposals for dogma. That is, our theologies are not the Word of God.

George Lindbeck highlights what doctrine does in the Christian life. Like grammatical rules that govern the writing and speaking of a language, doctrines govern the Christian life. He describes doctrines as "communally authoritative rules of discourse, attitude, and action."[b]

Robert Jenson makes a distinction between doctrine and dogma, a distinction "most clearly marked by the notion of irreversibility. Every theological proposition states a historic choice. 'To be speaking the gospel, let us henceforward say "F" rather than that other possibility "G."' A dogmatic choice is one by which the church so decisively determines her own future that if the choice is wrongly made, the community determined by that choice is no longer in fact the community of the gospel."[c]

Serene Jones describes doctrines "as imaginative lenses through which to view the world. Through them, one learns how to relate to other persons, how to act in community, how to make sense of truth and falsehood, and how to understand and move through the varied terrain of life's everyday challenges."[d]

Finally, Dorothy Sayers insists on the reality of dogma: "It is worse than useless for Christians to talk about the importance of Christian morality unless they are prepared to take their stand upon the fundamentals of Christian theology. It is a lie to say that dogma does not matter; it matters enormously. It is fatal to let people suppose that Christianity is only a mode of feeling; it is vitally necessary to insist that it is first and foremost a rational explanation of the universe."[e]

a. Karl Barth, *Church Dogmatics*, I/1, trans. G.W. Bromiley (Edinburgh: T&T Clark, 1975), 304.
b. George Lindbeck, *The Nature of Doctrine: Religion and Theology in a Postliberal Age* (Louisville: Westminster John Knox, 1984), 18.
c. Robert Jenson, *Systematic Theology* (New York: Oxford University Press, 1997), 1:17.
d. Serene Jones, *Feminist Theory and Christian Theology* (Minneapolis: Fortress, 2000), 16.
e. Dorothy Sayers, *Letters to a Diminished Church: Passionate Arguments for the Relevance of Christian Doctrine* (Nashville: W Publishing Group, 2004), 46.

the interconnectedness of doctrine and to recognize the ways that different theologies are affected by it. Theological training also helps us to see which doctrines are central for particular theologians.

Human attempts to articulate doctrine are always limited by our finitude and brokenness. Within these limits, Christians recognize a spectrum of authoritativeness in Christian teaching. The term **dogma** is used for Christian teaching at the highest level of authority and trustworthiness. Dogmas are teachings that are shared ecumenically across Christian communities, teachings that we have good reason to trust, teachings most central to the faith. At a less universal level of authority, particular Christian communities treat doctrine within those communities as authoritative. For example, Lutherans grant authority to Lutheran doctrine or a local congregation grants authority to a doctrinal statement. These doctrines might not be recognized or considered authoritative in another church context. Still, the doctrine is recognized as authoritative in its community.

Doctrinal proposals are also made at an individual level. Throughout the history of the church, individual Christians have done theological work, trying to articulate doctrine in their own times and places. Those individual theologies, then, have been subject to the discernment of the wider body. When Martin Luther wrote about justification by faith, he was not writing authoritative Lutheran doctrine. Later, communities of Christians came to recognize Luther's theology as authoritative, and his individual work informed the authoritative doctrine of Protestant Christianity. The ongoing work of individual theologians continues to inform the authoritative doctrine of the people of God.

Resources for Theology

As we learn to speak well about God and attempt to formulate faithful doctrine, we are going to look for resources to help us in the task. One model for thinking about sources and authority for theology is found in the **Wesleyan Quadrilateral**.[2] This model is named for John Wesley, one of the eighteenth-century revivalists at the roots of evangelicalism. Imagine a shape with four sides, with each side representing a resource that informs the Christian life: Scripture, tradition, reason, and experience. The four sides of this quadrilateral should not be understood as four equal sources for theology. It is better to think of Scripture as the source of Christian doctrine and to think of tradition, reason, and experience as resources for

2. The association of this model with John Wesley can be misleading. Wesley appealed to all four of these resources, but he did not use the term "quadrilateral" to describe his theological method. See William Abraham, *Waking from Doctrinal Amnesia: The Healing of Doctrine in the United Methodist Church* (Nashville: Abingdon, 1996).

understanding that source. The quadrilateral brings these resources into conversation with each other and with Scripture, which, as the Word of God, stands as the proper authority for theology. Church tradition, human reason, and our own experiences stand under the authority of Scripture and help us understand it better. The quadrilateral functions as a rubric that helps us think about theological questions. By looking at each side of the quadrilateral in turn, we can gain a clearer picture of the unique way that theology functions in the Christian life.

Scripture and Theology

John Wesley was clear that the role of Scripture in doing theology is categorically different from any role that other resources might play. "I allow no other rule," Wesley wrote, "whether of faith or practice, than the Holy Scriptures."[3] No source for theology can operate independently of Scripture. When the Protestant reformers of the sixteenth century spoke about the best way to do theology, they used the phrase *sola scriptura*, "Scripture alone." Martin Luther wrote that "the Word of God shall establish articles of faith and no one else, not even an angel."[4] The reformers were opposing abuses in both belief and practice that plagued the church in their time. The call of *sola scriptura* came from recognition that other authorities—including tradition, reason, and experience—were easy to bend in any direction that sinful human beings desired. Protestant theologians were conscious of our tendency to try to force theology to fit with human desire. The *sola scriptura* principle is a check, a safety net meant to keep us from falling into false thinking about God. As the Word of God, Scripture rectifies all human words—words of tradition, reason, and experience. Church tradition is open to abuse, and it does not always speak with one voice. Christians have different experiences and often do not agree on whether something is reasonable or not. Conclusions drawn from tradition, experience, and reason vary between individuals and locations, but all Christians in all places have access to the same reliable Word of God in Scripture. The best practitioners of doctrine are always ready to be challenged and corrected by God's Word. Scripture is an external

3. "To James Hervey," in *John Wesley*, ed. Albert C. Outler (New York: Oxford University Press, 1964), 72.
4. "The Smalcald Articles," in *Martin Luther's Basic Theological Writings*, ed. Timothy F. Lull (Minneapolis: Fortress, 1989), 507.

authority that breaks into our world from God to us, and it opens our eyes
to help us recognize the truth about God.

These claims demand two sets of questions. The first set of questions
is about the risks of doing theology. If Scripture is the norm for Christian thought and life, why would theologians pay any attention to other
authorities? If tradition and reason are full of abuses, if experience is so
often selfish, should Christians turn away from them? For that matter, why
should we try to talk about doctrine at all? Why not simply read the Bible?
The problem is that it is not so easy to "simply" read the Bible, and this
raises a second set of questions about the difficult task of understanding
and being faithful to the Word of God in Scripture. Scripture has been
used to validate abuse, and Christians often disagree about the meaning of Scripture. We also misinterpret Scripture, and much of the history
of Christian theology involves correcting mistaken readings of the Bible.
The interpretations of Scripture found in the writings of the early church
heretics, the torturers of the inquisition, or evangelical slaveholders during the Civil War provide examples of such bad readings.[5] The discipline
of theology is about learning to read Scripture more faithfully. It is also
about speaking the truth of Scripture in ways that fit new contexts, new
times, and new places. It is true that human beings are very talented at
using reason, tradition, and experience to support our own sins. It is also
true that reading Scripture well is very hard work.

By putting Scripture into conversation with reason, tradition, and experience, we find help in understanding its meaning and guarding against
our tendency to misinterpret it. John Wesley illustrates how he held these
questions together in the life of faith. Wesley wished to be "a man of one
book." He longed for God's Word in Scripture, writing, "O give me that
book! At any price, give me the book of God!"[6] The more Wesley im-
mersed himself in that "one book" and the more he got to know the Bible,
the more he understood the gospel in his own life and strove to share the
good news with others. He relied on Scripture as the source of doctrine.
This "man of one book," though, read broadly from many books. He
asked the leaders of his movement to read a large library of Christian
sources drawn from the earliest centuries of the church to their own time.

5. Mark A. Noll, *America's God: From Jonathan Edwards to Abraham Lincoln* (New York:
Oxford University Press, 2002).
6. "Preface to *Sermons on Several Occasions*," in Outler, *John Wesley*, 89.

Describing his own practice, Wesley shows how there is no contradiction between the longing to be a people of "one book" and being willing to learn from other resources as we seek to be more faithful readers of Scripture. Wesley recounts how he loved to sit alone with the Bible, which he describes as sitting in the presence of God. When he did not understand the meaning of Scripture, he would pray for illumination. He also used a rule for reading Scripture that had been used by many Christians before him, the rule that "Scripture interprets Scripture." He would search other passages of Scripture to help him understand the passage he was reading. He expressed trust that God would make the Word clear to him. Then he would turn to the reason and experience of other Christians: "If any doubt still remains, I consult those who are experienced in the things of God and then the writings whereby being dead they yet speak."[7] He turned to the Christian tradition—to the voices of other faithful Christians. This method demonstrates how Scripture relates to tradition, reason, and experience: Christians are people of the "one book" who become better readers of Scripture by being in conversation with other Christians. We will discuss the doctrine of Scripture in greater depth in the next chapter.

Tradition and Theology

Many Christians undervalue the role of tradition in guiding Christian belief and life, and this is troublesome for the same reason that undue confidence in tradition is: human sin is very real. We need to be aware of the ways that sin may make us resistant to the truth of Christian tradition. The danger of undervaluing tradition is especially real in contemporary North American evangelicalism, where, as theologian Soong-Chan Rah points out, consumerism, individualism, and racism have negative effects on the practice of doctrine.[8] If we undervalue tradition, we run the risk of mistaking fleeting or sinful human experience as the universal way of following God. We do not have to read Scripture in isolation: we are able to learn from and with our brothers and sisters in Christ who are on the journey of faith with us. Christians are always in conversation with other Christians about the things of God. The discipline of theology can be seen as one long conversation—stretching over centuries and continents—about

7. Ibid., 90.
8. Soong-Chan Rah, *The Next Evangelicalism: Freeing the Church from Western Cultural Captivity* (Downers Grove, IL: InterVarsity, 2009).

how to read Scripture well. The best practitioners of doctrine take time to learn about this conversation by studying the Christian tradition.

The tradition is an essential resource for theologians seeking to better understand Scripture, but the word *tradition*, like the word *doctrine*, often does not carry warm connotations. Some people talk about "dead tradition," and others regard it as something to be overcome and rejected. We do not want to be chained to outdated practices that no longer apply to our situation. Theologians view tradition in a different way, because far from being "dead," the Christian tradition is very much alive—not least because, as Christians, we know that death is not the end. The authority of tradition does not come from repetition of old phrases or ideas, as if our task is to do things the way they have always been done. Rather, the authority of tradition rests in its consistency with the "living and active" (Heb. 4:12) Word of God. The Christian tradition gives us access to the best efforts of other Christians to think faithfully about Scripture and life. In listening to other Christians—past and present, near and far—we acknowledge that our own wisdom is limited, and we recognize and rejoice in the work of God in the lives of others. As we learn about past Christians, we find guidance and direction for our reflections in the present. Theologian Kathryn Tanner says that knowing Christian tradition is a way "of expanding the range of imaginative possibilities for theological construction in any one time and place. . . . Placing one's own efforts within this ongoing and wide stream, one grows in appreciation for the two-thousand-year, global history of efforts to say what Christianity is all about."[9] Listening to the tradition helps us practice humility. It helps us recognize our limits and lets us learn from others who share the faith.

The most widely shared and authoritative Christian tradition comes from early summaries of Christian doctrine, known as the **rule of faith**, which took mature form in ecumenical **creeds**. The Apostles' and Nicene Creeds are brief statements of Christian faith that enjoy broad recognition as faithful summaries of key scriptural teachings. Theologian Vincent of Lérins (d. ca. 445) suggested a rule that Christians ought to believe those things that are recognized as true always, everywhere, and for everybody. His point was that Christian truth extends across time and crosses borders. The creeds fit Vincent's rule; no other summary of Christian teaching has come

9. Kathryn Tanner, *Jesus, Humanity and the Trinity: A Brief Systematic Theology* (Minneapolis: Fortress, 2001), xviii.

so close to being accepted always, everywhere, and by all Christians. As such, the creeds provide us with standards of **orthodoxy**, or right Christian belief. Orthodox doctrine is contrasted with false doctrine or **heresy**, beliefs that have been rejected by the church as contrary to Scripture. While "heresy" can be a frightening word, a heresy is simply a doctrine that has been found, in the Spirit-guided judgment of God's people, to be wrong. The fact that someone is wrong does not mean that they are damned. Correct doctrine does not save us. Jesus saves us. This does not mean that heresy is not serious. Because doctrine matters, false doctrine matters. If right doctrine—true, beautiful, and good Christian teaching that is faithful to God's Word—is connected to faithful practice, if right doctrine can be a means of grace that shapes us as disciples, then false doctrine will also have consequences for practice and formation. Anyone can cite Scripture, and the most damaging heretics are often skilled at quoting verses to support their views. By leading us back to Scripture, the creeds help us discern the truth. They help us avoid making judgments about doctrine based on feelings, emotional responses, or personal reactions.

> ### The Apostles' Creed
>
> I believe in God, the Father almighty, creator of heaven and earth;
>
> And in Jesus Christ, His only Son, our Lord, Who was conceived by the Holy Spirit, born of the Virgin Mary, suffered under Pontius Pilate, was crucified, dead and buried. He descended to hell, on the third day rose again from the dead, ascended to heaven, sits at the right hand of God the Father almighty, thence he will come to judge the living and the dead;
>
> I believe in the Holy Spirit, the holy catholic Church, the communion of saints, the forgiveness of sins, the resurrection of the body, and the life everlasting. Amen.[a]
>
> a. "Textus receptus (c. 700)," in John H. Leith, ed. *Creeds of the Churches: A Reader in Christian Doctrine from the Bible to the Present*, 3rd ed. (Louisville: John Knox, 1982), 24–25.

Reason and Theology

While caricatures may portray faith and reason as opponents, reason is central to the practice of doctrine. The faithful exercise of reason is close to the very heart of theology as a discipline. God *is* reason, and because he has ordered the entire cosmos according to his rational plan (John 1:3),

Global Theologians Connecting Philosophy and Theology

The work of connecting theology with philosophy is both a global and a local enterprise. All theological work is done in context. The quotations that follow illustrate the ways that two contemporary theologians are thinking about the connections between specific contexts and the practice of doctrine. First, Kenyan theologian James Kombo writes about the doctrine of the Trinity in African and ecumenical thought.

> We (in African theology) must seek to understand what the Bible means by emphasizing one God, while at the same time teaching the divinity of the Son and of the Holy Spirit. We have to search for ourselves how the church fathers understood God when they formulated the creeds that have been inherited by us. . . . We cannot bypass these efforts in our own search for a reinterpretation that is appropriate for the African context. If we are going to engage in informed theological discourses with the wider theological fraternity, we cannot afford to short-circuit the contributions to the Trinitarian debate by individual theologians. . . . To listen to what these theologians say is to function within a universal Christian story. To function within the universal Christian story . . . is not to fall into Eurocentric formation. The African church is part of the universal church; it does not have another story. It is the same universal story that the African theologian must identify, listen to, and clarify for the African audience.[a]

Kombo articulates the doctrine of the Trinity in African philosophical forms, but he does not ignore the ecumenical context in doing so. Next, Chinese theologian K. K. Yeo talks about the relationship between Christian doctrine and Confucian thought.

> I believe that Christ completes or extends what is merely implicit or absent (theology, transcendence, spirit) in Confucius; without Christ, the Confucian ethic too quickly (even in early Chinese history) degenerates into a system of ritualistic behavior. But the Confucian ethic amplifies various elements of Christian theologies (for example, community, virtues) that are underplayed in Western Christianity. The Christ of God (in the Bible) can bring Chinese classics and cultures (such as Confucian ethics) to their fulfillment while protecting the universal church from aberrations of Chinese history, and while protecting China against the aberration of Christian history and interpretation in the West. CCT [Christian Chinese Theology] has something to say to the universal church that needs to be heard. CCT will discover its *global* mission if it can be allowed to find its own biblical interpretation.[b]

Yeo, like Kombo, sees the relationship between contextual and ecumenical theology as one that runs both directions. Both local and ecumenical Christian thought contain aberrations, and both contain riches.

a. James Henry Kombo, *The Doctrine of God in African Christian Thought* (Leiden: Brill, 2007), 271–72.
b. Khiok-Khng Yeo, "Christian Chinese Theology: Theological Ethics of Becoming Human and Holy," in *Global Theology in Evangelical Perspective: Exploring the Contextual Nature of Theology and Mission*, ed. Jeffrey Greenman and Gene Green (Downers Grove, IL: IVP Academic, 2011), 97–113.

reason is intrinsic to faith.[10] As creatures made in God's image, we are created to act reasonably in everything we do, especially in the way that we think and speak about God.

We exercise reason when we do such things as analyze facts and ideas, construct arguments, form judgments, and decide what is true or false. These actions assist us in the task of theology when we employ them to discern how Scripture holds together and what this requires of our lives. This often takes the form of drawing out implications from the teachings of Scripture. Reason helps us to better understand the things of God so that we may be more faithful in word and deed. Using reason for this purpose is part of what it means to show integrity in our teaching (Titus 2:7). As people called to love God with our minds, we have to be willing to do the hard work of thinking through the claims of faith so that we can understand what they mean and how they all fit together. The use of our reason is an act of discipleship. It enables us to share the good news more effectively and helps us love God more as we begin to see with increasing clarity the "depth of the riches and wisdom and knowledge of God" (Rom. 11:33).

The practice of doctrine thus involves stewardship of the intellectual gifts God has given us. The practice of doctrine also involves Christians in conversation with disciplines besides theology—the arts, sciences, and humanities—as we seek the truth of God. Christians are always in conversation with the intellectual riches of the day. The ancient Augustine found help in Platonic philosophy, and the medieval Thomas Aquinas brought the riches of Christian doctrine together with the best of Aristotelian thought. Both Augustine and Aquinas thought about these philosophical traditions as Christians. Intimates with the Scriptures, both understood that philosophy would not look the same once it encountered Jesus Christ, and both saw places where philosophy must be corrected by doctrine, but neither theologian let this stop him from learning from the philosophers. The contemporary practice of doctrine can find a model in Augustine and Aquinas. Christians have nothing to fear from learning, from knowledge, and Christians know that human learning will need to be challenged by the Word, but the riches of human knowledge are nothing to be despised. As we practice doctrine and learn faithfulness in our own intellectual contexts, we have much to learn from scientists, artists, and philosophers.

10. See Thomas Aquinas, *Summa Theologica*, trans. Fathers of the English Dominican Province (Allen, TX: Christian Classics, 1948), I.14.4.

We must also be aware that sin is stamped on our reason as it is on every other aspect of life, and reason cannot function rightly apart from God's grace. We cannot take it for granted that we know what is or is not reasonable apart from the revelation of God. Since there is no *logos* (reason) apart from the true *logos*, Jesus Christ, we have no foolproof standards by which we can judge what must be true about God apart from what God has shown us in revelation. Christians embrace reason, but we are not ruled by empiricism. We do not have to assume, for instance, that things must be measurable in order to be true. Christian belief is not restricted to what we can understand. God always remains beyond the limits of our ability to describe him, and God cannot be captured by our ideas. Reason is a vital resource for theology, but we must remember that we "know only in part" (1 Cor. 13:12). Sin often causes us to bend the truth, and the only cure for fallen reason is Jesus Christ. In the incarnation, the Son of God took on a human mind as well as a human body, and he shows us what a human life lived with perfect reason looks like. By connecting his life to ours, therefore, Jesus frees us to reason rightly about God. This is why Paul tells us to "let the same mind be in you that was in Christ Jesus" (Phil. 2:5).

Experience and Theology

The idea that experience ought to be a resource for theology is highly contested. One strand in contemporary theology has little patience with appeals to experience, seeing experience as hopelessly subjective, individualistic, and sinful. Another strand of theology seeks to make it clear that experience always and necessarily influences our practice of doctrine and prefers to make that influence clear rather than pretending objectivity. There are clear dangers in relying on experience as a resource for doctrine, but we also cannot discount the importance of experience.

Much of what worries theologians in appeals to experience arose during the Enlightenment. One of the hallmarks of the modern era is suspicion of authorities like tradition and Scripture. Instead of relying on such external authorities, Enlightenment thinkers taught that reason alone should serve as the primary authority for all areas of life. Friedrich Schleiermacher (1768–1834), a pastor in Berlin, recognized that this view destabilized the Christian faith, and he argued that faith should be understood in terms of our most basic "experience" of God, a concept he defined as a "feeling."[11] Schleiermacher tried to explain Christian faith without relying on the traditional authorities or limiting it to what we can prove, and the argument was effective. One can reject authoritative sources or argue against rational conclusions, but it is difficult to discount what someone *feels* about God. The problem, however, is that experience-based faith becomes subjective, individualistic, and, ultimately, private and detached from reality. The German philosopher Ludwig Feuerbach (1804–72) argued that everything we know about God is nothing more than a reflection of ourselves. "Knowledge of God is self-knowledge," he insisted. "By his God you know the man, and by the man his God; the two are *identical*."[12] In other

---

God Is Not . . . God Is . . .

Tertullian says, "That which is infinite is known only to itself. This it is which gives some notion of God, while yet beyond all our conceptions—our very incapacity of fully grasping Him affords us the idea of what He really is. He is presented to our minds in His transcendent greatness, as at once known and unknown."[a]

The tradition of apophatic theology is one that tries to do justice to the mystery and majesty of God and to recall that God cannot be pinned down by our doctrines. God is always more than we can express. Apophatic theology, then, uses a method of negation. Instead of trying to say what God is, the apophatic theologian makes statements about what God is not.

A cataphatic approach to theology makes positive statements about God, and cataphatic theology works with the confidence that comes from the fact that God has, in fact, made himself known to us.

a. Tertullian, *Apologeticus* 17, in *The Writings of Quintus Sept. Flor. Tertullianus*, ed. Alexander Roberts and James Donaldson, trans. S. Thelwall (Edinburgh: T&T Clark, 1869), 1:86.

---

words, if we know God through experience, then the subject matter of theology is no longer God but *us*. We end up making God in our image instead of the other way around, and this leaves us with an idol.

Schleiermacher's turn to experience was influential, and no theology is immune to the temptation to use experience in the wrong way. Part of the task of theology is to expose and reject bad appeals to experience. At

11. Friedrich Schleiermacher, *On Religion: Speeches to Its Cultured Despisers*, trans. and ed. Richard Crouter (Cambridge: Cambridge University Press, 1988), 22.

12. Ludwig Feuerbach, *The Essence of Christianity*, trans. George Eliot (New York: Prometheus Books, 1989), 12; emphasis added.

the same time, experience matters. Who we are and where we come from do influence our theologies, and God cares about our experiences. More, God can use experience in powerful ways, both in individual lives and in churches and communities. The Pietist theologian Philip Jacob Spener (1635–1705) focused on the Holy Spirit's work in transforming the lives of believers into reflections of God's grace. "It is not enough that we hear the Word with our outward ear," he argued, "but we must let it penetrate to our heart, so that we may hear the Holy Spirit speak there, that is, with vibrant emotion and comfort feel the sealing of the Spirit and the power of the Word."[13] In short, Christians must reflect what we believe in the way that we live. We cannot do so without the gift of grace as "guided by the Spirit" (Gal. 5:25).

This emphasis on the work of the Holy Spirit greatly influenced the evangelical movement. We see an example in John Wesley, whose life was changed by experience. Wesley wrote, "I felt my heart strangely warmed. I felt I did trust in Christ, Christ alone for salvation; and an assurance was given me that he had taken away *my* sins, even *mine*, and saved *me* from the law of sin and death."[14] Later, Wesley would emphasize the power that God works when faith comes alive in personal experience: "May every real Christian say, 'I now am assured that these things are so; I experienced them in my own breast. What Christianity (considered as a doctrine) promised, is accomplished in my soul.'"[15] In Wesley's theological context, resources for theology were often thought of as a "three-legged stool"—Scripture, tradition, and reason. The addition of "experience," turning three legs into four, can be viewed as both Wesley's genius and his flaw. Experience is powerful, but it is also slippery. It can transform lives, but it can also raise idols. Wesley builds safeguards around authoritative experience by defining it as a certain *kind* of experience: not just any feeling, but the converting, assuring, and transforming experience of the Spirit's work in our lives.

Many of us know the power of the experience of the Spirit both Spener and Wesley describe but may also recognize a burden that comes when Christians try desperately to *produce* this kind of heartfelt experience.

13. Philip Jacob Spener, *Pia Desideria*, trans. Theodore G. Tappert (Philadelphia: Fortress, 1964), 117.
14. Outler, *John Wesley*, 66.
15. Ibid., 191.

Contemporary Experience Theologies

In 1971 Peruvian theologian Gustavo Gutiérrez became the "father of liberation theology" as he wrote about the experience of the poor. Here, from the introduction to his book, we see a place for experience in theology that had not been acknowledged in quite this way before:

> This book is an attempt at reflection, based on the gospel and the experiences of men and women committed to the process of liberation in the oppressed and exploited land of Latin America. It is a theological reflection born of the experience of shared efforts to abolish the current unjust situation and to build a different society, freer and more human. . . . My purpose is not to elaborate an ideology to justify postures already taken. . . . It is rather to let ourselves be judged by the word of the Lord, to think through our faith, to strengthen our love, and to give reason for hope. . . . It is to reconsider the great themes of the Christian life within this radically changed perspective and with regard to the new questions posed by this commitment.[a]

Other theologians began to write from the perspectives of oppressed peoples. Black theology, for example, draws on the experience of black people as an important resource for theological reflection, and feminist theology draws on the experiences of women. It is inappropriate to make a general assessment of these experience theologies, because they are very diverse. It is possible to find examples of theologies that use experience as a warrant for silencing Scripture, but it is also possible to find experience theologies that are consciously orthodox and bound to God's Word. There is a sense in which every theology is an experience theology because theologians cannot leave their experiences at the door when they come to work.

a. Gustavo Gutiérrez, *A Theology of Liberation*, 15th anniversary ed. (Maryknoll, NY: Orbis Books, 1988), xiii.

Note how Wesley places emphasis on *God's* action, not his own. His heart is warmed, not by his own effort, but "strangely," by God. Paul's emphasis is similar when he criticizes the Galatians for relying on the law instead of upon the faith God has given them. He asks them a pointed question: "Did you experience so much for nothing?" (Gal. 3:4). The "experience" Paul points to here is not a "feeling" the Galatians produce but a gift of grace given to them through the work of the Holy Spirit. *This* experience is a fruitful resource for theology. God uses our experience of his grace to shape our understanding of Scripture. God uses our experience to enable us to see, know, and live the truth that "everything old has passed away" and "everything has become new" (2 Cor. 5:17). What we tend to think of as "experience," Scripture often speaks of in terms of "the heart," a concept that concerns the very center of the human self, including our emotions and desires. The heart matters to God in powerful ways. We need only to think of the psalmist's prayer that both his words and his heart "be acceptable" to God (Ps. 19:14), David's "integrity of heart" (1 Kings 9:4), and Jesus's command that we should love God with our "heart" (Luke 10:27).

Practicing Theology

Ephesians 4 displays some ways that the work of theology helps us to mature in the faith as "knowledge of the Son of God" is connected "to maturity, to the measure of the full stature of Christ" (Eph. 4:13). "Children" are "tossed to and fro and blown about by every wind of doctrine, by people's trickery, by their craftiness in deceitful scheming" (v. 14). As we grow in Christ, we try to make sense of our faith in order to live faithfully. As we speak truth in love, "we must grow up in every way into him who is the head, into Christ" (v. 15). Paul contrasts the way the gentiles live, "in the futility of their minds" (v. 17), "darkened in their understanding, alienated from the life of God because of their ignorance and hardness of heart" (v. 18), with those who have "learned Christ" (v. 20), those who "were taught to put away [their] former way of life, [their] old self, corrupt and deluded by its lusts, and to be renewed in the spirit of [their] minds, and to clothe [themselves] with the new self, created according to the likeness of God in true righteousness and holiness" (vv. 22–24). Here, the connections between bad doctrine (futile, insensate, alienated, and ignorant) and broken lives mirror the connections between truthful doctrine (learned of Christ) and transformed lives. Theology equips us for faithful living. Because we have "learned Christ" and been taught truth as it is "in Jesus" (vv. 20–21), our lives are forever changed.

Anselm of Canterbury (1033–1109) described the theological task as one of "faith seeking understanding" (*fides quaerens intellectum*). These words expressed his desire to appreciate the implications of the faith clearly, logically, and deeply. "For I do not seek to understand so that I may believe," he said, "but I believe so that I may understand."[16] There is postmodern appeal in Anselm's medieval description, an unapologetic honesty about

---

16. *Proslogion*, in *Anselm of Canterbury: The Major Works*, ed. Brian Davies and G. R. Evans (New York: Oxford University Press, 1998), 87.

Questions to Ask While Reading Theology

1. What are the key Christian teachings being articulated? What is the author's driving concern or main theme?
2. What counts for the author as authoritative (Scripture, tradition, reason, experience . . .)? Is the author's theological method implicit or explicit?
3. How does the author deal with the witness of Scripture?
   a. Implicitly? Explicitly?
   b. Does the witness of the Old Testament matter? The New?
   c. What biblical themes are privileged?
   d. What interpretative principles are at work?
4. How do these claims relate to other doctrines?
5. How does context (including gender, race, class, culture, and time) shape the theological voice? Is the theologian conscious of this? How does your context shape your evaluation of the piece?
6. Practice reading charitably. What is the best possible interpretation of how the piece reflects an attempt to be faithful to Jesus Christ?
7. How do these theological claims relate to the life of faith? Do you bring other questions from your experience?
8. If this theological proposal were taken seriously, how would it shape Christian practice? Would it affect our participation in spiritual disciplines? Our understanding of faithful living? Our practice of evangelism? Our life as the church?

the theologian's starting place in faith. Theology begins in God, who is unprovable, transcendent, and unutterable, and through grace and goodness it continues in a quest to understand matters of faith, matters that remain unprovable but nonetheless become visible and practical in lives transformed by the gospel. As we search for understanding, we become more faithful disciples of Jesus Christ.

2

Knowing God

Doctrines of Revelation and Scripture

The big reveal is a familiar trope in "reality" television. The woman or the living room gets an attractive makeover. New clothes. New curtains. If the budget is bigger, plastic surgery or a gut renovation. The production team keeps the person or the homeowner in the dark until the full transformation has been worked. Then, in the climax of the show, the viewers get to see the person's first reaction to the changes. We know the familiar reactions to the big reveal. Tears of joy. Shrieks of happiness. Wide-eyed disbelief. Reality television trades on our belief that this kind of revelation changes lives—that the ugly duckling will move in different circles now that she is a swan, the low self-esteem that led to awful choices will be blown away, the beautiful woman of the reveal is a new woman indeed. The sadness behind this warped version of reality is that, all too often, the staged reveal will not truly change anything. The big reveal of the reality show is a twisting of what revelation ought to be. Televised "revelation" depends on money, shock value, and manipulation. The changes that such revelation makes are external and temporary. It pretends to change lives, but it does not address what happens when the camera stops rolling.

Divine revelation is altogether more powerful. When God reveals divine reality to us, real transformation takes place. When we truly know the things of God, we will be changed—body, soul, and spirit. The deepest truth of our reality, what Scripture sometimes speaks of as the heart, will be transformed. The transformation worked in divine revelation is eternal.

This chapter introduces the doctrines of divine revelation and Scripture, which Christians recognize as the key locus of God's gift of revelation. The doctrine of revelation explores how it is that God makes himself known to us. The doctrine of Scripture examines what Christians believe about the Bible as God's revelation. Since theology is a conversation about the things of God, we will be much more sensitive practitioners of doctrine if we have thought well about divine revelation and, especially, about the gift of Scripture, in which God has made himself known to us.

In Christian theology, "revelation" is an enormous category. When we use the word, we imply that the things of God are—or were—hidden. We also imply that God chose not to leave us in the dark. God acts to reveal himself to us. God uncovers the things that were hidden, allowing us to know him and inviting us into relationship with him. This is part of the goodness of who God is—God is a revealing God, a God who wants us to have knowledge. But our access to revelation is not always straightforward. We are finite creatures, and God's revelation to us is appropriate to our limits. Protestant Reformer John Calvin speaks of this in terms of accommodation. God makes accommodations for us, which fit what we can know. Calvin compares this to the way someone cares for an infant. Calvin suggests God's revelation is something like the lisping way we speak to small children, that "God is wont in a measure to 'lisp' in speaking to us," and that "such forms of speaking do not so much express clearly what God is like as accommodate the knowledge of him to our slight capacity."[1] God's revelation to us fits with the kind of creatures we are. We are creatures who learn through our senses, through materiality, and we are creatures who dwell in history, in time and space. So, God reveals himself in history and materiality. Revelation is thus shaped by the kind of creatures we are, but there is a much more serious limitation on our ability to know God: the limitation of sin. Though God gives revelation, we are sinners, and this

1. John Calvin, *Institutes of the Christian Religion*, ed. John T. McNeill (Louisville: Westminster John Knox, 1960), 1.13.1.

influences the way that we know God. We are prone to selfish knowing and to self-deceit. We who would know God are biased, sinful knowers.

No Christian theology can forget these difficulties, but we also cannot stop seeking God. God's action forbids us to despair. True knowledge of God is available to us, not because we are perfect knowers, but because God is a good God, a God who wants us to know him. Our finitude is not, for the creator God, a problem. It is part of God's good intention for us, and we have a God who can and does communicate with the finite. The fact that our knowledge of God must fit our finitude is only a problem if we rail against the sort of creatures God made us to be, if we seek knowledge that does not fit with who we are. Our sinfulness is, of course, a problem, but it is a problem that God addresses. God reaches out to self-deluded sinners, healing, among other things, our ability to know him. God rescues ignorant sinners, showing us his glory, "the glory as of a father's only son, full of grace and truth" (John 1:14). Glory has invited us to ask, to search, and to knock, and has promised that "everyone who asks receives, and everyone who searches finds, and for everyone who knocks, the door will be opened" (Matt. 7:8).

The Doctrine of Revelation

God is good and reveals himself to us. It would not, hypothetically, have to work like this. We could imagine a god who would deny us knowledge of divine things, who would leave us in the dark, who would have no interest in a relationship with us, the kind of relationship that requires knowing and being known. We could imagine a deceptive god, an obscuring deity who would not care about our ignorance. This is not the God Christians worship. Our God is a communicator. Our God is a revealer. We seek to know and can know God with confidence, a confidence that rests on God and not on ourselves.

Theologians distinguish between two types of divine revelation: general revelation and special revelation. **General revelation** typically refers to God's self-disclosure in creation and the human conscience. Psalm 19 points to this type of revelation: the "heavens are telling the glory of God, and the firmament proclaims his handiwork." Even though this revelation is not audible— "there is no speech, nor are there words"— creation's praise still "goes out through all the earth," and so everyone has access to it (Ps. 19:1, 3–4). Paul echoes this theme in Romans when he talks about how God's "eternal power and divine nature, invisible though they are, have been understood and seen through the things he has made." This revelation is made "plain" to all people, "because God has shown it to them" (Rom. 1:19–20). Paul also talks about how the human conscience "bears witness" to God's law to the extent that even gentiles "do instinctively what the law requires" (2:14–15).

General revelation is contrasted with **special revelation**, which refers to God's specific self-revelation in the history of Israel, the incarnation of Jesus Christ, and Scripture. The key distinction between general and special revelation is that special revelation is not available to everyone automatically; rather, it is revealed in a unique event as something new. Often special revelation is described as the "Word of God,"

Key Scripture

We declare to you what was from the beginning, what we have heard, what we have seen with our eyes, what we have looked at and touched with our hands, concerning the word of life—this life was revealed, and we have seen it and testify to it, and declare to you the eternal life that was with the Father and was revealed to us—we declare to you what we have seen and heard so that you also may have fellowship with us; and truly our fellowship is with the Father and with his Son Jesus Christ. We are writing these things so that our joy may be complete.

This is the message we have heard from him and proclaim to you, that God is light and in him there is no darkness at all. If we say that we have fellowship with him while we are walking in darkness, we lie and do not do what is true; but if we walk in the light as he himself is in the light, we have fellowship with one another, and the blood of Jesus his Son cleanses us from all sin. (1 John 1:1–7)

---

which can refer to Jesus Christ, the Bible, or even to a prophetic or proclaimed word that witnesses to Christ and reflects the truth of Scripture.

The Relationship between General and Special Revelation

Most theologians affirm the existence of these two categories of revelation. There are disagreements, however, about the nature of the relationship between them. Where should we begin when seeking knowledge of God, and what status does general revelation have in relationship to special revelation? Theological positions on these questions can be grouped, loosely, into four possible categories: (1) general revelation takes priority; (2) special revelation takes priority; (3) there is ongoing continuity between the two types of revelation; (4) sin has veiled the continuity between the two, but God, the revealer, can lift the veil. Descriptions of each position, along with the issues at stake, follow.

The Primacy of General Revelation

At one end of the spectrum are those who defend the primacy of general revelation over special revelation. Eighteenth-century Deists and many modern thinkers fit within this position, holding that special revelation can be accepted only when it corresponds to what can be known by reflection upon the evidence given in general revelation. This means that a biblical teaching that does not match up to empirical observation and rational reflection must be reinterpreted or dismissed. The tendency to dismiss the biblical witness makes this view controversial. Evangelicals and other traditional theologians sharply criticize this view, believing that it offers a constricted view of God's freedom, undermines the authority of Scripture, and tends to make human reason the arbiter of what must be true about God. Even so, the assumptions undergirding this view remain influential, and theologians who speak from this position often do so from a desire to be able to speak in the public sphere. General revelation, the thinking goes, is available to all and so might be accepted in a public debate where Christian special revelation, which is only accepted as authoritative by Christians, may not get a public hearing. A theology drawn from general revelation is known as a **natural theology**, because its evidence comes from nature. Debates about the role of general and special revelation in theology are sometimes framed as debates about the possibility of doing natural theology.

The Primacy of Special Revelation

At the other end of the spectrum is the claim that special revelation should have primacy over general revelation, because general revelation does not give us any valid knowledge of God at all. Swiss theologian Karl Barth (1886–1968) is a well-known proponent of this position. His view developed, in part, as a reaction against Christians who defended questionable theological views on the basis of affirmations grounded in general revelation. Barth found the most damaging example among those who embraced the Reich Church, the official church of the German state, during the rule of the Nazi Party in the 1930s and 1940s. The Reich Church argued that God had established a certain order within creation that corresponded to Nazi teachings. This interpretation of general revelation allowed many to support Nazi policies as Christian. Barth rejected natural theology because he recognized the deep influence of sin on all human beings, and Barth's warning raises suspicions about all that we find "natural."

Barth spoke against allowing any knowledge acquired through general revelation to influence theology. He argued that our minds are twisted and destroyed by sin, and as a result, we do not retain an ability to accurately discern God's revelation in creation or our own consciences. For Barth, the *only* reliable and trustworthy revelation of God is found in the person of Jesus Christ revealed in Scripture. For all practical purposes, then, general revelation should have *no* role in theology, because it leads only to "abstract speculation concerning a something that is not identical with the revelation of God in Jesus Christ."[2] Scripture alone serves as a reliable source for our knowledge of God.

Barth's view has been a powerful force in theology since his time, reminding us that what we think of as "natural" or an appeal to conscience may in fact be distorted by sin. Barth's voice warns us that we may well be supporting what we want instead of what God wants. This is a warning we do well to take seriously, and while it is a harsh warning, it is also full of grace and goodness because it is meant to protect against the kind of sinful delusion and idolatry of power that so often hurt those who are weak. By giving strict primacy to special revelation, Barth's view suggests strong safeguards against human hubris and self-righteousness, and it forces Christians to grapple with the particularity of God's revelation in history. Many theologians welcome Barth's warning but would not want to take it as far as Barth does. If we truly reject all general revelation, then we may well undermine our ability to connect the truth of the Christian faith with anything or anyone outside the faith. If we reject all general revelation, then we will dismiss truth and beauty as found in the arts and sciences. Few Christians are willing to dismiss all insight from philosophy, poetry, science, and culture, and few are willing to deny that people who have never heard the Scriptures nonetheless recognize the existence of a creator and have a sense of good and evil. There are also many moments in Scripture that affirm God's revelation in creation, including Psalm 19 and Romans 1,

2. Karl Barth, "No! Answer to Emil Brunner," in *Natural Theology*, ed. John Baillie (London: Centenary, 1951), 75.

mentioned above. It is difficult to make sense of these passages if one follows Barth in a complete rejection of general revelation. For these reasons, many Christians look for a middle ground that accounts for both general and special revelation without discounting one or the other. Theologians occupying this middle ground can be grouped into one of two positions; the first is typically favored by Roman Catholics, the second by Protestants.

Ongoing Continuity between General and Special Revelation

One can picture both kinds of revelation in a relationship of **ongoing continuity**. General revelation remains an important and valid source of divine revelation, even under the condition of sin, because human sin does not cancel out God's "enduring witness to Himself in created realities."[3] This general revelation only lets us know *some* things about God, such as that God exists, but it does not let us know other things, such as that Jesus is God. Even though general revelation remains necessary and useful, it has to be supplemented by the fuller knowledge of special revelation. The claim that "grace does not destroy but supports and perfects nature"[4] affirms this idea. Nature—all that we may know through general revelation—is not opposed to grace. Both are the work of the same God. Special revelation does not replace general revelation but builds upon it. This view is similar to Barth's view in that it affirms that special revelation is necessary to come to full knowledge of God; it is different from Barth's view, however, because it holds that general revelation provides an ongoing source of divine revelation that is useful for Christian life even after sin.

In addition to providing a way to account for biblical passages such as Psalm 19 and Romans 1, there are two advantages to this view. First, it enables a strong **apologetics**, which is the rational defense of the Christian faith to those who are not believers. Since every human has access to the same general revelation in creation, it can be used as a shared starting point for conversation. Although the validity of such arguments is often questioned, the lasting influence of rational proofs for God's existence from such figures as Anselm and Thomas Aquinas illustrates the ongoing relevance of using God's revelation in creation to defend the Christian faith. This revelation also provides a point of connection between Christians and

3. Vatican II, *Dogmatic Constitution on Divine Revelation*, 1.3.
4. Thomas Aquinas, *Summa Theologica*, trans. Fathers of the English Dominican Province (Allen, TX: Christian Classics, 1948), I.1.8.

nonbelievers that can become a basis for sharing the gospel. Christians can meet others "where they are" by starting with general revelation. The second advantage centers upon the public benefit of being able to appeal to God's revelation in creation. Since this view affirms the ongoing validity of knowledge of God obtained through creation, it establishes a common basis for dialogue between Christians and non-Christians about issues of truth and morality. This explains why Catholic theologians often appeal to **natural law**, the idea that God built a moral framework into creation itself. Since this law can be discerned by reflecting upon general revelation, Christians can use it as a basis for partnering with non-Christians for the "common good." Such work plays an important part in establishing international law and standards of justice.

Unveiled Continuity

Despite these advantages, many Christians worry that viewing general and special revelation in unproblematic ongoing continuity fails to account for the vast reality of human sin. The fall has affected our human ability to read general revelation accurately, to see the truth of God that is there. What is more, the fall has affected nature itself, and so nature does not provide a pure vision of God's will. If we are to learn from nature, we will need ways to begin to discern where sin is at work, to separate God's good creative will from all that is fallen and broken. These concerns lead many Protestant thinkers to envision the relationship between general and special revelation as one of **unveiled continuity**. Both sorts of revelation are the truth about God, and both are continuous with one another, but we are unable to see this until God pulls back the veil that has clouded nature. Because of the damaging effects of sin, God's revelation in creation becomes clear when viewed through the corrective lens of special revelation. Calvin imagines Scripture as a pair of spectacles that allows us to see nature properly.

> Just as old or bleary-eyed men and those with weak vision, if you thrust before them a most beautiful volume, even if they recognize it to be some sort of writing, yet can scarcely construe two words, but with the aid of spectacles will begin to read distinctly; so Scripture, gathering up the otherwise confused knowledge of God in our minds, having dispersed our dullness, clearly shows us the truth of God.[5]

5. Calvin, *Institutes*, 1.6.1.

Notice that Calvin's image does not deny the goodness or value of general revelation, but it does recognize the effects of sin on our ability to know God. Sin has made us bleary-eyed, but Scripture lets us see. The relationship between general and special revelation is one of *unveiled* continuity; both are from God, but the grim realities of sin dictate that they must be seen in the proper order. The effects of sin, both on the world and on us as we seek to know the world, must not be underestimated. Only grace can pull back the veil that, under the condition of sin, blinds us to all that God reveals in creation. Calvin affirms general revelation, believing Scripture teaches that God "daily discloses himself" so there is "no spot in the universe wherein you cannot discern at least some sparks of his glory." The problem is not with God's revelation but with our ability to perceive it. Because of sin, we "have not the eyes to see unless they be illumined by the inner revelation of God through faith."[6] Even though God reveals himself to us in creation and our consciences, sin leads us to misinterpret this revelation and distort it into something false. With Scripture as our guide, we can look to general revelation and begin to interpret it correctly by seeing how it fits together with what we have been given in God's special revelation.

This is why Scripture is such a gift for the Christian life. Even though the whole of creation testifies to God, without God's special revelation, we are unable to truly know him. We see this reflected in the biblical writers' own reasons for writing their texts. For example, Luke says that he wrote his gospel "so that you may know the truth" (Luke 1:4), and John explains that he wrote his first epistle "so that you may know that you have eternal life" (1 John 5:13). These biblical writers believe that in order to know God, we will have to recognize the particular way he has revealed himself in history. Only then can we rightly recognize the ways that the entire created order corresponds to and reveals God's plan. God graciously reveals himself in Scripture and does so in ways that address our finitude and our sin.

Inspiration and Illumination of Scripture

Christians use two theological categories to name the Holy Spirit's relationship to Scripture: inspiration and illumination. The term **inspiration** refers to the Spirit's work as the author of the Scriptures, a work the Spirit did

6. Ibid.

in and with the human authors of the biblical texts. The term **illumination** signifies the ways that the Spirit continues to work in and with God's people, as readers of Scripture, to help us understand and be faithful to what we read there. Thus, inspiration names the Spirit's work, in the past, in getting Scripture written. The Spirit is *in* these words, but as theologian Stanley Grenz reminds us, the "Spirit's work within Scripture did not end in the distant past."[7] Illumination names the Spirit's work, in the present, in helping God's people, both individually and as the church, to read Scripture well. The Spirit casts light on (illumines) these words. The Bible, inspired by the Holy Spirit, is God's Word, and the Spirit's illuminating power helps us understand and embody that Word. Grenz describes Scripture as "one aspect of the Spirit's mission of creating and sustaining spiritual life. He both authors and speaks through the Bible, which is ultimately the Spirit's book. By means of Scripture he bears witness to Jesus Christ, guides the lives of believers, and exercises authority in the church."[8]

The authority of Scripture rests in its author, God the Holy Spirit. There are many theories about the *means* of the Spirit's work of inspiration. We can exclude a pair of problematic alternatives. Given the kind of text that Scripture is and the kind of Spirit we know, it cannot be the case that the Spirit inspired the words of the Bible through simple dictation. The Christian Scriptures are a complex collection of texts with human authors from various centuries, locations, and perspectives. When we read the Bible, we see that the Spirit, in inspiring these texts, did not erase or smooth over these differences between the human authors. For instance, the four Gospels, all inspired by the one Holy Spirit, reflect the different situations and community needs into which each of their four human authors wrote. The Spirit did not give us one gospel, by dictation. The Spirit's work of inspiration preserves and honors the four voices of the four evangelists, all of whom tell the one story of Jesus. God works in and with human artistry and diversity. Without understanding the exact means of inspiration, we can exclude wooden theories that would erase the human authors of Scripture.

On the other side of the spectrum, we should also exclude overly loose ideas of what it means to acknowledge the Spirit as the author of these words. In everyday conversation, we may use the word *inspiration* to

---

7. Stanley Grenz, *Theology for the Community of God* (Grand Rapids: Eerdmans, 1994), 382.
8. Ibid., 379.

The Biblical Narrative

The Christian theological tradition emphasizes the unity of Scripture. The whole canon is one book, and the Old and New Testaments must always be read together. One way to think of that unity is to look at Scripture's narrative unity, the way that it tells one story that begins with creation in the book of Genesis and ends with the final defeat of sin and death in the new creation of the book of Revelation. One way that Christians think about this narrative unity is to read Scripture as a story with four big movements:

1. Creation, in which we see God's original good intention and purpose
2. Fall, in which sin and death enter the world
3. Redemption, in which God's work in Israel is fulfilled in Christ the Lord, who brings salvation and healing
4. Glory, in which God's final good intentions and purposes are worked out for all of creation

These four major points in the plotline of Scripture show us a great deal about God and ourselves, and offer us an entryway into the story of Scripture, which becomes our story. Theologian Robert Jenson puts it well: "Not only is Scripture within the church, but we, the church, are within Scripture—that is, our common life is located *inside* the story Scripture tells."[a]

a. Robert W. Jenson, "Scripture's Authority in the Church," in *The Art of Reading Scripture*, ed. Ellen F. Davis and Richard B. Hays (Grand Rapids: Eerdmans, 2003), 30.

---

indicate a very weak connection between two people or ideas, but the Spirit's role as inspirer of Scripture should *not* be understood in such distant terms. While the Spirit has worked in and with the diverse human authors of Scripture, the canonical Scriptures exhibit a deep unity, which is the result of their common author in the Spirit and their common testimony to the Triune God. What is more, when we recognize the Scriptures as the Word of God, we are recognizing a reliable connection between these texts and the God whom we meet and know there. The Spirit's inspiring work is strong and true work, and it is work that—like other work we have seen the Spirit do—extends into history, particularity, and materiality. The Spirit's role in inspiring Scripture is not limited to the tone or theme of the text, but it extends to the words themselves. The phrase "verbal inspiration" gets at this idea. More, the Spirit is the inspirer of all of Scripture; inspiration is not limited to just some bits of the text. The phrase "plenary inspiration" is used to make this claim. The whole Bible,

Translation as a Key Aspect of the Doctrine of Scripture

Gambian theologian Lamin Sanneh (b. 1942) sees translation as central to understanding the doctrine of Scripture.

> Being the original Scripture of the Christian movement, the New Testament Gospels are a translated version of the message of Jesus, and that means Christianity is a translated religion without a revealed language. The issue is not whether Christians translated their Scripture well or willingly, but that without translation there would be no Christianity or Christians. Translation is the church's birthmark as well as its missionary benchmark: the church would be unrecognizable without it. . . . The missionary environment of the early church made translation and the accompanying interpretation natural and necessary. Mission in that sense was liberation, just as rejecting it was regressive. The general rule that people had a right to understand what they were being taught was matched by the view that there was nothing God wanted to say that could not be said in simple everyday language. God would not confound people about the truth, and that made the language of religion compatible with ordinary human understanding.[a]

Sanneh draws an interesting comparison between Muslim and Christian doctrines of Scripture. Islam understands the Qur'an as having been dictated in Arabic to the prophet Mohammed, and it must be in Arabic to be Scripture. Translations are not seen as Scripture but as paraphrases. For Christians, translations *are* still the Word of God. While it is informative to study the original languages, Christians still believe that we hear God's Word when we hear Scripture read in whatever language we speak. Sanneh reflects on the beauties of a doctrine of Scripture that truly belongs to the entire world and that meets people in the particularities of language and culture.

a. Lamin Sanneh, *Whose Religion Is Christianity? The Gospel beyond the West* (Grand Rapids: Eerdmans, 2003), 97.

from Genesis all the way through Revelation, is the Spirit's work. Just as we should not understand inspiration as a wooden, mechanistic process, neither should we see it as a loose, distant process. To put the same idea positively, the Spirit's work in inspiring the Scriptures is personal, cooperative, intimate, and particular.

The importance of Scripture does not stop with inspiration. We cannot just read these words. They will be useless to us without understanding. All Christians share the Holy Scriptures, and in many cases we share understanding of those Scriptures. Core doctrines like that of the Trinity or the identity of Christ rest on shared ecumenical interpretation of Scripture. Christians agree—across time, space, and culture—that the doctrine of the Trinity is a good interpretation of the biblical texts. One can make other claims, and one can find proof texts that suggest other understandings of who God is. To see that the God of Scripture is the Triune God requires sustained reading of the whole of the Bible. One verse plucked from here or there will not do. We have to read the whole story to see that the doctrine of the Trinity is biblical (more on this in the next chapter).

Christians share wide agreement on important principles for seeking understanding and interpretation of Scripture:

Read the whole book.
Seek to understand confusing passages in light of other parts of Scripture.
Listen to the interpretations of others who know the Lord.
Pray for the Spirit to cast light on the text.

The doctrine of illumination and the consensus that the Spirit works in readers of Scripture do not gloss over the difficulties and differences in biblical interpretation, but those difficulties do not stop the Spirit from working. The Spirit's illuminating power works in individuals and in the whole body of Christ. It works across time and space, across borders and centuries, because all time and space belongs to the Spirit. Illumination glorifies the Father and the Son, for such is the nature of the Spirit. It honors and deepens those who seek to know the Scriptures more and more. The Spirit's illuminating power shines forth, not just in helping us to understand the Bible, but also in transforming us into living witnesses to the truth that we read there, people who begin to look like Christ, to "bear the image of the man of heaven" (1 Cor. 15:49). Scripture is illuminated when the Spirit shapes people who have been disciplined and transformed by the Word, who live its truth in everyday life. It is one thing to understand that Jesus is Lord; it is quite another thing—one that tends to illumine Scripture more brightly—to encounter people whose lives embody that truth. The task of biblical interpretation, called **hermeneutics**, is complex, but it is full of rewards for those who will dig in deep.

Christians often connect the doctrine of inspiration to the words of 2 Timothy, in which Paul urges Timothy to live a godly life and to continue in the faith, reminding him "how from childhood you have known the sacred writings that are able to instruct you for salvation through faith in Christ Jesus. All scripture is inspired by God and is useful for teaching, for reproof, for correction, and for training in righteousness, so that everyone who belongs to God may be proficient, equipped for every good work" (3:15–17). Why is Paul confident that Scripture will be able to work like this in Timothy's life? The answer is that it is "totally 'God breathed,' that is, it is completely of divine origin."[9] New Testament scholar Gordon Fee identifies Paul's confidence in Scripture here as part of Paul's Jewish faith, "which understands the Old Testament as the writings of the 'prophets' (including Moses) and thus links those writings with the Spirit, the acknowledged source of prophetic inspiration."[10] Paul and Timothy, of course, knew the Scriptures as the Jewish Scriptures, the Christian Old Testament, but by extension Christians have always included the New Testament writings in that confidence, recognizing these words, too, as the Word of God. Confidence in Scripture and confidence in the Holy Spirit should go hand in hand, and this double confidence opens for us, as the people of God, the promise and possibility of wisdom and of intimacy with God.

Prayer for Illumination

Many worship traditions use a prayer for the Spirit's work of illumination before the Scriptures are read.

> Living God,
> help us so to hear your holy Word
> that we may truly understand;
> that, understanding, we may believe
> and believing,
> we may follow in all faithfulness and obedience,
> seeking your honor and glory in all that we do;
> through Christ our Lord. Amen.[a]

a. *The Worship Sourcebook*, Faith Alive Christian Resources and Calvin Institute of Christian Worship, 2nd ed. (Grand Rapids: Baker Books, 2013), 142.

Not Marcionism or Montanism but Canon

The Spirit's work is not limited to the authorship of the Scriptures. We also confess the Spirit's work in bringing the Scriptures to us, and we receive Scripture as a collection of texts. The books that make up the Christian Bible are together known as the **canon**. The word *canon* means "measure," and it refers to the whole of Scripture as the measuring stick for Christian

---

9. Gordon Fee, *God's Empowering Presence: The Holy Spirit in the Letters of Paul* (Peabody, MA: Hendrickson, 1994), 793.
10. Ibid., 794.

faith and life. Christians are sometimes surprised to learn that the process that gave us Scripture—canonization—involved human action and decision, but there is no contradiction in affirming that Scripture is the Word of God and also recognizing that the Holy Spirit worked through human beings to bring us that Word. God often works in surprising ways and is willing to use broken human beings in his work.

The books that make up the canon were received implicitly very early in the history of Christian faith, but it took some time for the contents of the canon to be settled. Around the year 140, a man named **Marcion** pushed for the church to adopt a coherent collection of texts, and he proposed his own list. Marcion's "canon" included the Gospel of Luke, several letters of Paul edited by Marcion, and a complete rejection of the Old Testament. Marcion's rejection of the Old Testament was consistent with his opinion that the character of God shown in the Old Testament could not be reconciled with the character of God revealed in Jesus Christ. The church rejected this opinion. Instead, the church—through the Spirit's power—recognized many more books as part of the canon of Scripture. The Christian canon has a kind of expansiveness that Marcion would have denied it. It includes more voices, more centuries, and more complexities than Marcion would have allowed. This is part of the goodness and richness of Scripture.

Some argue that the canon determined by consensus, though bigger than Marcion's, is still just a list reflecting the biases and opinions of those who had power at the time the New Testament was coming together. The expansiveness of the canon begins to speak against this, but it also helps to see that the early church recognized criteria as helpful to the process of recognizing which texts were inspired by the Spirit and intended by the Spirit to become Christian Scripture. Texts that had three characteristics became canonical: (1) texts written by the apostles, those who had first-hand knowledge of Jesus; (2) texts that were used broadly in the worship of faithful churches; and (3) texts that corresponded with the rule of faith, early shared summaries of Christian doctrine. Thus, the Spirit used these reasons to help guide the process of canonization. The judgment that the canon would include many books from Genesis to Revelation, two testaments and four gospels, means that we as Christians are not free to choose our own texts. The existence of the canon means that we are bound to all the texts included in it. We cannot limit God to only the texts that most easily make sense to us. We have to do the hard work of discerning who God is from the canon as a whole. The canon is expansive, but it also provides boundaries for the Christian life.

The canon of Scripture is one of the first and most universally agreed upon teachings of the Christian faith. Early Christianity emerged out of the heritage of early Judaism; it was natural that the church would continue to recognize the Jewish Scriptures as sacred. The God whom we meet in Jesus Christ is the same God we meet in the Old Testament. It was also natural that, given the new things God had done and was doing through Jesus Christ, people who knew Jesus and loved him, whose lives were changed by him, would write about him. Some of these writings would eventually be recognized as Christian Scripture and would become the New Testament. It made sense to the ancient church—as it does to most Christians in the present day—to grant special authority to the events and writings that came from Jesus's own time. Writings from apostles—those who knew Jesus in person and could give reliable testimony—were thus received as authoritative.

The **Montanist controversy** may be one catalyst that moved the Christian church toward the "closed" canon of Scripture that we know as the Old and New Testaments. The controversy swirled around the ecstatic prophecies of Montanus, Maximilla, and Prisca. Montanists claimed to speak for the Holy Spirit, raising questions about the relative authority of the written Scriptures versus new claims to truth.[11] Historian Margaret Miles explains that Montanism rejected "the view that the early days of Christianity were normative."[12] In rejecting Montanism as a heresy, the church was pointing to the authoritative status of the events of Jesus's life, death, and resurrection recounted in apostolic writings of disciples who were "eyewitnesses" of Jesus's "majesty" (2 Pet. 1:16). To claim the authority of the bounded canon over any new revelation is to give special authority to what God did in the years closest to Jesus's lifetime. The closed canon recognizes that God's revelation comes to us in history, in particularity, in time, and in space, and that, when God entered into that history in the person of Jesus Christ, revelation became a person. The closed canon witnesses to Jesus who is revelation in the flesh. The bounded canon prioritizes

---

11. Frances Young, *The Making of the Creeds* (Harrisburg, PA: Trinity Press International, 1991), 50.

12. Margaret R. Miles, *The Word Made Flesh: A History of Christian Thought* (Oxford: Blackwell, 2005), 49.

Jesus. It prioritizes the particulars surrounding his life. The rejection of Montanism, for the early church up to the church today, is not a rejection of the power and inspiration of God the Holy Spirit. It is, instead, always a rejection of false claims made in the Spirit's name. That the canon of Scripture is closed means it is not open to additions from Montanus, or from me, because the Spirit led the church to recognize these writings, and not others, as true testimonies of the faith.

We have already thought about the Spirit as the author of Scripture; it is also important to see the Spirit's work in superintending the process of canonization. The fact that Christians receive the Scriptures as a collection of texts, written by multiple human authors from many centuries and communities, is a testimony to the way the Spirit chooses to work among us. Some people suggest that the process of canonization shows that Scripture is not authoritative. This argument assumes that the facts of human authors and human involvement in assembling the canon must somehow mean that these books are not the Word of God. This position is insensible to the Spirit's characteristic ways of working in the world and with human beings. In a similar vein, some would suggest that rejecting Montanism and excluding postcanonical revelation from the Scriptures is simply a human power play, an imperialistic attempt to shut down dissenting voices. Again, this argument ignores the Spirit's ways of working. The Spirit is the Spirit of truth, and it should not surprise us that the Spirit sorts truth from falsehood. The Spirit is the Spirit of Jesus Christ, and it should not surprise us that the Spirit agrees with and testifies to Jesus. Christian theology does not reject people who claim to know the power of the Holy Spirit working in their lives and even revealing truth to them, but Christian theology will always insist that such testimonies require discernment. Wise discernment recognizes the compelling truth and beauty of the gospel; the centrality of Jesus's life, death, and resurrection; and the work of the Holy Spirit as the author of Scripture. God is true, and God is trustworthy. God does not engage in self-contradiction, and so we can be confident that the same Spirit who inspired the Scriptures and shepherded the process of canonization will, when working in our lives today, do work that is consistent with the Scriptures. The Bible, inspired by God the Spirit, is the primary authority for Christian faith and life and the key to spiritual discernment.

Behind this discussion of canon, there are important differences between Protestant and Catholic understandings of the relationship between

Scripture and church tradition. In the last chapter, I introduced the Protestant doctrine of *sola scriptura* and argued that Scripture must be our first resource for doing theology. Protestants see Scripture as coming, necessarily, before the authority of church and tradition. This is not a denial of the importance of tradition, but it is a judgment claim that we stand in need of an "external Word," a revelatory authority from God that is outside us and able to correct us. Protestant doctrines of Scripture and theological methodologies put Scripture above tradition as a "norming norm." For Catholicism, the **Council of Trent** clarified the relationship between Scripture and tradition for post-Reformation Catholicism. The council rejected the Protestant principle of *sola scriptura* and affirmed that Catholic theology relies on both Scripture and living tradition as interdependent and authoritative sources for theology. The Catholic church "receives and venerates with a feeling of reverence all the books both of the Old and New Testaments, since one God is the author of both; also the traditions, whether they relate to faith or to morals, as having been dictated either orally by Christ or by the Holy Ghost, and preserved in the Catholic church in unbroken succession."[13] In the twentieth century, the Catholic church reaffirmed this understanding of the equal value of Scripture and tradition at the **Second Vatican Council**, where official teaching describes both sacred Scripture and sacred tradition as coming from one source of revelation, the Word

---

Deuterocanonical Books

Many Christians are aware of differences between the accepted biblical canon as understood by Protestants, Roman Catholics, and Eastern Orthodox Christians. During the Protestant Reformation, a growing interest in studying the Bible in the original languages—Greek and Hebrew—drew attention to the fact that a portion of the Old Testament did not exist in Hebrew. The Roman Catholic canon, which includes the books Protestants view as deuterocanonical or apocryphal, was officially proclaimed at the Council of Trent against the Protestant exclusion of these books. These Latin books had long been used as Christian Scripture, but Protestants excluded them from the canon because they were not recognized as Scripture by the Jewish people. Most of the deuterocanonical books were written during the period between the Old and New Testaments, and these books are useful for understanding this time.

---

13. John H. Leith, ed., *Creeds of the Churches: A Reader in Christian Doctrine from the Bible to the Present*, rev. ed. (Richmond: John Knox Press, 1973), 402.

of God: Scripture "as it is consigned to writing under the inspiration of the divine Spirit," and tradition as "the word of God entrusted by Christ the Lord and the Holy Spirit to the Apostles."[14] The truth of tradition is seen as guaranteed through the **succession** of bishops from Peter to the current pope, who guard that tradition "in its full purity, so that led by the light of the Spirit of truth, they may in proclaiming it preserve this word of God faithfully, explain it, and make it more widely known." In Catholic theology, "both Sacred Tradition and Sacred Scripture are to be accepted and venerated with the same sense of loyalty and reverence."[15]

Protestant theologians tend to see this position as an overvaluing of tradition connected to undue optimism about human beings and human institutions. Protestants point to the vast distance in time between the resurrection of Jesus and the present day and to appalling abuses in the church as strong reasons for being far more suspicious of the authority of tradition. Protestant-Catholic differences about the relationship between Scripture and tradition are reflected in explanations of canon formation, for here we see Scripture (the texts of the canon) and tradition (the process of canonization) come together in very complicated ways. Where Catholic explanations point to the authority of the church in canon formation, Protestant explanations point to the texts themselves. Where Catholics see authoritative church tradition proclaiming a canon, Protestants see the church as recognizing the authority already inherent in the Scriptures. Christians were able to recognize that authority, in part, because their faith "had itself been shaped from an early time by many of the same documents which ultimately became canonical."[16] Theologian John Webster expresses a typically Protestant position when he says that "the church's judgment is an act of confession of that which precedes and imposes itself on the church."[17]

Defining and Defending Authority

Christians speaking about the doctrine of Scripture use specific terminology to indicate the authoritative nature of the text. This language is especially

14. *Dogmatic Constitution on Divine Revelation*, 2.9.
15. Ibid.
16. Harry Y. Gamble, *The New Testament Canon: Its Making and Meaning* (Philadelphia: Fortress, 1985), 69.
17. John Webster, *Holy Scripture: A Dogmatic Sketch* (New York: Cambridge University Press, 2003), 62.

important in conversations in evangelicalism in the United States. To claim that Scripture is **inerrant** is to make a strong claim about the truth and reliability of the texts. God does not err, and these texts are the Word of God; therefore, it makes sense to confess the inerrancy of Scripture. Other evangelicals, concerned that the term "inerrancy" suggests standards of historical and scientific precision that were foreign to the contexts in which the biblical authors wrote, prefer to speak of the **infallibility** of Scripture. To claim that Scripture is infallible is to state that Scripture will not fail. God intends Scripture to lead us to salvation and guide us in the Christian life, and it is infallible in this purpose. Both claims of inerrancy and claims of infallibility are statements about the authoritative nature of the Scriptures as the Word of God, and both terms may be seen in doctrinal statements of American institutions and churches. Logically, to confess inerrancy is also to confess infallibility. The way the debate is framed, however, means that the reverse is not always the case, and often a confession of infallibility is specifically intended to be an alternative to inerrancy. Both claims of inerrancy and claims of infallibility are statements of faith, statements about the kind of book given to us by God. Both terms take on particular meaning in twentieth- and twenty-first-century evangelicalism. The term "inerrancy" was not commonly used until the nineteenth century, but as historian Mark Noll notes, "The conviction that God communicates in Scripture a revelation of himself and of his deeds, and that this revelation is entirely truthful, has always been the common belief of most Catholics, most Protestants, most Orthodox, and even most sects of the fringe of Christianity."[18]

Among evangelicals in the United States, there is tension over the use of the words *inerrancy* and *infallibility*. Unfortunately, there is a great deal of misunderstanding between groups of Christians who make these doctrinal claims. Proponents of infallibility worry that the doctrine of inerrancy imposes "a modern standard on an ancient writing,"[19] but most Christians who believe that Scripture is inerrant are sensitive to differences between ancient and modern contexts and insist that it is not an error for Scripture to fit within its own time and place. For example, Carl F. H. Henry states that we cannot think "that modern technological precision in reporting

18. Mark Noll, "A Brief History of Inerrancy, Mostly in America," in *The Proceedings of the Conference on Biblical Inerrancy 1987* (Nashville: Broadman, 1987), 9–10.

19. Roger E. Olson, *The Mosaic of Christian Belief: Twenty Centuries of Unity and Diversity* (Downers Grove, IL: InterVarsity, 2002), 108.

statistics and measurements, that conformity to modern historiographic method in reporting genealogies and other historical data, or that conformity to modern scientific method in reporting cosmological matters, can be expected from the biblical writers."[20] In other words, the doctrine of inerrancy emphasizes the need to evaluate Scripture *on its own terms* rather than according to "standards of truth and error that are alien to its usage or purpose."[21] Mutual incriminations between inerrancy and infallibility camps are not uncommon, but a charitable reading of both doctrinal claims reveals much shared space here. Both are strong claims about the reliability of Scripture, a reliability that comes from God as Scripture's author. Both are statements of faith. That is, I cannot offer "proof" that Scripture is the authoritative text that I believe it is. My confession of biblical authority is a confession of faith, a confession about the kind of God I meet when I read Scripture. As we study Scripture, its truth will not always be immediately obvious, but in faith we continue to seek God's truth, trusting that Scripture is God's chosen means of revelation and that we will see more and more of that truth as we grow in intimacy with God. Theologian Alan Padgett says that "the truth of Scripture is about our relationship with Christ, for a personal truth requires a personal relationship."[22] While we do our best to articulate doctrines that are faithful to the nature of Scripture as God's Word, we finally know the truth of Scripture in relationship with the One to whom it gives testimony.

Practicing the Doctrine of Scripture

The doctrines of revelation and Scripture may be, on the surface, among the easiest doctrinal categories to put into daily practice, because that practice begins with reading and studying God's Word. Christians have long made it a practice to memorize portions of Scripture, to internalize the Word of God so that it becomes part of our very being. We can never be too familiar with the Scriptures, in which there is infinite depth and richness.

20. Carl F. H. Henry, *God, Revelation, and Authority* (Waco, TX: Word, 1979), 4:201.

21. Chicago Statement on Biblical Inerrancy, XIII. The full text of the Chicago Statement is available online at http://library.dts.edu/Pages/TL/Special/ICBI_1.pdf.

22. Alan Padgett, "'I Am the Truth': An Understanding of Truth from Christology for Scripture," in *But Is It True?*, ed. Alan G. Padgett and Patrick R. Keifert (Grand Rapids: Eerdmans, 2006), 111.

Sonnet on the Holy Scriptures

|||||||||||||||||||||||||||||||||||||||||||||||||||||||||||||||||||||||||||||||||||||||||||||||||||||||||||||||||||||||||||||||||

In this sonnet, poet George Herbert (1593–1633) meditates on the "infinite sweetness" of God's Word, which he calls "a mass of strange delights." Similar to Calvin's image of Scripture as spectacles, Herbert writes of Scripture as a lens "that mends the lookers eyes."

> OH Book ! infinite sweetnesse ! let my heart
>   Suck ev'ry letter, and a hony gain,
>   Precious for any grief in any part ;
> To cleare the breast, to mollifie all pain.
>
> Thou art all health, health thriving, till it make
>   A full eternitie : thou art a masse
>   Of strange delights, where we may wish and take.
> Ladies, look here ; this is the thankfull glasse,
>
> That mends the lookers eyes : this is the well
>   That washes what it shows. Who can indeare
>   Thy praise too much ? thou art heav'ns Lidger here,
> Working against the states of death and hell.
>
>   Thou art joyes handsell : heav'n lies flat in thee,
>   Subject to ev'ry mounters bended knee.[a]

a. *The Poetical Works of George Herbert* (New York: D. Appleton, 1857), 71–72.

Biblical scholar Richard Hays, in his study of Paul's use of Scripture from the Old Testament, concludes that "Paul's readings characteristically treat Scripture as a living voice that speaks to the people of God. The Bible for Paul is not just a chronicle of revelation in the past; the words of Scripture sound from the page in the present moment and address the community of believers with authority."[23] So it is for us. We are addressed by Scripture, and the Word of God in Scripture transforms lives. Again, in Hays's words,

> Because readers who discern the true message of Scripture behold the glory of God in Jesus Christ, Paul tells us, they are "changed into his likeness." No reading of Scripture can be legitimate, then, if it fails to shape the readers into a community that embodies the love of God as shown forth

---

23. Richard B. Hays, *Echoes of Scripture in the Letters of Paul* (New Haven: Yale University Press, 1989), 165.

in Christ. This criterion slashes away all frivolous or self-serving readings, all readings that aggrandize the interpreter, all merely clever readings. True interpretation of Scripture leads us into unqualified giving of our lives in service within the community whose vocation is to reenact the obedience of the Son of God who loved us and gave himself for us.[24]

At this second level, the practice of the doctrine of Scripture is one full of challenges. We are fond of "frivolous" and "self-serving readings," and we, as sinners, love readings that "aggrandize the interpreter." Only through the illuminating and sanctifying power of the Holy Spirit may we hope to be freed from such readings, but in God's grace the illuminating Spirit is adept in using the inspired words of Scripture to call us out of our sinful selves and transform us into the image of Christ our Lord. Eugene Peterson reflects, "Reading Holy Scripture is totally physical. . . . It is the practice of the Christian community to cultivate habits of reading that sharpen our perceptions and involve us in getting this word of God formatively within us." "The book is not written to flatter us," Peterson continues, "but to involve us in a reality, God's reality, that doesn't cater to our fantasies of ourselves."[25] When Scripture comes to us, when it addresses us from outside of ourselves, the transformative encounter can be frightening. The Word of God, says the author of Hebrews, "is living and active, sharper than any two-edged sword, piercing until it divides soul from spirit, joints from marrow; it is able to judge the thoughts and intentions of the heart. And before him no creature is hidden, but all are naked and laid bare to the eyes of the one to whom we must render an account" (Heb. 4:12–13). We may be tempted to hide from God and from ourselves, but God's Word is revelatory. If we will put ourselves in its path—reading, listening, meditating—it will bring truth to light and work to make us new.

24. Ibid., 191.
25. Eugene Peterson, *Eat This Book: A Conversation in the Art of Spiritual Reading* (Grand Rapids: Eerdmans, 2006), 61, 64.

3

|||||||||||||||||||||||||||||||||||||||||||||||||||||||||||||||||||

The God We Worship

Doctrine of the Trinity

For thus says the LORD, who created the heavens (he is God!), who formed the
earth and made it (he established it; he did not create it a chaos, he formed
it to be inhabited!): I am the LORD, and there is no other. I did not speak in
secret, in a land of darkness; I did not say to the offspring of Jacob, "Seek
me in chaos." I the LORD speak the truth, I declare what is right. Assemble
yourselves and come together, draw near, you survivors of the nations! They
have no knowledge—those who carry about their wooden idols, and keep
on praying to a god that cannot save.

Isaiah 45:18–20

Isaiah declares a powerful message: there is only one God, and only God
has power to save. There is "no other" Lord besides the true God, revealed
to us in Scripture. Because God speaks the truth to us about who he is,
God's identity is not secret. Worshipers of other gods—false gods—have
a double problem: first, they lack knowledge, and second, their "gods"
cannot save. In Scripture, the deeply practical problem of idolatry crops
up again and again. For sinful human beings, idolatry is a basic feature

of our situation. The human heart, according to John Calvin's diagnosis, is a "factory of idols."[1]

Idolatry has devastating consequences. It makes our thinking "futile" and darkens our "senseless minds" (Rom. 1:21). Idolatry also destroys human lives as we yearn for our false gods and act on that yearning (v. 26). Worshiping false gods shapes people who are "filled with every kind of wickedness, evil, covetousness, malice. Full of envy, murder, strife, deceit, craftiness, they are gossips, slanderers, God-haters, insolent, haughty, boastful, inventors of evil, rebellious toward parents" (v. 29–30). Repeatedly, Scripture warns that we become like the gods we serve; in the assessment of G. K. Beale, "worshippers reflect in their character the ungodly image of what they worship."[2] We are molded into the likeness of our false gods; people who make idols "are like them; so are all who trust in them" (Ps. 115:8). When caught in idolatry, we are without knowledge of God, our lives a mess, pitifully bowing before "gods" powerless to offer salvation. Idolaters are left "foolish, faithless, heartless, ruthless" (Rom. 1:31).

This is the situation God rescues us from in revealing his character and identity to us. Fleeing from idols, we run toward the Triune God, who has shown us his true character as the only God: Father, Son, and Holy Spirit. The doctrine of the Trinity calls us to return to the one true God as it teaches us to speak carefully about who God is. Because it teaches us God's identity and helps us to distinguish the living God from false idols, the doctrine of the Trinity is central to Christian faith. It provides basic teaching about God, letting us know *whom* we worship. The mystery of God's triune nature is revealed to us in Scripture, and this gracious gift is also a practical gift because it enables us to better love and serve God. When we turn away from idols and worship the Triune God, God transforms us in his image, and we become more like him.

One God, Three Persons

The mystery of God's being is God's triunity. The one true God—the only God—exists eternally in three persons, the same three persons we

1. John Calvin, *Institutes of the Christian Religion*, ed. John T. McNeill (Louisville: Westminster John Knox, 1960), 1.11.8.
2. G. K. Beale, *We Become What We Worship: A Biblical Theology of Idolatry* (Downers Grove, IL: IVP Academic, 2008), 240.

see at work when Jesus is baptized in the Jordan River by his cousin John. "Just as he was coming up out of the water," Jesus "saw the heavens torn apart and the Spirit descending like a dove on him. And a voice came from heaven, 'You are my Son, the Beloved; with you I am well pleased'" (Mark 1:10–11). Here, the Father speaks, the Son emerges from the water, and the Spirit descends. All three persons of the Triune God are active in this moment as at every moment. The Father is God. The Son is God. The Holy Spirit is God. And, in total continuity with the Old Testament, there is only one God. The Triune God is the one God of Israel; God did not *become* Trinity at some point in time. Rather, God is eternally Father, Son, and Holy Spirit. If we want to know the truth about God, we will have to turn to the Father, the Son, and the Spirit. We will have to study what the one God—Father, Son, and Holy Spirit—has done throughout history, from creation to today, and we will understand this teaching better if we look at how understanding of the Trinity developed in the early church.

Discerning the Doctrine

In the first centuries after Jesus's resurrection, the church faced transition. Christians needed to make sense of the new things God had done in Jesus Christ in light of the things God had done in centuries past. If what they knew about God in Scripture was true and what they knew about God in Jesus was true, then how could they put the whole picture together? What did they know about God now that Jesus had been raised from the dead? What would it look like to worship Jesus and be faithful to the one true God? How could the work of the Father, Son, and Holy Spirit make sense in light of the revelation that God is one? A foundational text comes from Deuteronomy.

> Hear, O Israel: The Lord is our God, the Lord alone. You shall love the Lord your God with all your heart, and with all your soul, and with all your might. Keep these words that I am commanding you today in your heart. Recite them to your children and talk about them when you are at home and when you are away, when you lie down and when you rise. Bind them as a sign on your hand, fix them as an emblem on your forehead, and write them on the doorposts of your house and on your gates. (Deut. 6:4–9)

Key Scripture

Jesus said to him, "I am the way, and the truth, and the life. No one comes to the Father except through me. If you know me, you will know my Father also. From now on you do know him and have seen him." Philip said to him, "Lord, show us the Father, and we will be satisfied." Jesus said to him, "Have I been with you all this time, Philip, and you still do not know me? Whoever has seen me has seen the Father. How can you say, 'Show us the Father'? Do you not believe that I am in the Father and the Father is in me? The words that I say to you I do not speak on my own; but the Father who dwells in me does his works. Believe me that I am in the Father and the Father is in me; but if you do not, then believe me because of the works themselves. Very truly, I tell you, the one who believes in me will also do the works that I do and, in fact, will do greater works than these, because I am going to the Father. I will do whatever you ask in my name, so that the Father may be glorified in the Son. If in my name you ask me for anything, I will do it. If you love me, you will keep my commandments. And I will ask the Father, and he will give you another Advocate, to be with you forever. This is the Spirit of truth, whom the world cannot receive, because it neither sees him nor knows him. You know him, because he abides with you, and he will be in you. I will not leave you orphaned; I am coming to you. In a little while the world will no longer see me, but you will see me; because I live, you also will live. On that day you will know that I am in my Father, and you in me, and I in you. They who have my commandments and keep them are those who love me; and those who love me will be loved by my Father, and I will love them and reveal myself to them." (John 14:6–21)

Through perennial struggles against idolatry, Israel had learned that there is only one God, "the Lord alone." There are no other gods besides this Lord, and we owe everything—heart, soul, and might—to this God. This truth was so important that it demanded daily practical reminders, reminders like words on doorposts and constant talk about it. The new Christians knew perfectly well, as Jesus also knew, that God is "Lord alone," a jealous God who permits no rivals. They knew this, and now they were worshiping Jesus and calling him "Lord" (Matt. 28:9; Luke 24:52; Heb. 1:6). God's people articulated the doctrine of the Trinity as they sought a way to hold together the truths that (1) there is only one God and (2) Jesus is God, worthy of worship. Historically, these questions focused first on how to think about Jesus, but it became apparent that the church also needed to answer these questions about the Spirit.

Trinitarian Heresies

It took theological work and careful reading of Scripture to learn that God is Trinity. Many ways of understanding Jesus, his Father, and the Spirit were proposed, and the church rejected several of these attempts at understanding as inadequate ways of identifying the God of Scripture. Those untrue ways of speaking about God are now recognized as heresies. Understanding these heresies will help us see why the doctrine of the Trinity is the best way to describe the God revealed to us in Scripture. Our next task, then, is to outline several heretical attempts to explain the reality of Father, Son, and Spirit. All three heresies—adoptionism, modalism, and Arianism—emphasize the oneness of God, and all three wish to reject idolatry. All rest on the same mistaken assumption: they take for granted that recognizing Jesus and the Spirit as God would undermine the oneness of God. They accept that the Father is God, but they wrongly assume that Jesus and the Spirit cannot actually be divine.

Adoptionism

Adoptionism is a form of **subordinationism**, which would make Jesus and the Spirit less than the Father. The **adoptionist** understanding of Jesus makes him into an ordinary human being who merited adoption by God, and it was his "moral progress that won for him the title Son of God."[3] Whatever special status this adoptionist Jesus has is not because he is truly divine but because God conferred it on him on the basis of his obedient life. This Jesus is not divine by nature; instead, he has been promoted to the level of sonship. At the core, adoptionism tried to defend the oneness of God by denying that Jesus is God. It eliminates him as a rival to the Father.

Although its impulse may be to work *against* idolatry, adoptionism fails because it ultimately leaves the Christian church *in* idolatry. Because the adoptionist Jesus is not truly God, anyone who worships him is caught up in the catastrophe of idolatry. Those who turn to the adoptionist Jesus as Lord and savior are left with nothing. Another human being, a creature like us, cannot save us. We need God to save us, and this need points us to another grave failure of adoptionism. It distorts the good news of salvation, making it into a story about rewards earned in exchange for a life well

---

3. Leo Donald Davis, *The First Seven Ecumenical Councils (325–787): Their History and Theology* (Collegeville, MN: Liturgical Press, 1983), 41.

lived. If Jesus is just one of us but lived in perfect obedience to the Father and so was adopted as God's son, it would seem that the rest of us are called to do the same. The good news of Jesus as savior is replaced with impossible demands for us to imitate a good man. No human example, no matter how good or wise, can offer salvation. In adoptionism, the good news becomes brutal news; the gracious hope of Christ the savior is replaced with a taunting offer of false hope, hope that can never be achieved. Adoptionism also creates problems for our understanding of revelation. When the adoptionist Jesus speaks, we hear a human word and not the Word of God. Christologies that, like adoptionism, deny Jesus's divinity also deny that he is the revealed truth of God.

Modalism

Also an attempt to protect the oneness of God, the heresy of **modalism** (sometimes called Sabellianism) is subtler than adoptionism. Instead of simply denying that Jesus is God, modalism would understand Father, Son, and Holy Spirit as three modes in which the one God works in the world. For modalists, Father, Son, and Spirit are not the deepest truth about God. Instead, they are like three masks God wears as he goes to work in the world. The real truth about God, for the modalist, is hiding behind those masks. The modalist God's work is understood as something like acting in a play. Imagine that an actor puts on a show about three characters. The same actor will play all three roles, switching between three masks whenever it is time to play another part. Imagine that after the curtain goes down, someone introduces us to the actor. We might praise the actor's talent or comment on the skill required to play three different roles. We would not, however, assume that the actor is the same as the three characters in the show, nor would we have any basis for thinking that we know this actor personally. The fact that we saw the actor portray three characters does not tell us the truth about who the person is.

This analogy helps us to see the problems with the modalist account of God. The modalist God appears to us as three but in reality is only one. In trying to protect the oneness of God, modalism denies that Father, Son, and Holy Spirit are the truth about who God is. In so doing, modalism relinquishes the beauty and the seriousness of all that Father, Son, and Spirit do in the world. If the Jesus who died on the cross was not the true

God but only a mode God was working in, if the crucifixion is only an act God was putting on, it just matters far less than if the crucified Jesus is the true God telling the truth about God's love for the whole world. If Jesus is a mode God works in, then his death makes it look like God loves us. If Jesus is truly God, then his death is the truth that God loves us. Modalism cannot offer an explanation for the relationships between the Father, Son, and Spirit, or even for moments in Scripture where more than one of the three is present at the same time. Modalism cannot make it clear why these three modes are special or different from other possible modes God might choose to work in. Might the modalist God act in a fourth or fifth mode? Finally, because the modalist God is not truly three, modalism leads to the problematic idea of **patripassianism**, or the suggestion that God the Father died on the cross. Either the cross is a ruse, or modalism would have the eternal God die.

Despite its intentions, modalism, like adoptionism, is also a form of idolatry. Because the modalist Father, Son, and Spirit are roles God plays in the world and not the real truth about God's character and identity, anyone who worships them is still caught in the idolater's trap. Worshiping a role instead of the true God still leaves us without true knowledge of God or a true relationship with the only One who is worthy of worship and has the power to save. In modalism, the good news becomes false news; the truth of God's love for the world becomes a publicity campaign. Instead of the Father loving us enough to send the Son to die on a cross and instead of the Son's true and willing sacrifice, the modalist God plays the role of a man being crucified. Instead of conquering death as Jesus is raised from the grave by the power of the Holy Spirit, the modalist God puts on a play for us in which it seems that death is defeated. Modalism puts a barrier between the truth about God and the magnificent things God has done in the world.

Arianism

In another attempt to protect the oneness of God, the heresy of **Arianism** taught that Jesus was God's first and greatest creature. Arius (d. 336) taught a form of subordinationism that was far more philosophically sophisticated than adoptionism. Recognizing that one of the most basic truths about God is his uncreated nature, Arius was willing to grant that Jesus was "like"

God in other respects. In fact, Arianism grants to Jesus as much as it thinks it can without affirming that he is eternal and uncreated. In this, Arianism goes far beyond adoptionism in the godlike status it gives to Jesus. Where adoptionism cannot explain the Word made flesh (John 1:14), Arianism tries to deal with this and other texts that speak of the greatness of Jesus by interpreting them in a subordinationist way. Arianism would offer a Jesus who was created before time began, but who, like other creatures, still had a beginning. Arian teaching about Jesus was summed up in the slogan, "There was when he was not." Though Arianism granted Jesus a godlike status, it denied that he is eternal, as only God can be. It insisted that if we could go back to the very beginning, before creation, we would arrive at the place where Jesus was not yet in existence. We would meet the "was" in which Jesus "was not." The Arian Jesus, however grand a creature he is made out to be, is not uncreated and eternal and so is not truly God.

At this point, a bit of Greek terminology was important to the debate about whether Jesus is truly God. The word *ousia* means "substance" or "essence"; it describes the very heart of something. God's substance or essence, we could say, is God-ness or the divine nature. The Arian party allowed that Jesus is the most perfect of creatures but insisted that Jesus could not share the *ousia* of the Father. Instead, for the Arians, Jesus was "like" God in essence, or *homoiousios* with the Father. The Arians maintained that Jesus's divinity is a gift he receives from the Father. The Arian Jesus is not God in his own right but is semidivine, eternally subordinate to the Father. The Arians understood the Spirit as eternally subordinate as well.

It is easy enough to use Scripture to proof text in favor of an Arian position. There are, after all, many subordinationist moments in the New Testament, moments where Jesus appears to be somehow less than the Father. Arians used texts like John 4:34, in which Jesus says, "My food is to do the will of him who sent me and to complete his work," to try to prove their point that Jesus could not really be God in the fullest sense. This moment in the history of Christian thought shows how important it is to read Scripture as a whole when trying to understand doctrine. Isolated verses may look like proof that the Arians had it right, but a reading of the whole Bible, from Genesis to Revelation, reveals the Arian claim as contrary to Scripture. One does not even have to leave the Gospel of John to see that a text like the one above has to be read in relation to those that testify to Jesus as God, texts like John 10:30, in which Jesus says, "The Father and I are one," or John 20:28, where Thomas cries out to the risen Jesus, "My Lord and my God!" Beyond verse and counter verse, though, the logic of the canon directs us to a Jesus who is God. For example, historian John Behr describes how the "divinity of Jesus is expressed in the New Testament primarily by ascribing to him all the activities and properties that, in Scripture [the Old Testament], belong to God alone."[4] Behr, here, is reading the deep unity between the Testaments and recognizing the portrait of Jesus in the New Testament as a portrait of none other than God. Subordinationist texts must be read in this light, as descriptive of the earthly relationship between the incarnate Jesus and his Father and not of the eternal relationships that are the very life of God.

Though it goes beyond adoptionism in what it would say about Jesus, Arianism fails just as adoptionism fails. Having made Jesus into a creature, Arian logic cannot simultaneously affirm the clear prohibition against idolatry that is worked through the whole Bible alongside the clear recommendation of Scripture that we, like the disciples and the angels, worship Jesus Christ (Matt. 14:33; 28:9; Heb. 1:6). If Arius were right about Jesus, then to worship Jesus would be idolatry. Since the Arian Jesus is not truly God, he does not have true knowledge of the Father, and he cannot truly reveal the Father to us. It does not matter how great or perfect the creature is; we need God and not a creature. Michael Thompson puts it this way: "The Son cannot be a bridge between God and humanity if the bridge doesn't fully reach to both ends."[5] In making Jesus less than God, Arianism also fails to take the essence of the Father seriously. If there was a time—even before time—when Jesus, the Son, had no existence, then there was also a time when the Father did not exist *as* the Father. God cannot *be*, in truth, the Father without the Son, because without the Son there is no father-son relationship in the life of God. Arianism thus distorts the Father of Jesus Christ into an idol by implying that the Father is a different God than the God we meet in Scripture, the God who is the Father of the Lord Jesus Christ.

4. John Behr, *The Way to Nicaea*, vol. 1 of *Formation of Christian Theology* (Crestwood, NY: St. Vladimir's Seminary Press, 2001), 57.
5. Michael Thompson, "Arianism: Is Jesus Christ Divine and Eternal or Was He Created?," in *Heresies and How to Avoid Them*, ed. Ben Quash and Michael Ward (Peabody, MA: Hendrickson, 2007), 20.

Nicene Trinitarian Doctrine

In the year 325, bishops from across the Christian church gathered at the ecumenical Council of Nicaea to confront the Arian challenge, and the council affirmed that Jesus is truly God. Against the Arian suggestion that Jesus is "like" God or *homoiousios* with the Father, Nicaea proclaimed with boldness that Jesus shares the divinity of the Father. God the Son is *homoousios* with God the Father, the same in essence or substance. The tiny *iota*, the one Greek letter difference between the Arian *homoi* (like) and the orthodox *homo* (same), marks the immeasurable difference between demoting Jesus to creaturely status and confessing that he is truly God. The struggle against Arianism continued, and the insights of the Council of Nicaea were reaffirmed in 381 at the Council of Constantinople. The affirmations of that council are summarized in the words of the Nicene-Constantinopolitan Creed. Usually known just as the **Nicene Creed**, the statement packs a great deal of theology into very few words. Those words distill the truth about God revealed in Scripture into a brief and teachable format, one that helps us know the character and identity of the Triune God.

First, the creed affirms that there is only one God, and it affirms this in full connection to the faith of Israel. The creed emphasizes the oneness of God and excludes the possibility of **tritheism**, the belief that there are three Gods. Far from being contrary to the monotheistic faith of Israel, the affirmation that Jesus and the Spirit truly are God is the only way to maintain that faith after it becomes clear that Jesus is savior. In light of God's revelation in Jesus, the best way to reject idolatry and affirm Israel's faithful confession that God is "Lord alone" is to recognize the mystery of the Trinity. This is why theologian Janet Soskice is right to make the counterintuitive claim that the doctrine of the Trinity is "the means by which Christianity stays closest to its Jewish roots."[6] If Jesus were anyone other than the true God, Christians would, indeed, have turned their backs on Judaism when they moved to bow before him. The one God confessed in the Nicene Creed is the same God we know from reading about creation in Genesis, the deliverance of Israel from Egypt in Exodus, or the commands of justice and obedience in the Prophets.

6. Janet Martin Soskice, "Biblical Trinitarianism," in *Heresies and How to Avoid Them*, ed. Ben Quash and Michael Ward (Grand Rapids: Baker Academic, 2007), 128.

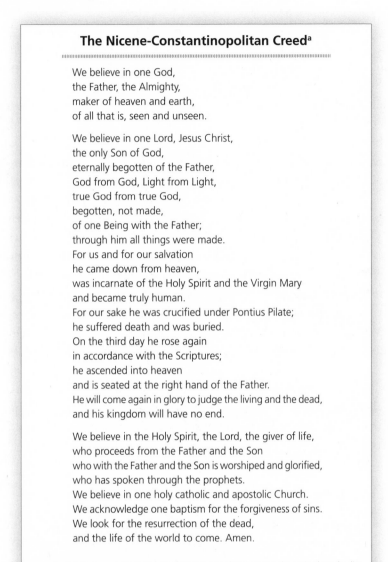

The Nicene-Constantinopolitan Creed[a]

We believe in one God,
the Father, the Almighty,
maker of heaven and earth,
of all that is, seen and unseen.

We believe in one Lord, Jesus Christ,
the only Son of God,
eternally begotten of the Father,
God from God, Light from Light,
true God from true God,
begotten, not made,
of one Being with the Father;
through him all things were made.
For us and for our salvation
he came down from heaven,
was incarnate of the Holy Spirit and the Virgin Mary
and became truly human.
For our sake he was crucified under Pontius Pilate;
he suffered death and was buried.
On the third day he rose again
in accordance with the Scriptures;
he ascended into heaven
and is seated at the right hand of the Father.
He will come again in glory to judge the living and the dead,
and his kingdom will have no end.

We believe in the Holy Spirit, the Lord, the giver of life,
who proceeds from the Father and the Son
who with the Father and the Son is worshiped and glorified,
who has spoken through the prophets.
We believe in one holy catholic and apostolic Church.
We acknowledge one baptism for the forgiveness of sins.
We look for the resurrection of the dead,
and the life of the world to come. Amen.

a. English Language Liturgical Commission translation. From the United Methodist Hymnal (Nashville: The United Methodist Publishing House, 1989), 880.

The confession that Jesus is *homoousios* with the Father is made against subordinationism. Jesus Christ is fully God, "Light from Light, true God from true God." We are able to know this Jesus by locating him in historical events. The Son is the man who was crucified under Pontius Pilate. We also confess that the Spirit is God, "the Lord, the giver of life." The Lord

God is "one God"—hear the echo of Deuteronomy—and Jesus and the Spirit, as well as the Father, are rightly called Lord. The creed also affirms, against both subordinationism and modalism, that God *is* relationship. The Son is "begotten" of the Father, and the Spirit "proceeds" from the Father. The loving relationships between Father, Son, and Holy Spirit go right to the heart and essence of God. Father, Son, and Holy Spirit all do the things that God does. All three persons are identified with God's work as Creator: the Father is "maker of heaven and earth," the Son is the one "through [whom] all things were made," and the Spirit is the "giver of life." The creed uses the three names—Father, Son, and Holy Spirit—that are revealed in Scripture and confesses that all three persons are eternal.

As limited human beings, we cannot grasp the fullness of God's triune nature, and no amount of practice with the doctrine can or should unravel the trinitarian mystery. Unfortunately, Christians sometimes suggest that this makes the doctrine of the Trinity meaningless. On the contrary, the doctrine exists to help Christians teach the identity of God, as revealed in Scripture, as faithfully and clearly as possible. We confess that God is Trinity in submission to the logic of what God—Father, Son, and Holy Spirit—has done in Scripture. The doctrine does not erase or explain the paradox of threeness-in-oneness. Instead, it acknowledges that God's oneness does not need protection from us, and it asks us to give up the pride that would claim to know what "must" be true and to rejoice in the goodness of God's unexpected triune life.

Scripture and Language about the Trinity

The confession of the Nicene Creed grew from a process of discernment in which Christians grappled with all that Scripture tells us about God and learned to speak about God in a way that makes sense in light of it. Sometimes people object to theological language because it is not the direct language of Scripture. John Calvin heard the same objection, and he responded by saying that theological terms like "Trinity" and "persons" are used for the purpose of pointing to the truth of Scripture. "Say that in the one essence of God there is a trinity of persons; you will say in one word what Scripture states, and cut short empty talkativeness."[7] The term "Trinity"

7. Calvin, *Institutes* 1.13.5.

James Kombo on the Trinity in African Thought

In chapter 1, we saw reflection from Kenyan theologian James Kombo on the relationship between particular intellectual contexts and doctrine. Here, we see him working out the doctrine of the Trinity using African categories in a way that parallels the Nicene Fathers' use of Greek categories to be faithful to the biblical witness in the language of the creed:

> Careful Christianization of the African concept of God should first fully accept that God is one. The Africans already know that God is one, and that that God is the explanation of the genesis of man and the entire created order. Moreover, God in the African context is not a static substance or essence, and neither is he mere man on an infinitely magnified scale. On the contrary, he is the "Great *Muntu*," a "subject" with the ultimate personality and thus distinct from everyone and everything else. . . . African Christian thought must "Yahweh-ize" the Great *Muntu* and name him in trinitarian terms. This is a significant point of departure that must be deliberately addressed. The African context, as we have noted, knows monotheism, but the idea of God as Trinity is a completely new concept. The beginning of the concept of the Trinity is the Incarnation. The Trinity is the focal point in Christian worship and the concept lays the claim that Jesus Christ is God. This thought is revolutionary to an African worshipper. Because the African knows God by his name, to tell him that Jesus is *Nyame, Leza* or *Nyambe* is similar to telling a Jew that Jesus is Yahweh! It is met with initial shock, surprise, and denial. But this, to be precise, is the scriptural position.[a]

a. James Henry Kombo, *The Doctrine of God in African Christian Thought* (Leiden: Brill, 2007), 235–36.

expresses biblical judgments about God's nature,[8] and the doctrine coheres with Scripture as a whole, and so it is not a teaching that we try to "prove" with some simple list of verses. Instead, the whole of Scripture, from Genesis to Revelation, testifies to the character and identity of the Triune God. We know God as Trinity because we read the New Testament in full continuity with the Old Testament. Certain New Testament passages are key to understanding God's triune nature, but those key passages do not stand alone. Consider these words of Jesus from the Gospel of John:

8. David Yeago, "The New Testament and Nicene Dogma," in *The Theological Interpretation of Scripture: Classic and Contemporary Readings*, ed. Stephen E. Fowl (Malden, MA: Blackwell, 1997), 87–102.

When the Spirit of truth comes, he will guide you into all the truth; for he will not speak on his own, but will speak whatever he hears, and he will declare to you the things that are to come. He will glorify me, because he will take what is mine and declare it to you. All that the Father has is mine. For this reason I said that he will take what is mine and declare it to you. (John 16:13–15)

This text does not describe the fullness of the doctrine of the Trinity, but it does include several of the characteristics of New Testament talk about God that eventually pushed Christians to articulate the doctrine. In these few verses, the Father and the Spirit are named by the Son. It is clear that Father, Spirit, and the speaking Son are closely linked and in very significant relationship with each other. It is clear that the Spirit, as the one who guides us in truth, has immense authority and that "all" the Father has belongs to Jesus. The things that belong to God belong to Father, Son, and Spirit. What is more, the truth the Spirit declares is Jesus's truth. This text and others like it, then, help teach Christians how to speak well about God.

The more practice we have in dwelling with the words of Scripture, the more familiar those words become, the more faithfully we are able to talk about Father, Son, and Spirit. In the Gospel of Matthew, Jesus prays and thanks the Father for making himself known, and then Jesus draws on his own relationship with the Father to talk about how we can know him. "All things have been handed over to me by my Father; and no one knows the Son except the Father, and no one knows the Father except the Son and anyone to whom the Son chooses to reveal him" (Matt. 11:27). Paul tells of the Spirit who searches "the depths of God" (1 Cor. 2:10). In Hebrews, we read that the Son has come to do God's will (Heb. 10:7–10). John's Gospel is flooded with rich language about the Triune God. There, we see that Jesus is the way to the Father (John 14:6) and that to see Jesus is to see the Father. "Believe me," Jesus says, "that I am in the Father and the Father is in me" (v. 11). The things Jesus does reveal the Father to us, and the Father is "glorified in the Son" (v. 13). We are not abandoned when Jesus goes to the Father, because he sends the Spirit who testifies on his behalf (15:26). Jesus makes the Father's name known, and he fills us with the Father's love and his own presence (17:26). Jesus does the Father's work, and he and the Father "are one" (10:30). The doctrine of the Trinity seeks faithfulness to the patterns and judgments about Father, Son, and Spirit reflected in Scripture.

Life as Relationship

As Scripture directs our language about God, it also gives us clues about the relationships between Father, Son, and Holy Spirit. When we recognize that God is Trinity, we see that being in relationship is inseparable from what it means to be God. As Thomas Aquinas (1225–74) puts it, "Relations exist in God really."[9] Thomas is not the sort of thinker who uses a word like "really" lightly. Relationship goes right to the reality of the truth about God, and relations involve "regard of one to another."[10] This means that when we recognize the relationships of Father, Son, and Spirit, we are able to speak about real threeness in God without violating the truth that God is one. Because Father, Son, and Spirit are God, everything that is true of the Father is true of the Son and the Spirit *except* for their particular relationships. Everything that is true of the Father is true of the Son, except that the Father is not the Son. Everything that is true of the Son is true of the Spirit, except that the Son is not the Spirit. This kind of careful language is not finicky hair-splitting; instead, it is our best attempt to speak faithfully about the wonder that God is truly one and truly three.

The trinitarian heresies fail to recognize the relational nature of God in Scripture. For Arians, there was a time when Jesus did not exist, and so the relationship between Father and Son did not exist. The Arian god is not eternally, fundamentally relational. In modalism, God only *seems* to be Father, Son, and Spirit, but there is no relationship at the heart of the divine life. Thomas's insight into biblical trinitarianism is that the eternal life of God is a life of relationship. This helps us to better know the specific nature of God's greatness and glory. It means that God, as a community of abundant love, is complete in his own life. Because God is relationship, God does not need us in order to be in relationship. The New Testament accounts of Jesus's life give us privileged glimpses into God's existence in relationship. When Jesus prays to the Father, for example, we are not reading about an act he was putting on for our sake. We are reading the truth about God. The term **perichoresis**, meaning mutual indwelling, is used in theology to point to the relational nature of God. Father, Son, and Spirit exist in unique relationship, and perichoretic relationship has no

9. Thomas Aquinas, *Summa Theologica*, trans. Fathers of the English Dominican Province (Allen, TX: Christian Classics, 1948), I.28.1.
    10. Ibid., I.28.3.

parallels outside of God. The three persons of the Trinity all dwell in each other. Some theologians talk about perichoresis as the eternal dance of the Triune God. The word hints at both the oneness and the threeness of God. Recognizing this oneness and threeness is part of the joy of knowing the true God. In Calvin's words, "He so proclaims himself the sole God as to offer himself to be contemplated clearly in three persons. Unless we grasp these, only the bare and empty name of God flits about in our brains, to the exclusion of the true God."[11]

Speaking Well of Threeness and Oneness

In summary form, the doctrine of the Trinity is the recognition that God is eternally

One God
In three persons: Father, Son, and Holy Spirit

This language of "persons" is not perfect, and the body of Christ agreed to use it only after a great deal of difficulty. Christians recognized that the term could wrongly imply tritheism or that the persons of the Trinity are just like human persons, but the church agreed to talk about Father, Son, and Spirit as persons because we needed a way to talk about the personal nature of triune relationship. Naming the three as persons does *not* mean that the three are persons in the sense that you and I are persons. In fact, you and I may be quite confused about what it means to be a person. Father, Son, and Spirit are not, for example, three separate centers of consciousness. But Father, Son, and Spirit are truly *personal* in a deep and wonderful sense of the word. Shirley Guthrie's description is helpful: the "oneness of God is not the oneness of a distinct, self-contained individual; it is the unity of a *community* of persons who love each other and live together in harmony."[12] Guthrie continues, "'Personal' means by definition *inter*-personal; one cannot be truly personal alone but only in relation to other persons. Such is the unity and personal character of God the Father, Son, and Holy Spirit."[13] The three persons of the Trinity exist

---

11. Calvin, *Institutes*, 1.13.2.
12. Shirley C. Guthrie Jr., *Christian Doctrine*, rev. ed. (Louisville: Westminster John Knox, 1994), 92; emphasis Guthrie's.
13. Ibid.

in real relationship to each other, and because they are personal, we, their creatures, can have personal relationships with them. One of the gifts of the personal God is to relate personally to us. The doctrine of the Trinity teaches that we know and are loved by a personal God.

The threeness and oneness of God is not something that we can fully grasp, and it is not something that we can talk about perfectly. Instead, the doctrine of the Trinity gives us safeguards against mistaking the true God for false idols. Inherent in the doctrine are rules that help us to speak truthfully about God. First, an ancient rule governing trinitarian speech helps us to talk about God's oneness: *the works of God are indivisible.* This rule recognizes that God's unity is such that any work that God does is the work of all three persons of the Trinity. Father, Son, and Spirit all, for instance, do the work of creation. All three do the work of redemption. Father, Son, and Spirit are one in work and one in purpose. We should resist the temptation to slice the things of God up into threes. This rule reminds us not to lean into the kind of modalism that would reduce God from three persons to three functions. Father, Son, and Spirit are three personal realities, *not* three jobs God has to do.

The **doctrine of appropriations** helps us to talk about God's threeness. In reading the biblical accounts of the three triune persons, we see that it is appropriate to talk about the distinct work that each of the divine persons does in the world. While God's work of redemption is indivisibly the work of Father, Son, and Spirit, it is also wholly appropriate to talk about the Son's redemptive work on the cross or the Spirit's sanctifying work in the body of Christ. The work of each of the three persons in the world allows us to assign something that is true of all three persons to one of the persons. The one Triune God "is love" (1 John 4:8), and it also makes perfect sense to designate that love to the Second Person of the Trinity when Jesus acts with the greatest of love in laying down his life for his friends (John 15:13). In the words of contemporary theologian Eugene Rogers, "Because the three persons are distinct from one another, God can 'be' love."[14] The doctrine of the Trinity teaches us what it means and what it does not mean for God to be love. Samuel Powell explains, "Without the doctrine of the Trinity, our talk about God's love can be overly sentimental as we attribute human emotions to God. But in the context of the doctrine of the Trinity,

14. Eugene F. Rogers, *Sex and the Christian Body* (Oxford: Blackwell, 1999), 198.

Ways Not to Talk about the Trinity

"God, Jesus, and the Spirit." This way of talking implies that Jesus and the Spirit are less than God. More, it eliminates the Father.

"Three members of the Trinity." The Trinity is not a club, and language like "membership" implies that there is something beyond the three persons that the Father, Son, and Spirit might join up with. Father, Son, and Spirit are not members of God. They are God.

"The Trinity has three parts." Parts are not relational. Persons are. "Parts" implies a lack of fullness, but the three persons of the Trinity are fully God.

Augustine of Hippo wrote an enormous book on the Trinity in which he explains how various metaphors fail. This does not mean we have to flee from metaphor as we try to understand the doctrine, but it is wise to be aware of a metaphor's limits.

"I have three jobs: mother, wife, and teacher." This metaphor is modalistic. I am not my jobs, and my jobs do not have personal relationships with one another.

"It is like an egg; shell, white, and yolk make one egg." (Or an apple: peel, flesh, and core. Or a clover: one stem, three leaves.) These metaphors, like the "three jobs" metaphor, do not suggest the relationships between the triune persons. They also fail to help us worship the full divinity of all three persons. None of these images gets at the depth of the unity of the three persons, because each speaks of three parts that are quite distinct and easily separable; I have, in my kitchen, an egg separator and an apple corer.

God's love can mean only one thing—that the Father sent the Son to die as an atoning sacrifice and that the Holy Spirit has come to continue the ministry of Jesus and to bring about our response to God in the form of obedience and praise."[15] God's love is relational. God's love is self-giving, and this love transforms us in ways that match God's own love.

Practicing the Doctrine of the Trinity

At the beginning of Hebrews, the author draws a comparison between angels and the Son. Even though God gives great gifts to angels, angels

15. Samuel M. Powell, *Discovering Our Christian Faith: An Introduction to Theology* (Kansas City, MO: Beacon Hill, 2008), 332.

are still creatures. The definitive difference between creatures, angelic ones included, and the Son is that the Son is worthy of worship. Hebrews begins by worshiping the Son, whom God "appointed heir of all things" and "through whom he also created the worlds" (Heb. 1:2). The worshipful language for Jesus continues:

> He is the reflection of God's glory and the exact imprint of God's very being, and he sustains all things by his powerful word. When he had made purification for sins, he sat down at the right hand of the Majesty on high, having become as much superior to angels as the name he has inherited is more excellent than theirs. (vv. 3–4)

Unlike the angels, Jesus is the Father's begotten Son. Unlike the angels, Jesus is to be worshiped. Unlike the angels, the throne of Jesus "is forever and ever" (Heb. 1:8). The Father says to the Son, "Sit at my right hand until I make your enemies a footstool for your feet" (v. 13). At the beginning of Ephesians, Paul connects God the Father and Christ the Lord and offers up praise for who God is and what God has done, especially for the grace given to us in Jesus.

> Blessed be the God and Father of our Lord Jesus Christ, who has blessed us in Christ with every spiritual blessing in the heavenly places, just as he chose us in Christ before the foundation of the world to be holy and blameless before him in love. He destined us for adoption as his children through Jesus Christ, according to the good pleasure of his will, to the praise of his glorious grace that he freely bestowed on us in the Beloved. In him we have redemption through his blood, the forgiveness of our trespasses, according to the riches of his grace that he lavished on us. With all wisdom and insight he has made known to us the mystery of his will, according to his good pleasure that he set forth in Christ, as a plan for the fullness of time, to gather up all things in him, things in heaven and things on earth. In Christ we have also obtained an inheritance, having been destined according to the purpose of him who accomplishes all things according to his counsel and will, so that we, who were the first to set our hope on Christ, might live for the praise of his glory. In him you also, when you had heard the word of truth, the gospel of your salvation, and had believed in him, were marked with the seal of the promised Holy Spirit; this is the pledge of our inheritance toward redemption as God's own people, to the praise of his glory. (Eph. 1:3–14)

Come, Thou Almighty King

This trinitarian hymn attributed to Charles Wesley offers praise to the three persons in one God. It addresses each of the three persons as divine, and it connects the doctrine of the Trinity to worship and to personal relationship with the worshipers who call on God to rule their hearts.

> Come, thou almighty King,
> help us thy name to sing,
> help us to praise!
> Father all glorious,
> o'er all victorious,
> come and reign over us,
> Ancient of Days!
>
> Come, thou incarnate Word,
> gird on thy mighty sword,
> our prayer attend!
> Come, and thy people bless,
> and give thy word success;
> Spirit of holiness,
> on us descend!
>
> Come, holy Comforter,
> thy sacred witness bear
> in this glad hour.
> Thou who almighty art,
> now rule in every heart,
> and ne'er from us depart,
> Spirit of power!
>
> To thee, great One in Three,
> eternal praises be,
> hence, evermore.
> Thy sovereign majesty
> may we in glory see,
> and to eternity
> love and adore!

Here we learn to worship the Triune God for blessing us "in Christ" and choosing us "in Christ." We praise God's "glorious grace," a gift poured over us through Jesus. Because our hope is set "on Christ," we live in worship, "for the praise of his glory." The Spirit marks us as God's people, people who again praise his glory. The words of Ephesians are offered in worship of the Triune God, and the activity of worship is a joyful one. There is joy in knowing God. There is joy in being loved. There is joy in the magnitude and generosity of what Father, Son, and Spirit have done for us.

Julian of Norwich (1342–c. 1416) wrote of the joy she knew in worshiping the Triune God. In her words, "The Trinity filled me full of heartfelt joy, and I knew that all eternity was like this for those who attain heaven. For the Trinity is God, and God the Trinity; the Trinity is our Maker and keeper, our eternal lover, joy and bliss—all through our Lord Jesus Christ."[16] Practice in the doctrine of the Triune God yields bountifully in worship. The heart of the doctrine is about who we worship, and there is nothing more wonderful, life giving, or joyous than to worship the true and living God, recognizing that God is wonderfully different from and superior to any false god we might imagine. The most proper and important fruit of the doctrine is worship, and we cannot forget the truth that opened the chapter. If idolatry turns us into echoes of our idols, worship of the true God shapes us too, drawing us into God's own relational life of love and changing us into luminous reflections of God's true nature. John Wesley described the Christian life as the life in which, "above all, remembering that God is love," we are "conformed to the same likeness."[17] As we worship the Triune God, God unveils our faces, so that others may see in us "the glory of the Lord as though reflected in a mirror," as we are "transformed into the same image from one degree of glory to another" (2 Cor. 3:18).

God—Father, Son, and Holy Spirit—rescues us from dependence on false gods. God opens our eyes to see that idols are powerless to save. We are rescued from vague gods, from cruel gods, and from gods who are nothing but sad reflections of our own sinful desires. Instead of reflecting the generic fuzziness, the brutality, or the selfishness of those false gods, we are transformed into the image of the particular and loving God we know in the Father, the Son, and the Holy Spirit. We are transferred from the tyrannical authority of false gods who ask us to love the wrong things to the righteous authority of the Triune God, who shows us how to love.

16. Julian of Norwich, *Revelations of Divine Love*, trans. Clifton Wolters (London: Penguin, 1966), 66.
17. *John Wesley*, ed. Albert C. Outler (New York: Oxford University Press, 1964), 184–85.

Because God makes himself known to us through revelation, we know who we are speaking of when we talk about belief in God. We know whom we worship. We know who the God is who enables us to witness and serve in his name. We know what it looks like to be transformed in love, because we have seen love at work in the willingness of the Father to send us his only Son, of the Son to die for our sake, and of the Spirit to fill us with his holy power so that we become beacons of the triune love.

4

|||||||||||||||||||||||||||||||||||||||||||||||||||||||||||||||||||

A Delightful World

Doctrines of Creation and Providence

And he showed me more, a little thing, the size of a hazelnut, on the palm of my hand, round like a ball. I looked at it thoughtfully and wondered, "What is this?" And the answer came, "It is all that is made." I marveled that it continued to exist and did not suddenly disintegrate; it was so small. And again my mind supplied the answer, "It exists, both now and for ever, because God loves it." In short, everything owes its existence to the love of God.[1]

These words are from Julian of Norwich, a medieval Christian who recorded a number of revelations of God's love. The vision above, in which God shows "all that is made" to Julian in the form of "a little thing, the size of a hazelnut," is one of the most well known of Julian's revelations. In light of this vision of creation's fragility, of its utter dependence on God, Julian marvels that it exists at all, and she draws three truths from it.

The first is that God made it;
the second is that God loves it;
and the third is that God sustains it.[2]

1. Julian of Norwich, *Revelations of Divine Love*, trans. Clifton Wolters (London: Penguin, 1966), 68.
2. Ibid.

Key Scripture

Praise the LORD!
Praise the LORD from the heavens;
    praise him in the heights!
Praise him, all his angels;
    praise him, all his host!

Praise him, sun and moon;
    praise him, all you shining stars!
Praise him, you highest heavens,
    and you waters above the heavens!
Let them praise the name of the LORD,
    for he commanded and they were
    created.
He established them forever and ever;
    he fixed their bounds, which can-
    not be passed.

Praise the LORD from the earth,
    you sea monsters and all deeps,
fire and hail, snow and frost,
    stormy wind fulfilling his
    command!

Mountains and all hills,
    fruit trees and all cedars!
Wild animals and all cattle,
    creeping things and flying birds!

Kings of the earth and all peoples,
    princes and all rulers of the earth!
Young men and women alike,
    old and young together!

Let them praise the name of the LORD,
    for his name alone is exalted;
    his glory is above earth and
    heaven.
He has raised up a horn for his
    people,
    praise for all his faithful,
    for the people of Israel who are
    close to him.
Praise the Lord! (Ps. 148)

In these elegant points, Julian sums up the Christian doctrine of creation, and she does so in a way that gets at both head and heart. The doctrine of creation is not first about the obvious trigger points in the contemporary North American conversation, and this means that we may require some retraining in order to practice the doctrine well. When we hear the word *creation*, we have been primed to expect either a tribute to nature or a scientific account of the origins of the universe. We think of majestic wilderness and towering pines, or we think of evolution or dinosaurs or carbon dating. Christians may well have something to say about those things, but if we get hung up there, we miss the sweetness at the heart of the doctrine. Janet Martin Soskice notes that "the biblical discussions of creation" are "concerned not so much with where the world came from as with who it came from, not so much with what kind of creation it was in the first place as with what kind of creation it was and is *now*."[3] The doctrine of creation is about the dependence of all things on God the Creator and, as Julian saw, the love the Creator bears for all that he has made.

---

3. Janet Martin Soskice, *The Kindness of God: Metaphor, Gender, and Religious Language* (New York: Oxford University Press, 2007), 60–61.

This means that the doctrine of creation cannot begin with appreciation for natural beauty. Nor can it begin as a conversation with science. It must begin with the character of the God who is Creator, who made and loves and sustains all that is. This is why the chapter on the Trinity needed to come before this chapter. In relationship to creation, Christians tend to notice two things about the Triune God. First, God is not one of the things in this world, and so our doctrine about this world will have to take account of the unfathomable difference between it and God. God is utterly distinct from creation; that distinctiveness is behind the psalmist's cry, "Before the mountains were brought forth, or ever you had formed the earth and the world, from everlasting to everlasting you are God" (Ps. 90:2). Second, the same God who is not of this world is nonetheless intimately involved in it. Indeed, creation depends on God for its ongoing existence at every moment. The doctrine of creation is about God, and so our education about it should begin not with creation itself but with God's revealing Word. It is not by studying butterflies or stars but "by faith [that] we understand that the worlds were prepared by the word of God" (Heb. 11:3). The Triune God is not some generic god, and our doctrine of creation will have to be about the relationship between creation and *this* Creator, the Creator who is Father, Son, and Holy Spirit. "All things came into being through" the Word made flesh, Jesus Christ, "and without him not one thing came into being" (John 1:3). *This* is the personal God who lives in personal relationship with creation.

The doctrine of creation points us to faithful practice as creatures of a creator God, creatures who live in a world that exists for God's loving purposes: "For we are what he has made us, created in Christ Jesus for good works, which God prepared beforehand to be our way of life" (Eph. 2:10). We are created *in* Christ Jesus, and we are created *for* Christ Jesus: "For in him all things in heaven and on earth were created, things visible and invisible, whether thrones or dominions or rulers or powers—all things have been created through him and for him" (Col. 1:16). Jesus is both the source and the purpose of creation. We live in a world that has a point, a world that matters. The good news that "all things" are "for him" has enormous implications for the Christian life. The rest of this chapter expands on key points of the doctrine of creation in light of Julian's three truths quoted above.

God Made It: *Creatio ex nihilo* and the Power of God

Julian's categories show that talk about the doctrine of creation is not limited to the beginning of all things—God's original creative action in bringing all things into being—but Christian conversation certainly tends to start there. Scripture starts there too, as the familiar first line of Genesis invokes "the beginning when God created the heavens and the earth" (Gen. 1:1). The first chapters of Genesis show us a world in which God has made all things. Those first chapters set up a way of thinking about the God who created all that is and about God's relationship with creation. Old Testament scholar Sandra Richter sums up the theological vision of the creation story, highlighting its distinction from ancient Israel's neighbors.

> Yahweh was a god unlike the others of the ancient Near East, one who stood outside and above his creation, a god for whom there were no rivals and who had created humanity as his children as opposed to his slaves. Thus I think Genesis 1 was intended as a rehearsal of the creation event (where else would you start the story?) with the all-controlling theological agenda of explaining who God is and what his relationship to creation (and specifically humanity) looked like.[4]

Not just the first chapter of Genesis but also the whole of Scripture points to this creator God. The testimony of Genesis is that of the end of the Bible as well, of the book of Revelation, which praises God with the words, "You are worthy, our Lord and God, to receive glory and honor and power, for you created all things, and by your will they existed and were created" (Rev. 4:11). God the Creator has no rivals, yet all that is was made to be in loving relationship with the same sovereign God.

In the Christian tradition, the phrase "creation out of nothing" (in Latin, *creatio ex nihilo*) synthesizes and affirms the biblical testimony pointing to the kind of act with which God first created everything. God created all that is, the summary phrase announces, out of nothing. The phrase invokes the unchallenged majesty of the creator God, without whom nothing exists or ever has existed. The phrase also points, then, to the truth that all that exists, the totality of creation, is God's work and belongs to God. There are no exceptions. In the words of the Nicene Creed, "all that is, seen and

4. Sandra Richter, *Epic of Eden: A Christian Entry into the Old Testament* (Downers Grove, IL: InterVarsity, 2008), 95.

unseen," is God's. The implications of the doctrine of *creatio ex nihilo* can be better understood when we compare the doctrine to the false options that it excludes. If God created out of nothing, then God did not create out of something. Nor, if God created out of nothing, did God create out of his own divine being.

It is easy enough for us to think about acts of creation out of something. The sculptor creates from stone or clay, and the gods of Israel's ancient Near Eastern neighbors were understood to create out of preexisting chaos or even out of the bodies of their slain enemies.[5] Or, on certain understandings, a god might be understood to create from preexisting matter, from stuff that was already there alongside the god, primordial ooze or a hot, dense core of material that would later explode with a bang. The claim that God created, not out of something, but *ex nihilo* is a claim that nothing has status alongside God. The repeated testimony of Scripture is that only God is eternal; only God has no beginning; there is none like God.

To deny that God created out of preexisting stuff is to deny that anything, in all creation, has godlike status. In some ways, the doctrine of *creatio ex nihilo* is simply an implication of monotheism; it is one more way of affirming that "the LORD is our God, the LORD alone" (Deut. 6:4). And because the doctrine of the Trinity is a deeper understanding of this core Old Testament reality, *creatio ex nihilo* is an implication of trinitarian theology as well. There is none like the Lord, none alongside him. The doctrine of creation denies that God created out of something—be it chaos or a sea dragon, primordial ooze or a hot, dense core—but it does not deny that God, having already created, then works in and with all sorts of created things. God's initial act of creation is *ex nihilo*, but this does not preclude God's working with and through that which he has created already. So, the doctrine of creation may well coexist happily with contemporary evolutionary biology or cosmological theories, but it cannot exist alongside idolatry. Christian thought has no problem with scientific theories about how creation works, but it cannot bear the idolatry of scientism, which would reduce creation to what can be seen and measured. A world that God created from nothing cannot be a world of bare materialism, bereft of divine reality. A world that God created from

---

5. See John Walton, *Ancient Near Eastern Thought and the Old Testament* (Grand Rapids: Baker Academic, 2006); and Victor Harold Matthews and Don C. Benjamin, *Old Testament Parallels: Laws and Stories from the Ancient Near East*, 3rd ed. (New York: Paulist Press, 2006).

nothing cannot be the world of **deism**, in which God holds back, distant and standoffish, from what he has made. A world *ex nihilo* is, instead, a world full of God's presence and power.

To deny that God creates out of his own divine being is to recognize the difference between God and creation. This difference is fundamental to Christian thought, and being reminded of it is the ongoing stuff of Christian life. We can imagine acts of creation out of one's own being. Reproduction works as an analogy. An infant is formed from the stuff of her parents, hydras reproduce new hydras by budding, and both human babies and newly budded hydras are of the same species as their "creators." We could envision a god who fashioned creation out of his own being, making a creation that would itself be divine. The whole world as we see it in Scripture, though, which shows us the God who is more than we can conceive and beyond the things of this world, teaches us something else. So, Christian thought consistently rejects all forms of **pantheism**, the belief that the world is itself divine, and **panentheism**, the belief that God and the world are so bound together that God could not exist without the world.

Christians see, instead, a measureless and qualitative distinction between Creator and creature, between God and all that has been created. God is God, and we are not. We have already seen this theme in relation to the doctrine of the Trinity, and it is reinforced and expanded as we get practice in the doctrine of creation. This is another way in which affirmation of God as Creator *ex nihilo* is a reaffirmation of the biblical proscription against idolatry. Sinful human beings repeatedly confuse creature and Creator, treating the world as divine, exchanging "the truth about God for a lie" and worshiping and serving "the creature rather than the Creator" (Rom. 1:25), but the doctrine of creation trains us in another direction, reminding us that there is no god but God. The doctrine of creation affirms the goodness of what God has made (more on that below), but it makes no allowance for nature cults and zero room for worshiping human beings and pursuing selfish human ends. The doctrine of creation puts Creator and created in their proper places, insisting that created good things are always dependent, always finite, and always subordinate to the Creator.

In connection to this aspect of the doctrine, Christian theology recognizes and gives thanks for God's sufficiency and freedom. Divine sufficiency is the flipside of creaturely dependence. Where we depend on God for existence and all things good, God is enough for God. Another way to see this is to recognize that the God who is truly different from creation is not a needy God. Specifically, God does not need creation in order to be who God is; God is not lacking in love or goodness or relationship in any way that makes creation necessary. Theologian Stephen Long explicates, "God does not create because God is lonely. God does not create because God needs friends. God is not the lone patriarch, the strong silent type who secretly desires to 'open up' to us but cannot do so without our help. God does not create because God has to."[6] In this, we can appreciate a great gift. God creates, not because God needs us, but because God wants us. So, Rowan Williams asks us

> to bend our minds around the admittedly tough notion that we exist because of an utterly unconditional generosity. The love that God shows in making the world, like the love he shows towards the world once it is created, has no shadow or shred of self-directed purpose in it; it is entirely and unreservedly given for our sake. It is not a concealed way for God to get something out of it for himself, because that would make nonsense of what we believe is God's eternal nature.[7]

Creation is the overflowing of God's goodness and love outside of God's own life. Creation is excessive. Creation has all the characteristics of a good gift: it is freely given, without constraint; it is given in love for the other, without selfishness; it is not a grasping, grudging thing, with so many strings attached. Creation is the free work of an all-sufficient God of abundance, the God whose love and mercy is always more than we can imagine. Athanasius (c. 296–373) rejoices: "For God is good—or rather, of all goodness He is Fountainhead, and it is impossible for one who is good to be mean or grudging about anything. Grudging existence to none therefore, He made all things out of nothing through his own Word, our Lord Jesus Christ."[8] Creation is made for relationship with this gift-giving God, and "its basis," says theologian Kathryn Tanner, is "in nothing but

6. Stephen Long, "God Is Not Nice," in *God Is Not . . . : Religious, Nice, "One of Us," an American, a Capitalist*, ed. D. Brent Laytham (Grand Rapids: Brazos, 2004), 51–52.

7. Rowan Williams, *Tokens of Trust: An Introduction to Christian Belief* (Louisville: Westminster John Knox, 2007), 12–13. Thanks to David Lauber for drawing my attention to this quotation.

8. St. Athanasius, *On the Incarnation*, trans. A Religious of C.S.M.V. (Crestwood, NY: St. Vladimir's Seminary Press, 2003), 28.

Harmony and the Doctrine of Creation

Paul Schultz and George Tinker draw connections between biblical themes about creation and elements of Native North American culture.

> For we celebrate first the gift of wholeness and life that God has bestowed upon us and all the rest of the world. If we take that seriously, we have to image ourselves not as somehow above creation and in charge of it, but instead as one of God's created beings, related to all the rest of God's creatures: other people, the four-leggeds, the winged, and even the trees and streams and mountains. . . . The primary value for Native People has always been the need for harmony and balance, health and wholeness, not just for the individual, but for the community, for all people, for all of creation. This is the work to which our ancestors committed themselves, because it was and is the response the Creator demands to the gracious act of creation.[a]

Terry LeBlanc sees, in Native American culture, challenges to hierarchical dualism. LeBlanc connects the doctrine of creation to the doctrine of salvation.

> The Christian Scripture, as well as our own experiences if we take the time to reflect on them, is abundantly clear that redemption through Jesus's work on the cross has implications far beyond our generally limited focus on the restoration of human beings alienated from their Creator. The creation itself, Paul makes quite clear, groans in travail awaiting its own redemption (Rom. 8:18–25). Yet, even as we give tacit assent to this in our Christian theologies, we fail miserably to account for the work of the Spirit—dare I say, the gifts of the Spirit—so abundantly evident in the rest of creation through which that groaning is becoming increasingly unmistakable and from which we might learn something about the means and trajectory of salvation if we were to listen more carefully.[b]

a. "Rivers of Life: Native Spirituality for Native Churches," in *Native and Christian: Indigenous Voices on Religious Identity in the United States and Canada*, ed. James Treat (New York: Routledge, 1996), 59.
b. Terry LeBlanc, "New Old Perspectives: Theological Observations Reflecting Indigenous Worldviews," in *Global Theology in Evangelical Perspective: Exploring the Contextual Nature of Theology and Mission*, ed. Jeffrey P. Greenman and Gene L. Green (Downers Grove, IL: IVP Academic, 2012), 168–69.

God's free love for us. The proper starting point for considering our created nature is therefore grace."[9]

The doctrine of creation out of nothing is thus the Christian alternative to other possible ways of understanding the origins of all things. Christian faith is not pantheistic, nor does it subscribe to bare materialism or cold deism. Rather, Christians worship the God who is truly other than the world but, far from disdaining that world, inhabits it powerfully and personally. The God who creates *ex nihilo* is Lord over and lover of creation. The same

9. Kathryn Tanner, *Christ the Key* (Cambridge: Cambridge University Press, 2010), 116.

God who made the light and the darkness, the waters and the sky, is the one who raised Jesus from the dead, who "gives life to the dead and calls into existence the things that do not exist" (Rom. 4:17).

God Loves It: Relishing Goodness, Being Beloved

The creation account in the book of Genesis is about beginnings, but it is also about the nature of what God creates. We glimpse this world, these creatures, that God has made, and we learn what kind of world this is and what kind of creatures God has crafted: the good kind. In the first chapter of Genesis, the word *good* is repeated seven times. The goodness of creation is declared in the steady drumbeat of that word, a repetition not to be ignored. The "light was good" (Gen. 1:4). God saw that the earth and waters were "good" (v. 10) and the plants and trees were "good" (v. 12). The sun ruling the day and the moon ruling the night were "good" (v. 18). The "swarms of living creatures" in the water and the birds flying "across the dome of the sky" were "good" (vv. 20–21). The creatures of the earth—"wild animals," "cattle," and "everything that creeps"—were seen by the Creator God to be "good" (v. 25). Human beings, created "male and female" in God's own image, and the life God set before them—a life of fruitfulness, dominion, and blessing—were "very good" (vv. 27–31).

In the practice of Christian doctrine, the goodness of creation is a non-negotiable truth. As Christians, we live in and with this reality. Creation is good because it is the good work of the Triune God. It is not nature's beauty—dappled sunlight falling through leaves, rolling ocean waves, the intricacies of genes—that comprises the reality of created goodness. If that were the case, creation's goodness would be undone by the ugliness of a hurricane, a predatory creature, or a damaging mutation. Nor is it the good things that human beings do—designing buildings, baking confections, or loving children—that secures the goodness of creation. If that were the case, creation's goodness would be undone by the building of bombs, the misuse of resources, or the terrible abuses we human beings inflict on one another. In the Christian life, the goodness of creation is a present, living, and unshakable reality because God is the author and goal of it. Because, in Julian's words, "God loves it," we too must recognize and love the good of all God has made. We confess creation's goodness because it is the work of a good God who called it good and reveals that goodness to us. We see

---

Gerard Manley Hopkins on God's Grandeur

The world is charged with the grandeur of God.
It will flame out, like shining from shook foil;
It gathers to a greatness, like the ooze of oil
Crushed. Why do men then now not reck his rod?
Generations have trod, have trod, have trod;
And all is seared with trade; bleared, smeared with toil;
And wears man's smudge and shares man's smell: the soil
Is bare now, nor can foot feel, being shod.

And for all this, nature is never spent;
There lives the dearest freshness deep down things;
And though the last lights off the black West went
Oh, morning, at the brown brink eastward, springs —
Because the Holy Ghost over the bent
World broods with warm breast and with ah! bright wings.[a]

a. "God's Grandeur," in *Selected Poems of Gerard Manley Hopkins*, ed. Bob Blaisdell (Mineola, NY: Dover, 2001), 20.

---

that goodness in the sevenfold "good" of the first chapter of Genesis, and we see it throughout Scripture. Even as the sinful nations rebelled, God never "left himself without a witness in doing good—giving you rains from heaven and fruitful seasons, and filling you with food and your hearts with joy" (Acts 14:17). In Christ, we are to receive creation with thanksgiving because "everything created by God is good, and nothing is to be rejected, provided it is received with thanksgiving" (1 Tim. 4:4).

It may seem like a simple thing to affirm the goodness of creation, but this affirmation, when viewed in light of other common ways of understanding the world, is revolutionary. The reality of created goodness is central to the Christian way of living in the world. Very early in the history of the church, Christian thinkers met opposition to the goodness of creation in the form of gnosticism, and this has proved to be a recurring temptation to God's people. The word **gnosticism** refers to a variety of groups in the ancient world that claimed to have access to a special form of *gnosis*, a secret knowledge available only to the gnostic in-group, a knowledge that would open up the doors of salvation. There was a fair amount of diversity among these ancient groups, but the designation "gnostic" indicates features they shared. When contemporary theologians see gnostic tendencies in twenty-first-century cultures or churches, they are not claiming that the historical gnostic sects of the first century are still active. The claim is, instead, that contemporary cultures and churches sometimes share important features with ancient gnosticism. Those shared features include the claim to secret knowledge and, even more important in light of the doctrine of creation, a worldview rooted in hierarchical dualism.

Gnostic **hierarchical dualism** divides creation in two: material and spiritual. This dualism is hierarchical because the two are not viewed as different yet equally valuable; instead, there is a clear difference in value. The spiritual is good; the material is bad. Gnostic hierarchical dualism divides all that is according to this hierarchy. That is, everything may be identified with either the material or the spiritual, either the bad or the good. Bad, problematic materiality is associated with bodies and bodily functions like birth, eating, and death. Everything physical and tangible is seen as part of the problem. Good, salvific spirituality is associated with rationality and the invisible, with things that, like spirituality, cannot be seen or touched. Gnosticism imports this hierarchical dualism into teachings about God and creation. Kurt Rudolph describes gnostic dualism as "'anti-cosmic'; that is, its conception includes an unequivocally negative evaluation of the visible world together with its creator; it ranks as a kingdom of evil and of darkness."[10] Materiality is bad, and so, in the logic of gnosticism, it cannot be the work of God, who is good. Ancient gnostic groups often taught that God could not be the author of creation and proposed that the good God created spiritual reality while material reality was the work of some lesser being. Alternatively, gnostic groups might see God as the creator of spiritual reality and explain the existence of material reality as a result of sin. In either case, material creation was written off as something other than God's, something other than good.

The Christian doctrine of creation, recognizing God's goodness and power as well as God's loving intention toward all things, insists on a view of the world that runs counter to gnosticism. The Christian God—Father, Son, and Holy Spirit—is the Creator of all that exists. This is true, we saw above, without exception. God is the Creator of seen and unseen, heaven and earth, spiritual and material, body and mind and soul. Nothing exists that is not God's good work. Not time. Not angels. Not the laws of nature.

10. Kurt Rudolph, *Gnosis: The Nature and History of Gnosticism*, ed. Robert McLachlan Wilson (Edinburgh: T&T Clark, 1984), 60.

And certainly not matter. All of it is God's work, and God who is goodness itself made it all good. This anti-gnostic insight totally reorients our way of being in the world. To practice the Christian doctrine of creation is to relish the goodness of all that God has made and to recognize all creation's status as beloved by God and intended for Christ. Christian teaching is clear that materiality—in all of its tangible, physical, sensory particularity—is included in this. When gnostic-type thinking has resurfaced over the centuries, the church, guided by Scripture, has always corrected back toward affirmation of creation's goodness. This explains the unusual defense offered by a medieval man accused of heresy. "I am not a heretic," he said, "for I have a wife and sleep with her. I have sons, I eat meat, and I lie and swear, and I am a faithful Christian."[11] The last bit of evidence he offers (the lying and swearing) may be a bit off, but the first several fit solidly within the Christian practice of relishing the goodness of creation. In fact, our defendant is not far from quoting from 1 Timothy.

> Now the Spirit expressly says that in later times some will renounce the faith by paying attention to deceitful spirits and teachings of demons, through the hypocrisy of liars whose consciences are seared with a hot iron. They forbid marriage and demand abstinence from foods, which God created to be received with thanksgiving by those who believe and know the truth. For everything created by God is good, and nothing is to be rejected, provided it is received with thanksgiving; for it is sanctified by God's word and by prayer. If you put these instructions before the brothers and sisters, you will be a good servant of Christ Jesus, nourished on the words of the faith and of the sound teaching that you have followed. (1 Tim. 4:1–6)

In relishing creation's goodness, we will embrace the many aspects of created life as good gifts from a good God, and we will eschew any squeamishness about including, among those good gifts, the seemingly vulgar bits that turn up gnostic noses. Bodily life is good. Temporal life is good. Christians cannot give up on the world or attempt to isolate ourselves from it.

There is a deep **holism** inherent in a doctrine of creation that recognizes the goodness of all that God has made. Unlike the gnostics, who would divide the world into good and bad, Christians live in a unified world, a world in which

11. Thomas F. Madden, *The New Concise History of the Crusades* (Lanham, MD: Rowman & Littlefield, 2005), 124.

all things are included under the heading of created goodness. The Christian world is one in which all things exist under God's reign. This holism is the dramatic and life-changing opposite of gnostic dualism. Sometimes, though, in pushing against hierarchical dualism, a theology will lean so heavily on holism that it threatens to deny the existence and goodness of difference. Christian theology, with all its holism, embraces the reality of difference within creation. The litany of goodness in Genesis 1 is also a litany of difference made by God: the difference between the light and the dark, the waters and the dry land, and the differences between the fruits and the animals of "every kind." Even more fundamental is the difference between God and creation. Difference is one of the good things of God's creation. It is impor-

> ## "All Creatures of Our God and King"
>
> This hymn, based on words by Francis of Assisi (c. 1182–1226), calls for all creation—human and not—to join in praise of the Triune God.
>
> All creatures of our God and King,
> lift up your voices, let us sing:
> Alleluia, alleluia!
> Thou burning sun with golden beams,
> thou silver moon that gently gleams,
> *O praise him, O praise him,*
> *Alleluia, alleluia, alleluia!*
>
> Thou rushing wind that art so strong,
> ye clouds that sail in heaven along,
> O praise him, Alleluia!
> Thou rising morn, in praise rejoice,
> ye lights of evening, find a voice.
>
> Thou flowing water, pure and clear,
> make music for thy Lord to hear,
> Alleluia, alleluia!
> Thou fire so masterful and bright,
> that givest man both warmth and light.
>
> And all ye men of tender heart,
> forgiving others, take your part,
> O sing ye Alleluia!
> Ye who long pain and sorrow bear,
> praise God and on him cast your care.
>
> Let all things their Creator bless,
> and worship him in humbleness,
> O praise him, Alleluia!
> Praise, praise the Father, praise the Son,
> and praise the Spirit, Three in One.

tant to recognize that, in denying gnostic dualism, classic Christianity does not deny the existence of difference. What Christianity denies is that the existence of difference demands hierarchical rule of one over the other. Where gnosticism assumes that the difference between body and soul requires the denigration of the body and the elevation of the soul, Christian thought attempts a much more difficult but more hopeful way of living with difference. God can love the whole of creation in its magnificent diversity.

God Sustains It: Living under Caring Providence

Jesus, in unity with the Father and the Spirit, is "the Alpha and the Omega, the beginning and the end" (Rev. 21:6), but he is also the middle who "sustains all things by his powerful word" (Heb. 1:3). We, his creatures, live in that blessed middle, and God's creative care for the world is just as real here in the middle as it was at the beginning and will be in the end. Along with beginnings, the doctrine of creation treats the continuing work of God as the Lord of all creation, God's caring reign over and involvement in the world. Christian teaching about God's continuing work in creation is a subset of the doctrine of creation, the doctrine of **providence**. Scripture testifies to God's providential care for creation in many different ways. Proverbs enjoins the reader to "commit your work to the LORD, and your plans will be established" (Prov. 16:3), and claims that "the LORD has made everything for its purpose" (Prov. 16:4). The psalmist lifts up his eyes, looking for help that "comes from the Lord, who made heaven and earth," and trusts that "he who keeps Israel will neither slumber nor sleep" (Ps. 121:2, 4). Jesus assures his listeners that even the smallest things are in the care of God, that no sparrow will "fall to the ground apart from your Father" (Matt. 10:29).

Confidence in God's providential care for creation is a motif in Scripture. The God of the Bible is active, involved with creation. Often in Scripture, God is identified by and praised for his mighty works in history. Here, we can note just one example, a speech from the prophet Ezra, who explicitly connects God's work as initial Creator to God's ongoing work in the history of Israel.

> You are the LORD, you alone; you have made heaven, the heaven of heavens, with all their host, the earth and all that is on it, the seas and all that is in them. To all of them you give life, and the host of heaven worships you. You are the LORD, the God who chose Abram and brought him out of Ur of the Chaldeans and gave him the name Abraham; and you found his heart faithful before you, and made with him a covenant to give to his descendants the land of the Canaanite, the Hittite, the Amorite, the Perizzite, the Jebusite, and the Girgashite; and you have fulfilled your promise, for you are righteous. (Neh. 9:6–8)

The God who makes all things is also the God who chooses, brings, and gives. This God knows hearts and makes covenants. This is a faithful God who keeps promises. Ezra goes on to invoke God's deeds in bringing the people of Israel out of slavery in Egypt, leading them "by day with a pillar of cloud, and by night with a pillar of fire" (Neh. 9:12), giving the law at Sinai, sustaining the people for forty years in the wilderness, and leading them into the promised land. Ezra claims, as God's providential work, not just the gift of life in the land, but also the people's defeat and exile, in which God gave a people who rebelled against him "into the hands of their enemies" (v. 27). Ezra praises God for hearing the suffering people crying out. Ezra's God is not only a God of mighty acts. His action is just and merciful.

In Ezra's speech, we see the characteristic voice of Scripture, a voice that speaks confidently of God's work in the world. This voice trusts in God's providence. Here, we also read testimony to a providence that works in and with people for good purposes. Ezra's speech also raises a human difficulty in relation to the doctrine of providence. How are we to understand God's providence when we are faced with evil? Ezra's answer, in the face of Israel's exile, is to express faith in God's justice and mercy, even when, especially when, people act outside of God's will. The prophet praises God as "ready to forgive, gracious and merciful, slow to anger and abounding in steadfast love"; though the people turned away, God still "did not forsake them" (Neh. 9:17). The prophet continues, "You have been just in all that has come upon us, for you have dealt faithfully and we have acted wickedly" (Neh. 9:33). God's providence is real, caring, just. There is much that we do not understand about God's providential work in the world, and Christians disagree about how best to describe that work. Still, affirmation of God's providence, along with trust in God's continuing good work in the world, is a central feature of Christian thought. We have confidence in God's providence, and, with Julian, we can give thanks that God sustains what has been made.

Studies of doctrine sometimes divide talk about providence into three categories: preservation, concurrence (or conservation), and governance. **Preservation** refers to God's work and will in upholding all of creation. **Concurrence** describes God's work in and with all that he has made. Finally, **governance** indicates God's work in guiding all things to the purpose for which they have been made and God's active rule over creation. In practice, it is difficult to distinguish what acts of providence might best be described by each of the three terms, but the three are helpful in pointing to the extent of God's providence. That extent is total. God sustains all that is, God works with all that is, and God is bringing all that is to God's good ends. God is Lord of all creation, Lord of all places, all times, all of reality. In a modern world, a world in which we tend to have mechanistic expectations about the universe, this view of the extent of providence challenges expectations. We are trained to treat the world as 100 percent understandable and to act as though creation is fully in our control. We are trained to act as though the world were independent from God. Affirming God's providence in preserving all that exists, moment to moment, in concurring in and with his creatures, and in governing all things opens our eyes to a world that is full of God's presence and power. Charles Wesley speaks of such a world: "God is also the supporter of all things which he has made. He beareth, upholdeth, sustaineth all created things by the word of his power; by the same powerful word which brought them out of nothing. As this was absolutely necessary for the beginning of their existence, it is equally so for the continuance of it; were his almighty influence withdrawn, they could not subsist a moment longer."[12] This world is not ours to control, nor will we ever unfold all of its mysteries.

When we ponder the extent of God's providential care, we may find ourselves first disoriented and then reoriented as creatures suddenly aware of being in a world that is, in the words of poet Gerard Manley Hopkins, "charged with the grandeur of God."[13] Hopkins sees the same world as that of the Psalms, in which

> the word of the LORD is upright, and all his work is done in faithfulness. He loves righteousness and justice; the earth is full of the steadfast love of the LORD. By the word of the LORD the heavens were made, and all their host by the breath of his mouth. He gathered the waters of the sea as in a bottle; he put the deeps in storehouses. Let all the earth fear the LORD; let all the inhabitants of the world stand in awe of him. For he spoke, and it came to be; he commanded, and it stood firm. (Ps. 33:4–9)

A world under providence is one in which we recognize that nature truly belongs to God. The laws of nature are God's providential work just as miracles are.

More than Conquerors

Affirmation of God's providence raises questions about what God is up to when things go terribly wrong. Why would God, who is goodness and power,

12. Quoted in H. Orton Wiley and Paul T. Cuthbertson, *Introduction to Christian Theology* (Kansas City, MO: Beacon Hill, 1963), 146–47.
13. Hopkins, "God's Grandeur," 20.

allow evil and suffering? This is the question addressed in **theodicy**, which tries to justify God's actions in light of the existence of evil. There are many attempts, philosophical and theological, to explain the problem of evil. Some describe evil as a teacher or emphasize the ways that God may use evil for some superior purpose. Some explain the existence of evil as a result of God's good choice to give true freedom to his creatures, including the freedom to rebel against God's goodness. There is something of help in these strategies, but none will "solve" the problem of evil, and such strategies fall especially flat when they are depersonalized. No suffering person wants to hear trite clichés that bypass the depth of pain. This does not mean, however, that Christians have nothing else to say on the subject. For theologian Colin Gunton, evil cannot be "explained," but we do see, in God's providence, "something of the way in which its overcoming is begun and promised."[14] Our response to evil, in faith, will not be a neat, logical solution but a living into the narrative of Scripture in which sin and death are *not* God's good intention for creation and in which evil is overcome through the work of Christ. There is comfort in God's choice to be truly with us, to suffer with us and for us, and we live in confidence of God's final victory over sin, evil, and suffering.

Julian, with whom we began this chapter, was intimate with suffering. In her lifetime, she saw the plague sweep through her town twice, cutting great swaths of grief through Norwich. Amy Frykholm reflects on the effects this had on Julian: "Julian did not doubt the reality of sin. She could not deny the reality of suffering. . . . She carried from the pestilence's devastation an irrevocable image of putrid and rotting flesh and a set of hard and seemingly unanswerable questions about God's grace. The greatest mystery was sin."[15] Going forward, Julian would bring those questions into her life of faith, and she would later write with a pastoral concern that "while we may believe in the power of God, we might doubt God's love."[16] Julian's contemplation of the suffering of Christ, suffering that she describes in intimate and physical terms, convinced her that God's power and love are wrapped together in the body of Christ on the cross, that, as Frederick Bauerschmidt describes it in his book on Julian, "God's power is the power of the cross, and in her

---

14. Colin E. Gunton, *The Christian Faith: An Introduction to Christian Doctrine* (Oxford: Blackwell, 2002), 26.

15. Amy Frykholm, *Julian of Norwich: A Contemplative Biography* (Brewster, MA: Paraclete Press, 2010), 28.

16. Frederick Christian Bauerschmidt, *Julian of Norwich and the Mystical Body Politic of Christ* (Notre Dame, IN: University of Notre Dame Press, 1999), 61.

bodily sights Julian looks upon the reality of the divine nature, shown in God's redemption of humanity."[17] Julian recounts how she wondered why God allowed sin to enter the world, how the question gave her great sorrow. Meditating on God's love embodied on the cross, she saw that

> the Passion of our Lord is comfort for us against all this, and so is His blessed will. And because of the tender love that our good Lord has to all that shall be saved, He comforts quickly and sweetly, meaning thus: "It is true that sin is cause of all this pain,
>
>> but all shall be well,
>> and all shall be well,
>> and all manner of thing shall be well."
>
> These words were said most tenderly. . . . It would be a great unkindness to blame God for my sin, seeing He does not blame me for sin. In these same words I saw a marvelous, high secret hidden in God, which secret He shall openly make known to us in heaven. In this secret knowledge we shall truly see the reason why He allowed sin to come, and in this sight we shall endlessly rejoice in our Lord God.[18]

Julian's "all shall be well" is made all the more remarkable by the devastation she had known. It is a statement of faith and of confidence in God's love for us and victory over sin, a statement consistent with the biblical testimony to God's creative and providential love. The trick, though, to dwelling with Julian here is not to do so lightly. "All shall be well" is not a catchphrase to be thrown at suffering. It is a truth of faith that we learn throughout life, that can be stated only from where Julian stated it: a place of full knowledge of sin's horror and greater knowledge of God's goodness and faithfulness as bigger than that horror. It can be stated, as Julian stated it, only while gazing on the crucified and risen One, who is God's personal response to evil and suffering. From just such a place—aware of sin but trusting in God in Jesus Christ—Paul offers up his own words of faith in the face of suffering.

> What then are we to say about these things? If God is for us, who is against us? He who did not withhold his own Son, but gave him up for all of us,

17. Ibid.
18. *The Complete Julian of Norwich*, ed. Fr. John-Julian, OJN (Brewster, MA: Paraclete Press, 2009), 149.

will he not with him also give us everything else? Who will bring any charge against God's elect? It is God who justifies. Who is to condemn? It is Christ Jesus, who died, yes, who was raised, who is at the right hand of God, who indeed intercedes for us. Who will separate us from the love of Christ? Will hardship, or distress, or persecution, or famine, or nakedness, or peril, or sword? As it is written, "For your sake we are being killed all day long; we are accounted as sheep to be slaughtered." No, in all these things we are more than conquerors through him who loved us. For I am convinced that neither death, nor life, nor angels, nor rulers, nor things present, nor things to come, nor powers, nor height, nor depth, nor anything else in all creation, will be able to separate us from the love of God in Christ Jesus our Lord. (Rom. 8:31–39)

Practice Being Creatures

Our practice of doctrine is a *creaturely* practice, a practice that makes sense only in relationship to our Creator. The practice of the doctrine of creation extends into every area of the Christian life. The whole of that life is God's creation. The doctrine of creation is about our work and our leisure, our souls and our bodies. It is about the daily and particular details of our lives: eating, playing, sleeping, and timekeeping. In light of the doctrine of creation, we learn to see all of this, the little things and the big, as God's, as good, and as purposeful. As we become practiced in the doctrine of creation, we will find ourselves reoriented in life. We will learn to turn, by the Spirit's power,

- from disdain for creation to Christian delight in its goodness;
- from the gnostic impulse to escapism to a commitment to presence and participation in the world;
- from proud attempts at meticulous control to grateful openness to God's work in our lives;
- from frustration with our finitude to appreciation of its graciousness;
- from fatalism and resignation to active involvement in God's world, fighting against sin and injustice;
- from doomed determination to be independent in all things to gratitude for our dependence on God and acceptance of interdependence with others;
- from despair over sin to awe of God's sovereignty and trust in God's purpose;
- from possessiveness to stewardship;

- from greed to giving;
- from abstemiousness to joy;
- from heeding the inner voice that calls us worthless to a new self-assurance that comes from the worth we have in God;
- from cynicism to a place where we cultivate the habit of wonder; and
- from entitlement to care of creation.

Because God embraces us as creatures, we can embrace creation rightly, taking on the voice and stance of the psalmist who sings, "Great are the works of the LORD, studied by all who delight in them. Full of honor and majesty is his work, and his righteousness endures forever" (Ps. 111:2–3).

Selections from "On the Care of Creation: An Evangelical Declaration on the Care of Creation"[a]

Because we worship and honor the Creator, we seek to cherish and care for the creation. Because we have sinned, we have failed in our stewardship of creation. Therefore we repent of the way we have polluted, distorted, or destroyed so much of the Creator's work. Because in Christ God has healed our alienation from God and extended to us the first fruits of the reconciliation of all things, we commit ourselves to working in the power of the Holy Spirit to share the Good News of Christ in word and deed, to work for the reconciliation of all people in Christ, and to extend Christ's healing to suffering creation. . . . God calls us to confess and repent of attitudes which devalue creation, and which twist or ignore biblical revelation to support our misuse of it. . . . Our God-given, stewardly talents have often been warped from their intended purpose: that we know, name, keep and delight in God's creatures; that we nourish civilization in love, creativity and obedience to God; and that we offer creation and civilization back in praise to the Creator. We have ignored our creaturely limits and have used the earth with greed, rather than care. . . . We believe that in Christ there is hope, not only for men, women and children, but also for the rest of creation which is suffering from the consequences of human sin. . . . We urge individual Christians and churches to be centers of creation's care and renewal, both delighting in creation as God's gift, and enjoying it as God's provision, in ways which sustain and heal the damaged fabric of the creation which God has entrusted to us.

a. "On the Care of Creation: An Evangelical Declaration on the Care of Creation," Evangelical Environmental Network, accessed January 29, 2013, http://www.creationcare.org/blank.php?id=39.

5

Reflecting God's Image

Theological Anthropology

We are interested in questions about what it means to be human, since those questions are immediately relevant to our lives, but if the human being becomes the main subject of theology, we are not doing theology anymore. When Christian theologians talk about human beings, we do so in terms of our relationship to God. This means that humans are not center stage in our own story: even here, perhaps especially here, the story is about God first, and only then about us. Because theology is about the things of God, theologians have always had to approach the subject of human life and existence with humility.[1]

The doctrine of the human being—what sort of creatures we are and what we are like—is known as **theological anthropology**. Cultural anthropologists immerse themselves in the lives of certain peoples in order to study their habits, practices, and customs. Through joining people in eating, in worship, in sadness, and in celebration, anthropologists can provide a snapshot of the life of a small tribe in a rain forest, a unique church congregation, or some mysterious cohort of individuals like college freshmen.[2] The cul-

1. See Kathryn Tanner, "The Difference Theological Anthropology Makes," in *Theology Today* 50, no. 4 (January 1994): 567–80.
2. See Rebekah Nathan, *My Freshman Year: What a Professor Learned by Becoming a Student* (Ithaca, NY: Cornell University Press, 2005).

Key Scripture

O LORD, our Sovereign, how majestic is your name in all the earth! You have set your glory above the heavens. Out of the mouths of babes and infants you have founded a bulwark because of your foes, to silence the enemy and the avenger. When I look at your heavens, the work of your fingers, the moon and the stars that you have established; what are human beings that you are mindful of them, mortals that you care for them? Yet you have made them a little lower than God, and crowned them with glory and honor. You have given them dominion over the works of your hands; you have put all things under their feet, all sheep and oxen, and also the beasts of the field, the birds of the air, and the fish of the sea, whatever passes along the paths of the seas. O LORD, our Sovereign, how majestic is your name in all the earth! (Ps. 8)

tural anthropologist points out differences and similarities between cultures, helping us to know humanity better. The task of the theological anthropologist is different. Our job is to describe, not a slice of humanity, but *all* of it—and to do so in light of humanity's relationship with God.

The theological anthropologist works to understand humanity both as God intends it to be and as it actually is—and the two are often very different. As theological anthropologists, we take very seriously the fact that God created us. To know what it means to be human, we must know what it means to be created in the "image of God." The doctrine of creation is not the only movement in this story, though, and theological anthropologists must also take human sin seriously, accounting for the distortion and twisting of human nature under sin. Mercifully, our story does not end there either. A study of the human as sinner leads us inexorably to the One who saves human beings from sin: Jesus Christ. This raises a key point for theologians thinking about human beings: we take humanity seriously because *God* takes it seriously—seriously enough to become human in the person of Jesus Christ. Indeed, to talk about the Triune God is to talk about the God who became human for us and for our salvation, and this means that any doctrine about human beings must find its basis in one human being, Jesus of Nazareth. When we look at Jesus, we know what it means to be truly human, because he shows us what a human life looks like when it is lived in perfect relationship with the Father by the power of the Holy Spirit. The shape of Jesus's life challenges our understanding of our own lives, undermining our self-absorption and our presumptions about what our lives mean. Because he shows us what *true* humanity looks like, Jesus Christ alone enables us to practice being human. This chapter introduces theological anthropology by looking at the human as creature, as sinner, and as new creation in Christ.

Human as Creature

The human being is a creature who stands irrevocably with the rest of creation. We belong on the creaturely side of the distinction between God and all that is created. So, our study of the doctrine of creation in the previous chapter applies directly to human beings. As creation is good, so humanity is "very good" (Gen. 1:31). As creation is utterly dependent on the sovereign God for its existence, so is humanity. Unlike God, we humans are characterized by finitude. In contrast to God, who is all in all, we are limited, bound, and dependent.[3] Humanity is not God and must never be worshiped.

The dependent nature of human existence is a gift in itself. Christians in individualistic cultures have much to learn about the practice of interdependence from Christians in cultures that understand the human being as communal. "I exist because I belong to a family," writes African theologian John Pobee, who states that "family relationships determine"[4] how we view theological anthropology. While finitude, vulnerability, and dependence are realities contemporary North America tends to struggle against, these are also realities of human existence that are central to God's good intentions for us. Philosopher Alasdair MacIntyre speaks of the "virtues of acknowledged dependence."[5] Our created finitude means that we need each other, that we receive the gift of learning to live with and for another, and, above all, that we need God. The church father Irenaeus of Lyons (c. 130–202) put it like this:

> People who do not wait for the period of growth, who attribute the weakness of their nature to God, are completely unreasonable. They understand neither God nor themselves; they are ungrateful and never satisfied. At the outset they refuse to be what they were made: human beings who are

3. See Thomas Aquinas, *Summa Theologica*, trans. Fathers of the English Dominican Province (Allen, TX: Christian Classics, 1948), I.44.1.

4. John Pobee, *Toward an African Theology* (Nashville: Abingdon, 1979), 49.

5. Alasdair MacIntyre, *Dependent Rational Animals: Why Human Beings Need the Virtues* (Chicago: Open Court, 1999), 8.

subject to passions. They override the law of human nature; they already want to be like God the creator before they even become human beings. They want to do away with all the differences between the uncreated God and created humans.[6]

Irenaeus is unsympathetic with us when we are unable to accept the gift of our creatureliness. His words suggest that we pray for the grace to cultivate a way of being human creatures that does not fight against our finitude. Instead, we may, precisely as creatures, seek to be both grateful and fulfilled in our limitedness. Irenaeus speaks of being human, not as something that we can take for granted, but as something that we must become.

Middle Creatures

If human beings as creatures share important features with the rest of God's creation, what is it that makes us uniquely *human*? What sets us apart from birds, dogs, monkeys, and butterflies? What specific kind of creature is the human being? From the broad consensus of Christian thought, we can draw one partial answer. The human being is a kind of *middle* creature. Neither purely spirit, like the angels, nor purely physical, like the beasts, the human being stands in the middle of spiritual and physical creation. Scripture witnesses to our constitution by God as a **psychosomatic unity**, a creature who is always both physical and spiritual. We can think of the human being as an amphibian of sorts—like the newt that lives both on land and in water—except that in our case we live and relate to God both spiritually and physically. The claim that the human being is a middle creature is, practically, quite important. We can see the payoff of this aspect of doctrine if we compare it to two other possibilities: hierarchical dualism and reductive materialism.

Scripture does not divide human beings into pieces in our relationships with God. Christian thought about the human creature, like Christian thought on creation, rejects hierarchical dualism. The human being is not a soul in hostile relationship with a body. The human being is always one thing, one creature, in life before God. We are both bodily and spiritual, and the bodily and the spiritual are united in us. Compare this with the dualist

6. Irenaeus of Lyon, "Against Heresies," in *Theological Anthropology*, ed. J. Patout Burns (Philadelphia: Fortress, 1981), 25.

concept of the human being in which body and soul are antagonistically associated, with the body irrelevant to what it means to be truly human. Hierarchical dualism pits body against soul, and the body is understood as an obstacle or burden. Christians reject Platonic dualism in which the soul is "bound and glued to the body, and is forced to view things as if through a prison."[7] Christians know the body is not a prison. It is integral to God's good intentions for us. The body is for God's glory (1 Cor. 6:20). For the influential philosopher René Descartes (1596–1650), "while the body can very easily perish, the mind is immortal by its very nature."[8] But in Christian thought, we recognize that only God is "immortal by nature" or truly eternal. The eternal life that humans long for, resting in God's promises, will be ours, not by nature, but by the gift of God. When Jesus came to dwell among us, he came in the fullness of human psychosomatic unity. The Word was made flesh and Jesus cared about the flesh. His body was and is extremely important to what God is doing in the world. And so are our bodies.

Our problem as human beings is not our bodies. Our problem is that our whole beings, as psychosomatic unities, are subject to sin. Paul testifies to the way the incarnation and resurrection of Jesus Christ work for the whole human being, spiritually and physically. He expects our redemption to include the body when he writes, "If the Spirit of him who raised Jesus from the dead dwells in you, he who raised Christ from the dead will give life to your mortal bodies also through his Spirit who dwells in you" (Rom. 8:11). In a world influenced by Plato and Descartes, a dualist concept of what it means to be human has creeping roots buried deep within us. Our default understandings of human being, therefore, are often more Platonic, Cartesian, or gnostic than they are Christian. We speak all the time as though the really important part of who we are is an immaterial, spiritual, or even purely cognitive thing. Christian doctrine helps us practice speaking of ourselves as wholes, to lean against the habit of splitting ourselves into parts. The important theologian Augustine (354–430) recounts the brokenness of his youth, in part, as a time in which he lost his unity—his personal integrity—as the reign of sin in his life threatened to dissolve him into bits. He attempts to write honestly of his past: "I will try now to give a coherent account of my disintegrated self, for when I turned away from

7. Plato, *Phaedo*, trans. David Gallop (New York: Oxford University Press, 1999), 35.

8. René Descartes, *Meditations of First Philosophy: With Selections from the Objections and Replies*, trans. John Cottingham (Cambridge: Cambridge University Press, 1996), 10.

Gustavo Gutiérrez on Sin

Writing about poverty and oppression, Gutiérrez draws attention to the devastation of sin, reminding us that sin is bigger than we would sometimes like to pretend. Notice Gutiérrez's critique of a dualism that would ignore sin against bodies. Gutiérrez writes that sin is not

an individual, private, or merely interior reality—asserted just enough to necessitate "spiritual" redemption which does not challenge the order in which we live. Sin is regarded as a social, historical fact, the absence of fellowship and love in relationships among persons, the breach of friendship with God and with other persons, and, therefore, an interior, personal fracture. When it is considered in this way, the collective dimensions of sin are rediscovered. This is the Biblical notion that José María González Ruiz calls the "hamartiosphere," the sphere of sin: "a kind of parameter or structure which objectively conditions the progress of human history itself." Moreover, sin does not appear as an afterthought, something which one has to mention so as not to stray from tradition or leave oneself open to attack. Nor is this a matter of escape into a fleshless spiritualism. Sin is evident in oppressive structures, in the exploitation of humans by humans, in the domination and slavery of peoples, races, and social classes. Sin appears, therefore, as the fundamental alienation, the root of a situation of injustice and exploitation.[a]

a. Gustavo Gutiérrez, *A Theology of Liberation*, 15th anniversary ed. (Maryknoll, NY: Orbis Books, 1994), 102–3.

you, the one God, and pursued a multitude of things, I went to pieces."[9] Only God could put the pieces back together for Augustine, and as we seek wholeness, integrity, and unity as human beings who follow the integrity of Christ, God will make these gracious gifts real in our lives too.

On the other end of the spectrum from dualism, Christian theological anthropology also rejects any **materialism** that would deny the existence of the spiritual or reduce the human being to a constellation of body parts and nothing more. While popular thought is often dualist, the assumptions of empiricist scientism are materialist. Christians reject reductive understandings of human life that would insist we can be reduced to a series of responses to stimuli or a complicated system of nerves and synapses. In rejecting materialism, Christian thought is not rejecting scientific thought. Many faithful Christian thinkers are working to make sense of the human being as a physical-spiritual creature while also learning from the sciences. The fact that our spiritual lives are unified with our neurons should not surprise Christians who recognize that God created us as psychosomatic

9. Augustine, *Confessions*, trans. Maria Boulding, OSB (New York: Random House, 1997), 2.1, 25.

unities. But, in rejecting materialism, Christian thought firmly rejects any notion that the human being exists only as a kind of biological machine, as if human being can be explained in a mechanical way that leaves no room for a spiritual relationship to God. Wendell Berry (b. 1934) offers a powerful critique of reductive understandings of human being. Berry looks at how we identify human beings with machines and reads this as "the human wish, or the sin of wishing, that life might be, or might be made to be, predictable."[10] There are practical, moral implications in reducing the human being to a machine. Human life, says Berry, "cannot, except by reduction and the grave risk of damage, be controlled. It is . . . holy. To think otherwise is to enslave life, and to make, not humanity, but a few humans its predictably inept masters."[11]

The biblical witness bars us from dismissing either our physicality or our spirituality, but there is plenty of room for intramural debate in Christian thought about the exact constitution of the human being as psychosomatic unity. Christians—in conversation with philosophy, psychology, biology, and ethics—propose different understandings of human nature. Some argue for **nonreductive physicalism**, a kind of materialism that still recognizes the human being in relationship to God.[12] Others work with the language of body-soul dualism, differentiating a Christian **holistic dualism** from the hierarchical dualism that degrades the body.[13] Despite these different accounts, there is widespread agreement that Christian doctrine and practice must reject both hierarchical dualism and reductive materialism. This agreement rules out the dualist who denigrates the body by placing little value on the fleshliness of daily human life and the materialist who denies that human life is intended to be spiritual life lived in vibrant relationship with the living God. In contrast, the Christian claim that the human being is a middle creature, both material and spiritual, is coherent with a different kind of human practice. Josemaria Escriva (1902–75) speaks of

> the temptation . . . to lead a kind of double life: on the one hand, an inner life, a life related to God; and on the other, as something separate and distinct, their

10. Wendell Berry, *Life Is a Miracle: An Essay against Modern Superstition* (Washington, DC: Counterpoint, 2000), 6.

11. Ibid., 9.

12. Warren S. Brown, Nancey Murphy, and H. Newton Malony, eds., *Whatever Happened to the Soul? Scientific and Theological Portraits of Human Nature* (Minneapolis: Fortress, 1998).

13. John W. Cooper, *Body, Soul, and Life Everlasting: Biblical Anthropology and the Monism-Dualism Debate* (Grand Rapids: Eerdmans, 1989).

professional, social, and family lives, made up of small earthly realities. No, my children! We cannot lead a double life. We cannot have a split personality if we want to be Christians. There is only one life, made of flesh and spirit. And it is this life which has to become, in both soul and body, holy and filled with God: we discover the invisible God in the most visible and material things.[14]

As Christians practice being human creatures, we must learn from Jesus to rightly value both flesh and spirit. We learn that Escriva's "small earthly realities" matter. Human beings are not free to compartmentalize our lives, offering part to God but not the whole. The recognition that we are middle creatures, that whatever God intends for human beings is intended for us as psychosomatic wholes, helps us see that the whole of human life is about and for God.

Creatures in the Image of God

As psychosomatic wholes, human beings are created in the image of God (in Latin, *imago Dei*). The doctrine of the image of God begins with Genesis 1:26–27.

> Then God said, "Let us make humankind in our image, according to our likeness; and let them have dominion over the fish of the sea, and over the birds of the air, and over the cattle, and over all the wild animals of the earth, and over every creeping thing that creeps upon the earth." So God created humankind in his image, in the image of God he created them; male and female he created them.

There is something about being human that reflects God's own identity. But what is that something? Christians have suggested a variety of answers to this question throughout history, and theologians often group those answers into one of three categories: the image as a substantial likeness to God, the image as a function in relation to creation, and the image as relational to other human beings.

First, some Christians locate the *imago Dei* in our human likeness to something about God's own nature. They describe that image as residing in some capacity or feature of our existence that lets us relate to God in

---

14. Josemaria Escriva, "Passionately Loving the World," in *Conversations with Josemaria Escriva* (New York: Scepter, 2003), 177.

a way that other animals cannot. This is sometimes called a **substantial view** of the image of God, because it sees human beings as sharing in some aspect of God's substance. Theologians often talk about the human soul as that which makes us unique. Does the presence of a soul explain the image of God in us? What if other creatures have souls as well? It could be that humans are unique because our souls are *different* than animal souls. Perhaps the human soul is different because it gives the human unique characteristics such as the capacity for rational thought, the ability to pursue "the good," a special capability to love others, or an innate sense of God. Perhaps characteristics like these make humans distinct from all other animals, and they make us uniquely able to relate to God.

We could also have a **functional view** of the image of God, emphasizing the unique function human beings have in caring for God's creation. This view draws on the words of God in granting Adam and Eve "dominion over the fish of the sea, and over the birds of the air, and over the cattle, and over all the wild animals of the earth, and over every creeping thing that creeps upon the earth" (Gen. 1:26). The image of God is reflected in the God-given authority and responsibilities that humans have. As ancient Near Eastern kings would set up images to represent their royal power, God places human beings in creation as divine representatives. As such, our function is to remind creation of the presence, power, and character of the true King. The psalmist points to this as part of what makes humans unique and gives us special dignity: "Yet you have made [humans] a little lower than God, and crowned them with glory and honor. You have given them dominion over the works of your hands; you have put all things under their feet" (Ps. 8:5–6). The *imago Dei* here is in what humans *do*, not what we *are*. Perhaps humans are unique because we were created to function or act like God in the way that we live in creation; this unique responsibility means that humans have a way of being that beasts and butterflies simply do not have.

Many contemporary theologians propose a **relational view** of the image of God. This view often begins with God's triune nature, emphasizing God's life as perfect relationship between the Father, Son, and Holy Spirit. To be in the image of God, therefore, might mean that humans are, at our core, beings created to exist in relationship with others. No human can truly be human alone. Not only that, but unlike all other animals, human sociality reflects—or ought to reflect—God's love. Many think that the creation account in Genesis points to the paradigmatic example of this relational love in human life. Right after God says, "Let us make humankind in our image," we read that "God created humankind in his image, in the image of God he created them; male and female he created them" (Gen. 1:27). The mention of "male and female"—and the implication of the relationship between the two—suggests that part of what it means to reflect the image of God is to be in loving *relationship* with others. Neither Adam nor Eve can truly be what he or she is—that is, can truly be a human in the image of God—apart from his or her relationship with and love for the other (2:18–24).

How are we to sort through these ways of understanding the *imago Dei*? All three are suggestive for Christian practice, and all three draw on biblical themes. Certainly, it is true that humans possess qualities that make us different from other animals. It also is true that humans have been given a certain purpose in God's created order. And, again, it is true that humans are truly human in the midst of relationships with God and others. All three ways of thinking about the image of God imply practices for Christian life. For example, the relational model of the *imago Dei* suggests ways for Christians to model their relationships with others—such as those that occur in the home, church, or society at large—upon the pattern of relationality we see in the Trinity.[15] The functionalist model could press us to act rightly as stewards of God's good creation and witnesses to God's love. A substantive account that focuses on the soul's ability to relate to God could offer us ways to direct human capacities like reason or language toward the glorification of God. All of this is exciting for Christians who want to think about the shape of our lives as God's creatures.

But it has often proved dangerous to believe that we can pin down the capacity, the function, or the relationship that makes us human. Such thinking has been used to exclude some human beings from sharing in what it means to be human.[16] For instance, when rationality has been elevated as *the* thing that makes us human, it has been easy enough for us sinful creatures to suggest that anyone who is less rational is probably less human as well. Christians have long supposed that infants, for instance, are actually

15. For two very different proposals of this sort, see Miroslav Volf, *After Our Likeness: The Church in the Image of the Trinity* (Grand Rapids: Eerdmans, 1997); and Bruce Ware, *Father, Son and Holy Spirit: Relationships, Roles, and Relevance* (Wheaton: Crossway, 2005).
16. Ian A. McFarland examines these problems in *Difference and Identity: A Theological Anthropology* (Cleveland: Pilgrim Press, 2001).

human. But if rationality defines what it means to be human, it is an easy step to suggesting that a red-faced, screaming, wiggly creature in a cradle is not so very human after all. Some contemporary advocates for the moral permissibility of abortion use precisely this logic.[17] Accounts of human dominion over creation have been wrenched out of the biblical context that helps us see what dominion ought to look like. They have been used to justify careless and even violent abuses against God's creation. Relational accounts do not always consider that our human relationships are broken. Instead of mirroring God's love, our human sociality is marked by violence, greed, and exploitation. Specific recommendations about modeling human relationships on God's love run a disorientating gamut. Does loving like the Trinity look like an egalitarian democracy, or does it involve submission to authority? Accounts of how human sociality should mirror triune love can easily devolve into justifications for our pet politics or policies. Such accounts also sometimes fail to recognize the ways that human loving simply cannot parallel triune loving because humans are not triune.

It seems clear that we are missing something when we try to understand the human in the image of God any of these ways. In reality, we have a significant problem when we try to connect the doctrine of the *imago Dei* to Christian practice. The problem is this: each one of these views of the *imago Dei* focuses on the human being *as created* by God—that is, human being *before* sin. We cannot talk about how our creation in the "image of God" affects Christian practice without first acknowledging the brutal fact that the image of God has been distorted and broken by sin. In truth, if we want to speak about humans as we really are—which is how we must speak if we want to practice our doctrine—then we must speak about the *sinful* human who is not, in the fullest sense, living as an image of God in the way God intended. Human beings are sinners. We are those who have denied our true being, forfeited our God-given role as the caretakers of creation, and broken our relationships with God and others. Does this mean that we can no longer talk about humans in the image of God? No—as we will see, there is a way to talk about the *imago Dei* as it relates to the human even under sin. We need to understand the true nature of both our sin and its remedy. Only then will we be able to glimpse what it means to bear God's image.

17. For an overview, see J. P. Moreland and Scott B. Rae, *Body and Soul: Human Nature and the Crisis in Ethics* (Downers Grove, IL: InterVarsity, 2000).

Human as Sinful

The very same humans who were made in the image of God have corrupted that image through sin. Theological anthropology needs to take account of that sin, to recognize that "all have sinned and fall short of the glory of God" (Rom. 3:23). The Genesis account of Adam and Eve shows us humans blessed by intimate relationship with God. God gives them dominion over the creatures of the earth (Gen. 1:26) and tells them they can eat the fruit of any tree in the garden but one: "Of the tree of the knowledge of good and evil you shall not eat, for in the day that you eat of it you shall die" (2:15). God's word is tested when a serpent, a figure often associated with Satan, claims that eating the forbidden fruit will make humans "like God, knowing good and evil" (3:4). Will Adam and Eve seize the serpent's lure or trust in God? Their choice has tragic consequences for their relationships with God, creation, and one another. Overcome by shame, they hide from God. Their intimate relationship with God is broken, and their lives will now be subject to death. "Thorns and thistles" (v. 18) will mark the broken relationship between human beings and the rest of creation. The marriage relationship, a preview of all relationships between human beings, is also marked by sin; Eve's desire will be for her husband, and he will rule over her (v. 16). Whether the image of God in human beings is substantive, functional, or relational, it is broken by sin.

For Christians, the story of Adam and Eve's fall into sin is *our* story. Paul speaks of the way human beings participate in far greater realties than our own individuality. We are truly "in Adam" (1 Cor. 15:22). Adam and Eve's story is the story of humanity as a whole. It is also the story of each one of us. Will we trust in God's word, or will we try to make ourselves into gods and choose our own way? The reality of the **fall** has changed what is possible for human beings. Broken by sin, we want to go our own way; we choose to go our own way. We are the kind of creatures who truly want to live in sin even though sin makes us inhuman. The sin recounted at the beginning of Genesis is *our* sin, and we rightly share both the guilt and the dreadful consequences of it.

The Nature of Sin

Sin is many-layered and dense. It is both individual and corporate, infecting individual human beings and human institutions. Sin is both personal and systemic. While it belongs to humans in a special way, it also injures creation, which groans under its weight (Rom. 8:22). Sin extends into every aspect of human life: into body and soul, our ways of knowing and our emotions, work and relationships, hopes and desires. Sin separates us from the holiness of God.

Describing the nature of sin, many theologians emphasize the role played by pride.[18] The root of Adam and Eve's sin lies in their desire to be "like God," to assert self-sufficiency and autonomy over their dependence on and accountability to God. Many Christians connect this desire to the human tendency, noted by Paul, to base our righteousness in ourselves rather than in God (Rom. 10:3). If we think, here, of the worst connotations of "self-righteousness," we will have some sense of the point. Pride plays a role in Adam and Eve's decision as they willfully defy God with the goal of making themselves godlike. John Calvin suggests that the root of sin is unbelief, and "the beginning of the ruin by which the human race was overthrown was a defection from the command of God."[19] In other words, the prideful desire to be "like God" was a result of lack of trust in God's word. This distrust affects our willingness to follow God, and it also strikes at the core of our understanding of our own being as creatures.

If Adam and Eve doubted God's command about the tree, did they also doubt God's judgment that they were "very good" (Gen. 1:31)? We can read Adam and Eve, seeking their own knowledge of good and evil, as doubting God's judgment about them. Their sin shows disbelief in God's word, not only about the tree, but also about themselves. Sin involves a lack of trust in God, and this leads us to a deeper aspect of the nature of sin, which is about untruth.[20] Adam and Eve not only failed to believe God; they believed the false word of the serpent. This points to the treacherous nature of sin: it takes that which is good and negates it, distorting it into something evil. God's creation is good. Sin has to take what is good and bend it in the wrong direction, twisting it away from God. C. S. Lewis points to this when he imagines one demon instructing a junior tempter, "Everything has to be twisted before it's any use to us. . . . Nothing is naturally on our side."[21]

18. See, for example, Augustine, *City of God*, 14.13.
19. John Calvin, *Genesis*, ed. Alister McGrath and J. I. Packer (Wheaton, IL: Crossway, 2001), 43.
20. For an account of sin as "untruth," see Eberhard Jüngel, *Justification: The Heart of the Christian Faith; A Theological Study with an Ecumenical Purpose*, trans. Jeffrey F. Cayzer (London: T&T Clark, 2001), 100–115.
21. C. S. Lewis, *The Screwtape Letters* (New York: HarperCollins, 2001), 118–99.

Seeing sin as untruth helps us understand what it means to say that the human being is a sinner. On one level, the fact that sin is a *false* word means that it cannot be the most basic truth about human existence. Even under sin, the truth about human beings is still that we are "very good" creatures made in God's image. The fact that we are sinners does not undo God's good creation, as if humans could destroy the work of God. The fact that we are sinners does mean that humans are living a lie. In Eberhard Jüngel's (b. 1934) words, "The sinner's life becomes a sham existence."[22] Paul speaks on this theme when he connects human "wickedness" to those who "suppress the truth" (Rom. 1:18). Sin suppresses God's Word to us and about us by twisting it into something false. The consequence is that humans have "exchanged the glory of the immortal God for images resembling a mortal human being or birds or four-footed animals or reptiles" (v. 23). Note the reversal of God's original intention for humans: instead of having dominion over creatures, we are now worshiping them as gods!

Sinful humans have become a parody of what God intended us to be. We have, as Paul says, "exchanged the truth about God for a lie" (v. 25). Under sin, we are unfaithful to God and we become unfaithful bearers of the divine image, false witnesses to the God who made us to bear the divine image. We live a life of falsehood, marked by selfishness, the worship of false gods, and "every kind of wickedness" (v. 29). This life harms us, and it is an affront to God. We are estranged from God, and as we reject the Creator and source of all life, we sinners exist, in Athanasius's words, "in the state of death and corruption."[23] Sin is literally dehumanizing. Death, both physical and spiritual, is the consequence of sin (Rom. 6:23). Because no human is without sin, we are all subject to death. "There is no one who is righteous," Paul says, "not even one" (3:10).

Original Sin

Christians use the language of **original sin** to describe the reality that all human beings are born under the condition of sin, are sinners bound and chained. To understand what it means to be born into sin, we can look at the connection Paul makes between Adam's sin and the sin of all humanity:

22. Jüngel, *Justification*, 110.
23. St. Athanasius, *On the Incarnation* (Crestwood, NY: St. Vladimir's Seminary Press, 1993), 29.

"Sin came into the world through one man, and death came through sin, and so death spread to all because all have sinned" (Rom. 5:12). The idea that sin and death "spread" from Adam to all of humanity means that sin is not just about specific *acts*—either Adam's or ours—but is also about a sinful nature. All of us are included in Adam's sin, and all of us share in sinful human nature, human nature that has been damaged by the fall. Sin is *original* because every human is born under its reign. We are unable to enter into right relationship with God.

Pelagius (c. 390–418), a late ancient monk who lived in what is now Great Britain, insisted that humans do not inherit a corrupted or sinful nature. He taught that each of us stands in the same position as Adam, and each sinful act results from a decision either to obey or disobey God's command. For Pelagius, human nature is basically neutral, not sinful, and each of us is responsible for our own moral choices. So Pelagius says, "We do either good or evil only by our own will; since we always remain capable of both, we are always free to do either."[24] For Pelagius, then, every human has the power to act righteously or sinfully. When humans act righteously, it is because they choose to do so. When they sin, it is because they choose to sin. The key to the Christian life is to break the habit of sin. We are inspired to do so, Pelagius argues, by the example of Jesus Christ who lived a righteous life by choosing not to sin.

This horrified Augustine, who saw that Pelagius's view of human nature distorted the truth of the gospel. Augustine was very aware of his own struggles with sin, of the way it dug its claws deep into him and locked him in its grasp. He thought that Pelagius's account of human nature was cruel because it offered a false gospel, that it taunted broken sinners with false hope. Pelagius, Augustine believed, was telling people chained at the bottom of a deep, deep hole to climb on out. Augustine read the biblical witness to testify that, under the condition of sin, we humans are in a hole from which we cannot escape by our own power. The Council of Orange concurred in rejecting **Pelagian** thought as a heresy.

If anyone says that the whole person, that is, in both body and soul, was not changed for the worse through the offense of Adam's transgression, but that only the body became subject to corruption with the liberty of the

24. Pelagius, "Letter to Demetrias," in *Theological Anthropology*, ed. J. Patout Burns (Philadelphia: Fortress, 1981), 49–50.

soul being unharmed, then he has been deceived by Pelagius's error. . . . If anyone asserts that the transgression of Adam harmed him alone and not his progeny, or that the damage is only by the death of the body which is a punishment for sin, and thus does not confess that the sin itself which is the death of the soul also passed through one person into the whole human race, then he does injustice to God.[25]

Here we see the claims that sin does, in fact, damage human nature, and the punishment due for sin justly applies to the whole human race. This is *good* news because it means we can surrender our sad attempts to do something we cannot do, to save ourselves by righteous acts. We are free to throw ourselves instead on the mercy of Jesus Christ. That, for Augustine and most of Western Christian thought after him, is the very best of news. "Know your disease!" preached John Wesley. "Know your cure! Ye were born in sin; therefore 'ye must be born again,' 'born of God.' By nature ye are wholly corrupted; by grace ye shall be wholly renewed."[26]

Christians have offered at least two interpretations of the means by which all humanity is included in the guilt and punishment of original sin. The first describes the transmission of sinful nature as a kind of hereditary disease passed down from generation to generation.[27] This idea does not remove our responsibility for sin; in Augustine's explanation, we are responsible for our sin because sin is precisely what we want. We desire sin. The fact that sin traps us, that its effects are felt in our lives like an incurable disease, doesn't make sin any less our *own*. Another approach uses a legal explanation to describe the way Adam's sin, and the damage it causes, applies to humans now.[28] Adam's story is the story of every human because he stands as the representative of the entire human race in a legal relationship. As Paul puts it, "one man's trespass led to condemnation for all" (Rom. 5:18). Some explain this concept by using the idea of imputation. To each human being, God imputes, or applies, the guilt for Adam's sin. On this view, our legal guilt inevitably leads us to make the same decision Adam made and commit sins of our own, but the decision is still *our* decision and we are responsible for it.

25. See "Canons of the Council of Orange," in Burns, *Theological Anthropology*, 113.
26. "Original Sin," in *John Wesley's Sermons: An Anthology*, ed. Albert C. Outler and Richard P. Heitzenrater (Nashville: Abingdon, 1991), 334.
27. See the Belgic Confession, Article 15.
28. See, for example, the Westminster Confession, 6.3.

Which Human Nature?

Augustine's theological anthropology, worked out against Pelagianism, makes distinctions between what is possible for human nature as originally created, as fallen, as redeemed, and as it will be in the end. For Augustine, if we want to talk about what it means to be human, we always have to ask what state of humanity we are talking about. Augustine describes this in terms of our relationship to sin.[a]

Augustine sees created human nature as existing in a state of **original righteousness**, in which we were free to choose or not choose to sin:

Created human nature: **posse peccare** (able to sin)

The fall, though, changed the conditions of possibility for humanity, binding the human will to sin:

Fallen human nature: **non posse non peccare** (not able to not sin)

The redemptive work of Jesus opens up new possibilities for human nature and human willing:

Redeemed human nature: **posse non peccare** (able to not sin)

In this life, though, our freedom from sin is partial. Augustine expects the freedom of glory to be full freedom from sin:

Glorified human nature: **non posse peccare** (not able to sin)

a. See Augustine, *Enchiridion* (Washington, DC: Regnery, 1961).

However we conceive the means by which we are included in original sin, it is the case that each and every human being is born into a world dominated by sin and death. Sin precedes our lives, and we live with its effects from our very first breath until our last. In between, we will make our own contributions to this sinful world by committing sinful acts of our own, and these acts will, in turn, affect others. We thus share in the guilt of Adam and Eve not only because we follow in their sinful footsteps but because our sin, like theirs, has tragic consequences for the world around us. Mercifully, this is not the end of the human story. Indeed, sin is not the last or the most important word about us. We are also those who have been made new by the work of Jesus Christ.

The Human as New Creation in Christ

All of this brings us back to the question of how we are to practice the doctrine of the image of God. Given that human nature as we know it is sinful, where can we find a picture of true humanity that applies to us? The answer is that we must look to Jesus of Nazareth, the Messiah. Christians confess that *this* human being is the image of God (2 Cor. 4:4). This means that we need to rethink notions of the *imago Dei* that are based only on God's act of creation. We cannot understand our own humanity if we stop with Adam. This pushes us past the understandings of the *imago Dei* examined above, understandings that are helpful but that nonetheless meet their limits in sin. Adam is merely "a type of the one who was to come" (Rom. 5:14), the forerunner of Jesus Christ. This means that if we want to know what true humanity looks like, we should look not to Adam but to Jesus. Indeed, we must look to Jesus first, because he is the one who is "the image of the invisible God, the firstborn of all creation" (Col. 1:15). Jesus is the true human being, more human than we are.

Practicing Being Human

The New Testament promises that Jesus's true humanity can be applied directly to us so that it becomes our own. We can, in other words, become truly human beings and live truly human lives through Jesus. We become human through *resurrection*. "For since death came through a human being, the resurrection of the dead has also come through a human being; for as all die in Adam, so all will be made alive in Christ" (1 Cor. 15:21–22). We are all sinners who have fallen away from God's original intention for us. Through our sin, we have corrupted God's image in us. But God did not allow sin to define us. "Just as one man's trespass led to condemnation for all, so one man's act of righteousness leads to justification and life for all" (Rom. 5:18). Where our lives were marked by death because of sin, now they are marked by the life of Christ. His righteousness undoes our sinfulness. This means that who we really are as human beings is not defined solely by what God created us to be; nor is it defined by our sin. Rather, Jesus Christ defines our humanity. Our human being will be made complete when we become "like him" (1 John 3:2), remade in the image of his perfect humanity. Or as Paul puts it, "Just as we have borne the image of the man of dust, we will also bear the image of the man of heaven" (1 Cor. 15:49). In the truest sense, we are what we are becoming in and through Christ.

We practice theological anthropology when we ask God to transform our lives here and now into a foretaste of what we will become in the end. This takes place as our lives begin to be transformed into the likeness of Christ.

> You were taught to put away your former way of life, your old self, corrupt and deluded by its lusts, and to be renewed in the spirit of your minds, and to clothe yourselves with the new self, created according to the likeness of God in true righteousness and holiness. (Eph. 4:22–24)

> Do not lie to one another, seeing that you have stripped off the old self with its practices, and have clothed yourselves with the new self, which is being renewed in knowledge according to the image of its creator. (Col. 3:9–10)

Note how Paul is using the term "image" here. The image of God is not something we have as a possession, and it is not limited to a role we play in God's kingdom nor constituted only by our relationships. The image is something we receive in Christ. It means that we are no longer "clothed" with our sinful nature but with the human nature of Jesus (Gal. 3:27). *This* is what it means to exist in the "image of God." The *imago*, contemporary theologian David Kelsey (b. 1932) claims, is not a "what" but a "Who." "'Who is the "image"?' . . . The answer is, 'Jesus Christ.'"[29] As we practice theological anthropology, we learn that *true* human being is a gift, and we receive it through Christ by the power of his resurrection. We learn to base our hopes for what it means to be human on what God has done and is doing among us in Jesus. We will learn, in the power of the Holy Spirit, to be faithful bearers of the image of God, to be transformed—body and soul—into Christlikeness. Human being is not something that we have or are; it is something we *become* in the midst of relationship with God. As we practice theological anthropology, we might make our prayer that of Charles Wesley.

> Now display thy saving power,
> ruined nature now restore;

29. David H. Kelsey, *Eccentric Existence: A Theological Anthropology* (Louisville: Westminster John Knox, 2009), 2:938.

now in mystic union join
thine to ours, and ours to thine.
Adam's likeness, Lord, efface,
Stamp thy image in its place.
Second Adam from above,
Reinstate us in thy love.
Let us thee, though lost, regain,
Thee, the life, the inner man:
O, to all thyself impart,
Formed in each believing heart.[30]

30. Charles Wesley, "Hymn for Christmas-Day," in *Hymns and Sacred Poems (1739)* (London: Strahan, 1739), 206–8. A collection of Charles Wesley's published verse, standardized for scholarly citation, is available at http://divinity.duke.edu/initiatives-centers/cswt/wesley-texts/charles-wesley.

6

||||||||||||||||||||||||||||||||||||||||||||||||||||||||||||||||||||

The Personal Jesus Christ

Christology

The image of God is a person, Jesus Christ. Jesus Christ is God in the flesh, the living, personal center of the Christian faith. Jesus Christ is also the eternal God, the Son, the Second Person of the Trinity. Jesus Christ is Jesus of Nazareth, a first-century Jewish man, the person locals identified by his family relationships, asking, "Is not this the carpenter's son? Is not his mother called Mary? And are not his brothers James and Joseph and Simon and Judas?" (Matt. 13:55). He is the person who gives Christian faith shape and identity. Jesus has shown us who he is by coming, in the flesh, as one of us, "and we have seen his glory, the glory as of a father's only son, full of grace and truth" (John 1:14). He has shown us his person in words and in action and, most tellingly, in giving himself up to death on the cross, which biblical scholar Richard Hays calls "the central *defining* act for his identity."[1] In raising him from the dead, the Spirit and the Father have further revealed who the person Jesus is: "God raised him up, having freed him from death, because it was impossible for him to be held

---

1. Richard Hays, "The Story of God's Son: The Identity of Jesus in the Letters of Paul," in *Seeking the Identity of Jesus: A Pilgrimage*, ed. Beverly Roberts Gaventa and Richard B. Hays (Grand Rapids: Eerdmans, 2008), 189; emphasis Hays's.

Key Scripture

Who has believed what we have heard? And to whom has the arm of the LORD been revealed? For he grew up before him like a young plant, and like a root out of dry ground; he had no form or majesty that we should look at him, nothing in his appearance that we should desire him. He was despised and rejected by others; a man of suffering and acquainted with infirmity; and as one from whom others hide their faces he was despised, and we held him of no account.

Surely he has borne our infirmities and carried our diseases; yet we accounted him stricken, struck down by God, and afflicted. But he was wounded for our transgressions, crushed for our iniquities; upon him was the punishment that made us whole, and by his bruises we are healed. All we like sheep have gone astray; we have all turned to our own way, and the LORD has laid on him the iniquity of us all.

He was oppressed, and he was afflicted, yet he did not open his mouth; like a lamb that is led to the slaughter, and like a sheep that before its shearers is silent, so he did not open his mouth. By a perversion of justice he was taken away. Who could have imagined his future? For he was cut off from the land of the living, stricken for the transgression of my people. They made his grave with the wicked and his tomb with the rich, although he had done no violence, and there was no deceit in his mouth.

Yet it was the will of the LORD to crush him with pain. When you make his life an offering for sin, he shall see his offspring, and shall prolong his days; through him the will of the LORD shall prosper. Out of his anguish he shall see light; he shall find satisfaction through his knowledge. The righteous one, my servant, shall make many righteous, and he shall bear their iniquities. Therefore I will allot him a portion with the great, and he shall divide the spoil with the strong; because he poured out himself to death, and was numbered with the transgressors; yet he bore the sin of many, and made intercession for the transgressors. (Isa. 53)

in its power" (Acts 2:24). The Christian life is a life of relationship with this person, who is both God and human.

In practicing Christology, we learn more about Jesus's identity and more about what it means to live the Christian life, individual and corporate, in relationship with him. In the introduction to his book *Jesus of Nazareth*, Pope Benedict XVI (b. 1927) recounts the way modern developments "have produced a common result: the impression that we have very little certain knowledge of Jesus and that only at a later stage did faith in his divinity shape the image we have of him." Further, "this impression has by now penetrated deeply into the minds of the Christian people at large. This is a dramatic situation for faith, because its point of reference is being placed in doubt: Intimate friendship with Jesus, on which everything depends, is in danger of clutching at thin air."[2] Christology gives testimony against this crisis situation, helping us to know Jesus more, to learn his identity, and to deepen our relationships with the living Lord.

Jesus's identity has been a topic of discussion since his lifetime, and the biblical witness to this discussion reveals important principles for our practice of Christology. When "he asked his disciples, 'Who do people say that the Son of Man is?'" (Matt. 16:13), the disciples mentioned different theories that were out there: "Some say John the Baptist, but others Elijah, and still others Jeremiah or one of the prophets" (v. 14). Jesus does not seem particularly interested in speculation from outside. He wants to know what his disciples—people who know him on an intimate, personal basis—believe. "He said to them, 'But who do you say that I am?' Simon Peter answered, 'You are the Messiah, the Son of the living God.' And Jesus answered him, 'Blessed are you, Simon son of Jonah! For flesh and blood has not revealed this to you, but my Father in heaven'" (vv. 15–17). This story shows that the existence of a variety of theories about Jesus's identity is nothing new. We also find that those theories are not as important as what is known about who Jesus is by people who are in close relationship with him. Christological affirmations come from knowing Jesus. We meet him, personally, in the biblical accounts that testify to his identity.

The Person Jesus

As we grow familiar with the Scriptures, we are privileged to get to know Jesus. We read accounts of his life, his teachings, and his friendships. We see him identified in many ways, as in the story from Matthew just described, where Jesus is named the "Messiah," "the Son of Man," and "the Son of the living God." The claim that Jesus is the Messiah announces the continuity of God's work across the Old and New Testaments. Jesus the Messiah is the promised one, the anointed one, the savior. The title "Son of Man" looks like it refers to Jesus's humanity, but in the biblical context it is, even more, a pointer to his divinity. (There are plenty of New Testament markers of Jesus's humanity, but "Son of Man" has other connotations first.) In

---

2. Pope Benedict XVI, *Jesus of Nazareth: From the Baptism in the Jordan to the Transfiguration* (New York: Doubleday, 2007), xii.

the apocalyptic vision of the book of Daniel, the prophet sees one "like a human being coming with the clouds of heaven" (Dan. 7:13). In Matthew, Jesus echoes Daniel when he answers the high priest's accusation that he believes himself to be "the Messiah, the Son of God" with the words "You have said so. But I tell you, from now on you will see the Son of Man seated at the right hand of Power and coming on the clouds of heaven" (v. 64). The high priest hears this as a statement about Jesus's divine power and authority, a statement that, were it not true, would be just what the high priest declares it to be: "He has blasphemed!" (Matt 26:65).[3] The Son of Man is the one who has been "given dominion and glory and kingship, that all peoples, nations, and languages should serve him. His dominion is an everlasting dominion that shall not pass away, and his kingship is one that shall never be destroyed" (Dan. 7:14). Jesus the "Son of Man" *is* Jesus the "Son of God," who is so intimate with the Father, so beloved by the Father, that we know him to be "the reflection of God's glory and the exact imprint of God's very being" (Heb. 1:3).

Christian doctrine, born of reading and interacting with the New Testament witness, identifies Jesus as both divine and human. Jesus our savior is truly God, and he is truly one of us. In chapter 3, we saw the logic that led to the Nicene assertion that Jesus is fully God, *homoousios* with the Father. Jesus is the one in whom "the whole fullness of deity dwells bodily" (Col. 2:9). He claims identity with the Old Testament God, crying out, "Before Abraham was, I am" (John 8:58). Jesus, "full of the Holy Spirit" (Luke 4:1), acts with power and authority, performing miracles and forgiving sins and showing himself as Lord over creation, the one whom "even the wind and the sea obey" (Mark 4:41). Our relationship with him is the proper kind of relationship between humans and God; we are baptized in his name, worship him, and trust in him for salvation.

Christ the Lord, God's eternal Son, enters into the fullness of our humanity. He is born and is, like us, bodily. He grows, developing as human beings do, increasing "in wisdom and in years, and in divine and human favor" (Luke 2:52). He knows human limits, weakness, tiredness, and suffering. He has emotions, weeping at his friend's tomb (John 11:35) and grieving in Gethsemane (Matt. 26:36–40). Jesus is God, our Savior, Creator,

3. For a helpful discussion of issues related to the title "Son of Man," see Darrell L. Bock, "The Son of Man in Luke 5:24," *Bulletin for Biblical Research* 1 (1991): 109–21.

and Lord, and Jesus is a human being, who "had to become like his brothers and sisters in every respect, so that he might be a merciful and faithful high priest in the service of God, to make a sacrifice of atonement for the sins of the people" (Heb. 2:17). While this chapter focuses on Jesus's person, and the next chapter on salvation, this passage from Hebrews shows the interconnections between Jesus's identity and what he did for us in the cross and resurrection. "Because he himself was tested by what he suffered," we read, "he is able to help those who are being tested" (Heb. 2:18). This is the logic that drove christological discussion in the ancient church. In Jesus, in who he is, is our comfort and our hope. He is *with us* and *for us* right down to the very marrow, his and ours, in a way that is only possible because he is truly God and truly human. Jesus saves us by making our situation his own.

Most Christians have heard these basic affirmations about Jesus—he is God, he is human—but we may not recognize just how vital this christological teaching is to the beauty, truth, and goodness of what God has done for us in Jesus Christ. The development of the doctrine of the person of Christ helps us to understand these doctrinal claims at a deeper level. As we did with the doctrine of the Trinity—where we already encountered some of the most important truths about Jesus—we will look at the logic of the historical conversations that helped to clarify the doctrine of the person of Christ for the early church. This is not a strictly historical account of these matters.[4] Instead, I focus here on the ideas that drove this conversation, ideas about who Jesus is and why that matters for us as his followers.

The ancient church grappled with key questions about Jesus's identity in the christological controversies. The trinitarian doctrine of the Council of Nicaea (325), with its recognition that Jesus is fully and truly God, *homoousios* with the Father, became the shared backdrop against which further questions about who Jesus is could be considered. Given Jesus's divinity, given the rejection of Arian subordinationism that would have made Jesus less than the Father, how were Jesus's followers to understand his humanity? How could two such different realities—Creator and created, divine and human, eternal and finite—coexist in the person who stands at the center

4. For that, see Leo Donald Davis, *The First Seven Ecumenical Councils (325–787): Their History and Theology* (Collegeville, MN: Liturgical Press, 1983); John Behr, *The Way to Nicaea*, vol. 1 of *The Formation of Christian Theology* (Crestwood, NY: St. Vladimir's Seminary Press, 2001); John McGuckin, *Saint Cyril of Alexandria and the Christological Controversy* (Crestwood, NY: St. Vladimir's Seminary Press, 2004).

of the Christian faith? The church would wrestle with these questions at a profound level, and the result of that wrestling was articulated at the ecumenical Council of Chalcedon (451). Before we look at the doctrinal language of Chalcedon, it will first be helpful to consider the concerns that animated the christological controversies as Christians sought a doctrine of the person of Christ that is coherent with Scripture and with the realities of salvation.

Immutability + Finitude?

Why is it difficult to understand that Jesus is truly God and truly human at the same time? In the ancient world—and the logic extends into our present context—this raised concerns about the mixing of opposites, the coexistence of things that seem, by their very nature, to exclude each other. To appreciate the logical conundrums surrounding Jesus's identity, it is helpful to think about what it means to be God and what it means to be human. There is no doubt that Christian doctrine presses us to recognize the difference between divinity and humanity. This is a key implication of the doctrines of the Trinity and creation. The divine-human difference can be expressed in terms of characteristics that are contradictory with one another. God is eternal; human beings live in fleeting time. The psalmist trades on this divine-human difference in praise and supplication.

> Lord, you have been our dwelling place
>   in all generations.
> Before the mountains were brought forth,
>   or ever you had formed the earth and the world,
>   from everlasting to everlasting you are God.
> You turn us back to dust,
>   and say, "Turn back, you mortals."
> For a thousand years in your sight
>   are like yesterday when it is past,
>   or like a watch in the night. (Ps. 90:1–4)

God contains all space, all knowing, and all power (the classic "omni-" attributes listed below), but humanity is limited in all of these. We, in the words of a song many of us sang as children, are "weak but he is strong." The divine-human difference is deeper than the fabric of creation itself, and all this difference is the case before we have even begun to discuss the heartbreaking rift between God and human beings caused by sin. All of this should begin to illumine the problem faced during the Christology controversies. How could two such different realities both be the truth about the person Jesus?

Divinity	Humanity
eternal	temporal
omni-present, -scient, -potent	finite
holy	sinful
immutable	changeable

To call God "immutable" is to claim that God does not change. God is perfect, and God is the perfection of all good things. God's goodness is perfect. God is perfect kindness and perfect justice, and God's **immutability** is a corollary of this divine perfection. How can perfect goodness change? Can it become less good? More so? Different in its kind of goodness? So with the other perfections of God. If perfection implies completeness, fullness, and wholeness, then the idea of immutability makes sense as one way of pointing at God's greatness, one way of pointing at the difference between God and us.

Of the four sets of categories in the list above, the idea of immutability is the least intuitive to contemporary thinkers, but it was a key category in the ancient conversation, and it reaffirms differences named in the other pairings. The affirmation that God is immutable has taken heavy criticism in recent theology,[5] and some fear that to understand God as immutable is to make God into a cold, aloof sovereign with no real relationship to creation and people. These critics suggest that divine immutability is an import from Greek thought and has little to do with the God of the Bible or Christian theology. I think this critique is mistaken on two grounds. First, there is no such thing as a "pure" Christian theology, one that is unadulterated by the philosophies or intellectual contexts in which Christians are located. It is not only *inevitable* that Christian theologians will work with the intellectual resources of their contexts; it is *desirable* that we do so. Scripture is the norm for Christian thought, the norm that stands over other resources, because Scripture is unique as God's Word to us. All Christian theology is a conversation about Scripture, but the Reformation principle of *sola*

5. See, for example, Clark Pinnock et al., *The Openness of God: A Biblical Challenge to the Traditional Understanding of God* (Downers Grove, IL: InterVarsity, 1994). For more on this conversation, see D. Stephen Long and George Kalantzis, eds., *The Sovereignty of God Debate* (Eugene, OR: Cascade, 2009).

"Of the Father's Love Begotten"

This fifth-century hymn by Aurelius Clemens Prudentius sings praise to Christ.

> Of the Father's love begotten, ere the worlds began to be,
> He is Alpha and Omega, He the source, the ending He,
> Of the things that are, that have been,
> And that future years shall see, evermore and evermore!
>
> At His Word the worlds were framed; He commanded; it was done:
> Heaven and earth and depths of ocean in their threefold order one;
> All that grows beneath the shining
> Of the moon and burning sun, evermore and evermore!
>
> He is found in human fashion, death and sorrow here to know,
> That the race of Adam's children doomed by law to endless woe,
> May not henceforth die and perish
> In the dreadful gulf below, evermore and evermore!
>
> O that birth forever blessed, when the virgin, full of grace,
> By the Holy Ghost conceiving, bare the Savior of our race;
> And the Babe, the world's Redeemer,
> First revealed His sacred face, evermore and evermore!
>
> This is He Whom seers in old time chanted of with one accord;
> Whom the voices of the prophets promised in their faithful word;
> Now He shines, the long expected,
> Let creation praise its Lord, evermore and evermore!
>
> O ye heights of heaven adore Him; angel hosts, His praises sing;
> Powers, dominions, bow before Him, and extol our God and King!
> Let no tongue on earth be silent,
> Every voice in concert sing, evermore and evermore!
>
> Christ, to Thee with God the Father, and, O Holy Ghost, to Thee,
> Hymn and chant with high thanksgiving, and unwearied praises be:
> Honor, glory, and dominion,
> And eternal victory, evermore and evermore!

scriptura does not mean that Scripture stands isolated from the messy world. Scripture exists to speak in just that world. To dismiss divine immutability simply because it is a concept from Greek thought is to forget that all kinds of thought—Greek, Latin, American, African, medieval, modern, and all the rest—can be brought to the Bible. All kinds of thought, as the thought of sinful people estranged from God, will need to be disciplined by the Word of God, and all kinds of thought—inasmuch as there is truth, reasonableness, and beauty therein—may help us to understand the Bible in the thought worlds in which we dwell.

This leads to the second reason that I am unconvinced by contemporary dismissals of immutability. At its best, affirmation of God's immutability has always come from disciplined reflection on Scripture and has been disciplined by Scripture. The idea that God's difference from us might be expressed through a concept like immutability is a theme in Scripture. Psalm 102 contrasts impermanent created life with God's life: "They will perish, but you endure; they will all wear out like a garment. You change them like clothing, and they pass away; but you are the same, and your years have no end" (vv. 26–27). Malachi shows the contrast between God's faithfulness to the people of Israel and the faithlessness of people: "I the LORD do not change; therefore you, O children of Jacob, have not perished" (Mal. 3:6). The book of James celebrates God as faithful giver in "whom there is no variation or shadow due to change" (James 1:17).

Theologians like Augustine are thinking *with* Scripture when they affirm divine immutability and its close cousin, **impassibility** (not being subject to the passions or suffering). Augustine does not think that God has emotions that "disturb the mind," but he wants nothing to do with a cold, hard impassibility; if impassibility "is to be defined as a condition such that the mind cannot be touched by any emotion whatsoever, who would not judge such insensitivity to be the worst of all vices?"[6] Theologian David Bentley Hart (b. 1965) argues that, for the ancient church, immutability and impassibility were pastoral affirmations of God's goodness and faithfulness, comforting truth that "is also an affirmation that God is truly good, that creation is freely worked and freely loved."[7] The immutable, impassible God is the faithful God of the Bible, the God of the hymn "Great Is Thy Faithfulness," which references James 1:17 in the lyric "there is no shadow of turning with thee; thou changest not, thy compassions they fail not; as thou hast been, thou forever wilt be."[8] God is the faithful, steady, and sure God whose passions are truly *with* us. God's passions are unfailing compassions, seen in the passion of Christ, whose faithfulness led him to the cross for love of us.

6. Augustine, *The City of God against the Pagans*, trans. and ed. R. W. Dryson (Cambridge: Cambridge University Press, 1998), 14.9.600.

7. David Bentley Hart, "No Shadow of Turning," *Pro Ecclesia* 11, no. 2 (2002): 184–206.

8. Thomas O. Chisholm, "Great Is Thy Faithfulness," in *The United Methodist Hymnal* (Nashville: The United Methodist Publishing House, 1989), #140.

Divine immutability encapsulates the difference between God and us, and it is this difference that creates the christological "problem" of the ancient controversies. How could God, who is not us, become one of us?[9] How could God, who is perfect, eternal, and immutable, be identified with a human being, with human limits, and subject to change and suffering? To some, it seemed laughable or, worse, blasphemous to suggest that the Holy God had become a baby boy or that nails might be driven through God's hands to secure him to a cross. It is not for nothing that Paul preaches, "We proclaim Christ crucified, a stumbling block to Jews and foolishness to Gentiles" (1 Cor. 1:23). The mercy of the incarnation does not undo the paradox or clear away the mystery. It is not a purely rational solution to the seeming impossibility of the holy and eternal God becoming a vulnerable infant or bleeding sacrifice, but it *is* a recognition of what God has done in Jesus, of its beauty and its graciousness, which has the power to move us to praise. Squeamishness about the humanity of Jesus is not limited to the ancient context. New Testament scholar Raymond Brown (1928–98) writes, "Those who have problems with the humanity of Jesus are often not even aware of their bias. . . . Realistically, it may well be that most Christians *tolerate* only as much humanity as they deem consonant with their view of divinity."[10] God's mercy, though, goes deeper than what we think we are willing to tolerate, and "God's foolishness," as Paul goes on, "is wiser than human wisdom, and God's weakness is stronger than human strength" (1 Cor. 1:25). With the "foolishness," the "stumbling block" of the incarnation before us, we are in a place to consider several attempts to make that foolishness submit to human wisdom or to clear the stumbling block out of the way. These attempts are recognized as heresies because they do not make sense in light of the biblical testimony to the incarnation.

Christological Heresies

The christological heresies represent three attempts to rationalize or remove the gracious paradox of the incarnation. All of these heresies presuppose that God cannot truly be united with humanity, and so all propose that

9. Robert Louis Wilken summarizes Celsus's objections to the incarnation in *The Christians as the Romans Saw Them* (New Haven: Yale University Press, 2003), 102–5.
10. Raymond Brown, *An Introduction to New Testament Christology* (New York: Paulist Press, 1994).

Jesus, who is God, must be less than truly human or protected from the mess that is humanity. All were rejected in favor of the affirmation that the incarnation is the real union of the real God with the full reality of humanness.

Apollinarianism

Named for Apollinaris of Laodicea (c. 310–c. 390), **Apollinarianism** attempts to "solve" the problem of Jesus by suggesting that he must have been less than fully human. Apollinaris posited that, in Jesus, the divine Word replaced the human spirit. On the Apollinarian understanding of Jesus, the Word was "functioning in his body as mind and will,"[11] as if the Word had taken over a human body. John Behr describes this "understanding of the incarnation" as "ensouling."[12] If we were to imagine the incarnation as God's mind or spirit (Apollinaris uses the term *logos*) taking over or possessing a human body, we would have an Apollinarian idea of Jesus, an idea that is probably not far off from what many Christians imagine. Apollinarianism fashions a Jesus who is missing something essential to his humanity.[13] Apollinaris saw that humans are tricky, fickle things, often irrational and unreliable, and he could not imagine God sharing in that situation. His solution, then, was to imagine that in Jesus the problematic human spirit was swapped out in favor of the divine logos, giving us a Jesus who is less than fully human. Any Christology that tries to exempt Jesus from some aspect of being human is akin to the Apollinarian heresy.

Apollinarianism's most serious failing is that it cannot account for the way that Jesus saves. Earlier we noted connections between Christology and our understanding of salvation, and we will look at this in more depth in the next chapter. Salvation is tied up with Jesus becoming truly one of us. He makes our problem his own, and shares all that is his with us. Paul touches on these ideas when he reminds us of "the generous act of our Lord Jesus Christ, that though he was rich, yet for your sakes he became poor, so that by his poverty you might become rich" (2 Cor. 8:9). Because of the biblical testimony to the way Jesus redeems, challengers of Apollinarianism objected to any Christology that would excise some part of humanity

---

11. Margaret R. Miles, *The Word Made Flesh: A History of Christian Thought* (Oxford: Blackwell, 2005), 107–8.

12. Behr, *Way to Nicaea*, 240.

13. Miles, *Word Made Flesh*, 108.

from Jesus. If something is "ours," they reasoned, if something belongs to our human condition, then our hope rests in its becoming Jesus's as well. "What is not assumed is not saved," cried Apollinaris's opponents. Jesus assumes—he takes on—the fullness of the human condition and, in doing so, saves whole human beings. Jesus, wholly incarnate, is the savior of whole humans, in psychosomatic unity. Every aspect of our humanity is in need of salvation, and whatever makes us human—be it body, mind, soul, spirit, strength—is in need of Jesus. This critique of Apollinarian Christology was not new. It has biblical footings, and something similar had been articulated against gnostic concepts of Jesus, which denied that he truly had a body. Still, the rejection of the Apollinarian Jesus cemented Christian teaching about Jesus's full and true humanity. Jesus is no subhuman, no false human, and—most tempting of all—no superhuman.

Eutychianism

The next heresy imperiled Jesus's humanity in a different way. Where Apollinarianism imagines a less-than-human Jesus, **Eutychianism** presents a Jesus whose humanity has been undone by God. It is named for Eutyches (c. 380–c. 456), who taught that "Christ is of two natures before the Incarnation, of only one afterwards."[14] This heresy is also sometimes called **monophysitism**, because it sees the incarnate Jesus as having only one nature (*physis*). The error here is to assume that when divinity and humanity meet, divinity must trump humanity. If one imagines the incarnation as a cosmic collision between divinity and humanity, the divine nature, being omnipotent, holy, and so on, will either dramatically change or completely obliterate the human nature. In this way of thinking, Jesus's human nature, when it meets the divine, is either destroyed or so changed as to cease to be recognizably human. The human nature has been flattened or, in being mixed with the omnipotent divine nature, has become something other than human. Instead of divinity that is divinity and humanity that is humanity, Jesus's incarnate nature becomes some other thing, a mixture that is not true to either of the natures from which it came.

This Jesus can no longer claim to share in our humanity in any meaningful way; his humanity becomes, in Eutyches's analogy, like a drop of vinegar in the ocean of divinity. The result was that "the genuine humanity

14. Davis, *First Seven Ecumenical Councils*, 171.

of Christ and the importance of his historical reality were in danger of being swept away by an imprecise terminology."[15] Eutychianism is rejected because it denies the true humanity of the Lord. In rejecting the Eutychian heresy, the church recognized that God's dealings with humanity, in mercy, are not a matter of cosmic collision, and God does not solve the problem of human sin by destroying us or flattening us. In the gracious miracle of the incarnation, divinity unites with humanity while allowing it to be truly human. We, who are also human, have much to consider here in gratitude, for the rejection of Eutychianism is also the rejection of mistaken ideas that our salvation must basically destroy who we are. Not so. God's saving work in our lives is with us, not against us. When God works to save us, he does not wipe away our humanity, our particularity, or our personality. The mercy of God's salvation is to redeem his good work in us.

Nestorianism

The **Nestorian** heresy is the most subtle and pernicious of the christological heresies. It acknowledges the fullness of both Jesus's humanity and his divinity. This recognition, at first blush, *looks like* enough, and herein is the perniciousness of the heresy. Nestorius (c. 386–c. 450), bishop of Constantinople, saw that Jesus is divine and human, but he wanted to keep the two natures separate in important ways. Nestorian separation between Jesus's divine and human natures was meant to protect a certain idea of the sovereignty of God. In rejecting Nestorianism as heresy, the ancient church judged that this separation between Jesus's divinity and humanity leaves little hope for all of us humans, who trust in Jesus to undo the separation between God and us. Nestorius had internalized the truth of the vast difference between God and us, and he would have outlined that difference in much the same way we saw earlier.

God = holy, transcendent, immutable, savior
Humanity = finite, changeable, suffers

Nestorianism handled the question about how these two could meet by insisting that they would remain logically separable. Jesus's divine nature, for the Nestorian, did things appropriate for God. The Nestorian Jesus, in his

15. Ibid.

divinity, saves us, overcomes death, and is omniscient. Nestorius wanted to confine the human things that Jesus did to his human nature. So the Nestorian Jesus's human nature is the nature that did things like eat, cry, suffer, and die.

This kind of christological division appeals to a certain kind of piety and logic. It would dishonor God, Nestorius thinks, to attribute base human characteristics to him. Again, Nestorius thinks it is simply nonsense to suggest that God, who is eternal, might die. In the logic of Nestorianism, it "is as foolish to suggest that Jesus can raise someone from the dead as it is to suggest that the Logos can ever die. The man Jesus of Nazareth dies on the cross, therefore, as a man subject to mortality like all other men. God the Word raised him from the dead as himself one who was beyond the power of death. The distinctive spheres and capacities of both . . . were always preserved."[16] Nestorian Christology looks at Jesus's actions and tries to sort out which nature is responsible for each. Needs his diaper changed? Human. Miraculous healing? Divine. Crying at Lazarus's tomb? Human. Raising Lazarus from the grave? Divine. Bleeding on the cross? Human. Resurrection from the dead? Divine. This makes for a neat and tidy Christology, one that protects a piety that insists God must be beyond our troubles; but it is a heretical Christology because it undoes the mercies of the God who is powerful enough to have no need of our protection and loving enough to cry, suffer, and die for our sake.

Cyril of Alexandria (d. 444) was furious about Nestorius's move to separate the divine and human in Jesus, creating what seemed to Cyril to be two Jesuses and attacking the bridge that the incarnation builds between God and humanity. Nestorius began his thinking with the incompatibility of divinity and humanity and then tried to find a way to bring them together. Cyril's thinking started with the person of Jesus, in whom he saw revealed the fullness of divine and human natures. The fight between Cyril and Nestorius centered on a title for Jesus's mother: *theotokos*, the one who gave birth to God. Nestorius thought the title was inappropriate, even profane, for the eternal God cannot be born. For Nestorius, Jesus was born in his human nature, not in his divine nature. Nestorius spoke of Jesus's divine and human natures as associated with one another. Cyril recognized that this was simply not enough. Jesus, who is God and human, was born. What Jesus, who is God and human, does, he does as God incarnate. For Cyril,

16. McGuckin, *Saint Cyril of Alexandria*, 153.

the whole import of the incarnation, its truth and its significance, rests on this. Our desperate need is for God with us, not God associated with us. Cyril insisted that the two natures of Jesus are, in the incarnation, united. They are truly one person, the Lord Jesus Christ. All that Jesus does he does as that one divine and human person. In other words, Jesus (who is God and human) is born. Jesus (who is God and human) suffers and dies. Jesus (who is God and human) is our savior. Against Nestorius, Cyril therefore insisted that *theotokos*, because of the incarnation, is an appropriate title for Mary. The baby born of Mary is none other than God.

Theologian Thomas Weinandy explains Cyril's theology: "The Incarnation is not the compositional union of natures but the person of the Son taking on a new manner or mode of existence. . . . It can actually be said then that the person of the Son of God is truly born, grieves, suffers and dies, not as God, but as man for that is now the new manner in which the Son of God actually exists."[17] In other words, Jesus is not a composite or a sum of divinity plus humanity, and the incarnation was not a collision of a divine thing with a human thing. Neither is the incarnation a matter of God taking over a human being for his use. Jesus's humanity has no existence outside of the incarnation. It was not sitting around, waiting for the possibility that God might enter into partnership with it. Jesus's humanity came into existence only because God the Son came among us. In the incarnation, the eternal Son, who is fully divine, becomes human. This understanding lets Cyril, in writing on the unity of Christ, marvel at the goodness of the incarnation.

> Indeed the mystery of Christ runs the risk of being disbelieved precisely because it is so incredibly wonderful. For God was in humanity. He who was above all creation was in our human condition; the invisible one was made visible in the flesh; he who is from the heavens and from on high was in the likeness of earthly things; the immaterial one could be touched; he who is free in his own nature came in the form of a slave; he who blesses all creation became accursed; he who is all righteousness was numbered among the transgressors; life itself came in the appearance of death. All this followed because the body which tasted death belonged to no other but to him who is the Son by nature.[18]

17. Thomas G. Weinandy, *Does God Suffer?* (Notre Dame, IN: University of Notre Dame Press, 2000), 200.

18. Cyril of Alexandria, *On the Unity of Christ*, trans. John McGuckin (Crestwood, NY: St. Vladimir's Seminary Press, 2000), 61.

Chalcedonian Christology

The ecumenical **Council of Chalcedon** (451) worked through the questions raised by the christological heresies, and it resulted in a doctrinal statement defining boundaries for Christian talk about and understanding of the identity of Jesus Christ. The council affirmed that Jesus Christ has two natures, fully divine and fully human, and that those two natures are truly united in one person. Against Apollinarianism, Chalcedon affirms that Jesus is "complete . . . in his humanity" and "composed of a rational soul and a body." Against Eutychianism, Chalcedon states that the distinction of Christ's divine and human natures is not taken away by their union. Divinity remains divinity. Humanity remains humanity. Against Nestorianism, Chalcedonian Christology will not see the two natures of Christ as "divided or torn." Chalcedon stands as an important benchmark for the doctrine of Christology, and it provides a classic, orthodox statement about the identity of Christ. The definition of Chalcedon is a further clarification of the Nicene Creed, because at Chalcedon the church recognized that the one God, who exists eternally in three persons, worked decisively in the incarnation. The Second Person of the eternal Trinity became incarnate in Jesus Christ. Jesus is God, in truth, and he is one of us, in truth. We cannot explain the mystery, but we can affirm the beauty, love, and mercy that are here: God has become one of us.

Nicea, Doctrine of the Trinity	Chalcedon, Doctrine of the Person of Christ
One God	
Three persons	
Father	
Son ⟶	One person
	Two natures in unity: divine and human
Holy Spirit	

The language of "person" names both the Second Person of the Trinity and the historical person Jesus of Nazareth, God in the flesh. Eternally, this person is God. Beginning early in the first century in the womb of Mary, God became human. In this person, Jesus, are the fullness of divine nature and the fullness of human nature. In Jesus, we see divinity in its divine integrity, in no way less than truly God. In Jesus, we see humanity in its human integrity, in no way inhuman.

Thus, when Christians talk about the **two natures** of Jesus Christ, we affirm that he is both divine and human. The Christology of Chalcedon does not "solve" the supposed problem of the incarnation, nor does it tell us precisely what it means for divinity and humanity to be in unity in Jesus. Instead, the definition affirms what God has done in the divine-human Jesus while also maintaining silence about the deep mysteries of the incarnation. At Chalcedon, Christians identified ways of thinking about Christology that should be excluded as incoherent with the biblical narrative. On the one side, Jesus's divine and human natures are not to be confused

> ## The Definition of Chalcedon
>
> Following, therefore, the holy fathers, we confess one and the same Son, who is our Lord Jesus Christ, and we all agree in teaching that this very same Son is complete in his deity and complete—the very same—in his humanity, truly God and truly a human being, this very same one being composed of a rational soul and a body, coessential with the Father as to his deity and coessential with us—the very same one—as to his humanity, being like us in every respect apart from sin. As to his deity, he was born from the Father before the ages, but as to his humanity, the very same one was born in the last days from the Virgin Mary, the Mother of God, for our sake and the sake of our salvation: one and the same Christ, Son, Lord, Only Begotten, acknowledged to be unconfusedly, unalterably, undividedly, inseparably in two natures, since the difference of the natures is not destroyed because of the union, but on the contrary, the character of each nature is preserved and comes together in one person and one hypostasis, not divided or torn into two persons but one and the same Son and only-begotten God, Logos, Lord Jesus Christ—just as in earlier times the prophets and also the Lord Jesus Christ himself taught us about him, and the symbol of our Fathers transmitted to us.[a]
>
> a. "The Council of Chalcedon's 'Definition of the Faith,'" in *The Christological Controversy*, trans. and ed. Richard A. Norris Jr. (Philadelphia: Fortress, 1980), 159.

with one another, nor are they to be understood as somehow mixed together. On the other side, Jesus's natures cannot be understood as separated from or divided against each other. Theologian Sarah Coakley (b. 1951) suggests that a "playful case could be made" for reading Chalcedon as a riddle: "Q: What is 'without confusion,' 'without change,' 'without division,' 'without separation'? A: Two natures in one Person, Christ."[19] To

19. Sarah Coakley, "What Does Chalcedon Solve and What Does It Not? Some Reflections on the Status and Meaning of the Chalcedonian 'Definition,'" in *The Incarnation: An*

put the Chalcedonian exclusions in positive terms, the two natures of Jesus Christ are complete natures. They have integrity. At the same time, those natures are united. To affirm the integrity of the natures, of Jesus's divinity and humanity, is to reject any Christology (including Apollinarianism and Eutychianism) that would see Jesus's humanity as anything less than human or that would regard Jesus's divinity as anything less than divine. To affirm the unity of the natures, of Jesus's divinity and humanity, is to reject any Christology (including Nestorianism) that separates Jesus's humanity from his divinity or seeks to protect his divinity from becoming too heavily implicated in our human, creaturely mess.

Hypostatic Union

As we practice Christology, we use the language of **hypostatic union** to describe the unity of the divine and human natures in the person Jesus. That unity is real. It cannot be broken or torn asunder. It is such that all that belongs to each nature truly belongs to the person, Jesus. The term *hypostatic union* describes only the incarnation, and there is no other unity just like it. Still, the church has looked for helpful analogies, and Christians have often described the hypostatic union as not unlike the psychosomatic unity of body and soul in the human being. One person is truly physical and truly spiritual, and all that she does she does body and soul. The idea of hypostatic union is unity between the divine and human natures in the person of Jesus Christ that is real, unbreakable, and true. All that Jesus does, he does as God and as a human being.

Hypostatic union implies another important theological concept called the **communication of attributes** (*communicatio idiomatum*). The communication of attributes shows us how to think about the things that are appropriate to God (attributes such as eternality, immutability) and the things that are appropriate to humanity (attributes such as finitude and mortality) when we see those attributes in the incarnate Jesus. Before Jesus came to dwell among us, we understood the following:

God saves.
Humans suffer.

Interdisciplinary Symposium on the Incarnation of the Son of God, ed. Stephen T. Davis, Daniel Kendall, SJ, and Gerald O'Collins, SJ (New York: Oxford University Press, 2004), 155.

The doctrines of the Trinity and creation taught us to recognize the divine-human difference and to see why these sentences do not (except in the incarnation) work the other way around. God cannot suffer. Humans cannot save. But what happens after we meet Jesus, who is, in his person, the unity of divinity and humanity? The doctrine of the incarnation does not deny the difference between God and us. Instead, it recognizes that, in the incarnation, God has done something miraculous with that difference.

In the unity of Jesus's person, attributes are communicated. In the hypostatic union, the attributes appropriate to the divine nature must be attributed to the person Jesus. In the hypostatic union, the attributes appropriate to the human nature must also be attributed to the person Jesus. All those things that belong only to God are true of Jesus. Jesus, truly human, is really God. Human attributes that usually cannot describe God are true of Jesus. Jesus, truly God, is born, suffers, and dies. Everything Jesus does—from the moment of his conception in Mary's womb up to today—he does as God with us, God among us. When we meet Jesus, we meet God and humanity in person.

Nestorius wanted a Jesus with a separation of divine and human attributes, a Jesus whose divine nature did divine things, like miracles, and whose human nature did human things, like crying. By the grace of God, the incarnation does not work like that. In Jesus we see a communication of divine and human attributes. The one person Jesus is the one who commands the heavens and who weeps when his friend dies. Jesus, truly-God-and-truly-human, ate fish. Jesus, truly-God-and-truly-human, healed the man with the withered hand. Jesus, truly-God-and-truly-human, suffered on the cross. Divinity does not stand back from humanity. God is truly with us, in person, in Jesus. This is good news for us, for in it we meet the God who will not leave us estranged from life with him, the God who reaches across the divide between his holiness and our sin, to bring us into intimate relationship with him. In Cyril's words against Nestorianism, "When [the Son] became like us, even though he always remained what he was, he did not deprecate our condition. No, . . . he accepted, along with the limitations of manhood, all those things which pertain to the human condition, and he regarded nothing therein as unworthy of his personal glory or nature; for yes, and even so, he is God and Lord of all."[20] This is the wonder of

20. Quoted in McGuckin, *Saint Cyril of Alexandria*, 220.

Christology. It lies behind our ability to speak truths that are central to the good news of Jesus Christ, truths that seemed like blasphemies to Nestorius, truths that Jesus, in love for us, was willing to make his own:

God suffered.

Jesus saves.

Though he was God, Jesus

> did not regard equality with God as something to be exploited, but emptied himself, taking the form of a slave, being born in human likeness. And being found in human form, he humbled himself and became obedient to the point of death—even death on a cross. Therefore God also highly exalted him and gave him the name that is above every name, so that at the name of Jesus every knee should bend, in heaven and on earth and under the earth, and every tongue should confess that Jesus Christ is Lord, to the glory of God the Father. (Phil. 2:6–11)

	Monophysite	Nestorian	Orthodox
Number of natures	One	Two	Two
Relationship between the natures	Mixture of divine and human	Association of divine and human	Unity of divine and human
Humanity of Jesus	Flattened or overpowered	Fully human, but inappropriate for God to take on	Full humanity becomes God's own
Implications for salvation	Jesus is not truly one of us	Separation between God and us	Reconciliation and mediation between God and us
In practice	Jesus may seem distant and unattainable. We may believe that our own humanity must be destroyed if God is to transform us.	Our human messiness may be viewed as separating us from God. We may not believe that God is truly with us.	Jesus, our high priest knows and owns our human nature. Because of his true compassion and empathy with us, we can "approach the throne of grace with boldness, so that we may receive mercy and find grace to help in time of need" (Heb. 4:16).

Practicing Christology

As we gain practice in the doctrine of the incarnation, God will challenge our doubts about his love for humanity. In the incarnation, God is *with* us and *for* us in ways we could never have imagined without the Word made flesh. In Jesus, we see that God loves us as whole people—body, mind, and soul—because God took on our wholeness. Jesus, in becoming one of us, confirms the truth of the doctrine of creation that we are God's good work, that God considers us worth saving. In the incarnation, we meet God's desire for intimacy with us, seen in the fact that God came to us, among us, taking on our human particularity.

This word, **particularity**, is used in theology to point to the goodness of a God whose love extends to particulars. Jesus does not come among us as a generic human being; he comes as we do, with particulars. Jesus's particularity includes his maleness, his Jewishness, his location in first-century Palestine, and what Markus Bockmuehl calls his "bloody historical concreteness."[21] If any proposal for doctrine tries to offer us a non-Jewish Jesus, something has gone seriously wrong. Sometimes theologians talk about this particularity as a "scandal," because it offends our sense of fairness or propriety. The stumbling block of the incarnation is tied up in one package with the scandal of particularity. This package may look offensive—lumpy and oddly shaped—but for those who will look again, it contains the most precious of gifts: God's love for human beings who look at least as odd and are certainly offensive. God's love for us is not some idealized longing for a sanitized, universal idea of humanity. It is real love for real people: male and female, gentile and Jew, Middle Eastern and African and European and American and Asian—people from every nook of the planet. It is not just a love for ideas or for souls. It is a love that encompasses bodies as well as souls, a love concrete enough to become incarnate, to extend to fingers and toes: both Jesus's and ours. God's love is big enough to love specifics.[22]

Because God is with and for us, we are freed to be with and for others. Because God's love reaches into our specificity, our particularity, we

21. Markus Bockmuehl, "God's Life as a Jew: Remembering the Son of God as Son of David," in *Seeking the Identity of Jesus*, ed. Beverly Roberts Gaventa and Richard B. Hays (Grand Rapids: Eerdmans, 2008), 62.

22. M. Shawn Copeland draws attention to race and gender in *Enfleshing Freedom: Body, Race, and Being* (Minneapolis: Fortress, 2010).

Jesus and Particularity in Africa

Ghanaian theologian Mercy Amba Oduyoye reflects on Jesus's life and his work as redeemer seen in African context:

The human being is still an integrated person in Africa; the private and the political cannot be separated. Jesus exposed the structures of oppression that operated from temple and synagogue. . . . Jesus worked for the soundness of persons and structures, both religious and social. Just as in the Hebrew Scriptures, Yahweh rescued people from childlessness and disease, famine and fire, from flood and from the deep sea, so we find Jesus in the New Testament snatching women and men away from all domination, even from the jaws of death. He redeems by a strong hand all who are in the bondage of sin and who manifest their being in the service of sin by exploiting their neighbors. . . . The imagery of God in Christ as Redeemer is one that speaks clearly to Africa. . . . Christians see themselves as having been taken away from the slavery of a lifestyle that was painful to God to one that makes them the family of God.[a]

Oduyoye connects Christology to the particularities of her context, focusing especially on the suffering of African women:

In a continent where physical suffering seems endemic, a suffering Christ is a most attractive figure, for that Christ can be a companion. To the African mind, however, all suffering has to be like birth pangs: it has to lead to a birth, it has to lead to a new beginning. . . . In a continent where hunger, thirst, and homelessness are the continuous experience of millions, Jesus of Nazareth is a comrade. But women know that although Jesus took on hunger voluntarily, he never accepted deprivation as the destiny of humanity; rather he demonstrated that suffering is not in the plan of God, hence the emphasis of the victorious Christ in African women's spirituality.[b]

a. Mercy Amba Oduyoye, *Beads and Strands: Reflections of an African Woman on Christianity in Africa* (Maryknoll, NY: Orbis Books, 2004), 21–22.
b. Mercy Amba Oduyoye, *Introducing African Women's Theology* (Sheffield: Sheffield Academic Press, 2001), 57.

have hope that our love can follow suit. As we practice Christology, we draw nearer to Jesus Christ, and we begin to be transformed in him. Our love will move beyond feelings into concrete actions. Our love will be shaped in the image of Jesus's love. With Clare of Assisi (1194–1253) we will be inspired by "the love of the Lord Who was poor as He lay in the crib, poor as He lived in the world, Who remained naked on the cross,"[23] and we will learn to follow him in loving the vulnerable and the humble,

23. Clare of Assisi, "The Testament of Saint Clare," in *Francis and Clare: The Complete Works*, trans. Regis J. Armstrong, OFM Cap., and Ignatius C. Brady, OFM (New York: Paulist Press, 1982), 230.

the very specific folk who are "the least of these" (Matt. 25:40), the poor and the hungry and the naked who are treasured by Christ. As we become Christlike, our love, like his, will extend to particulars. Beverly Gaventa and Richard Hays speak about how we are changed as we learn the identity of Jesus

> *through long-term discipline*. This is already suggested by the shape of the Gospel narratives, in which Jesus calls disciples who follow him around for years without fully grasping who he is. Only after their extended exposure to him and after the shattering revelatory events of cross and resurrection do they even begin to grasp his identity. . . . Learning the identity of Jesus is a costly, lifelong process in which we grow, under the tutelage of Scripture and the church's disciplined practices of worship and service, toward a deeper comprehension of the Jesus we now know inadequately. . . . We come to know him rightly insofar as we are conformed to the pattern of his life. And, as Paul well knew, that will cost us not less than everything.[24]

Peter talks about the Christian life as a life of suffering. We are called to imitate Christ in suffering because Christ suffered for us. We suffer not because suffering is good but because God has defeated suffering and death in the resurrection of Christ. As participants in his resurrection empowered by the Spirit, we, like Christ, can live the truth that God's goodness and love are triumphant over suffering and death. This costly discipleship is not something we achieve. The practice of Christology is not about moralism and is not just about following in the footsteps of Jesus. Our Christology is incomplete if we do not follow in those footsteps, but we cannot hope to do so unless we are empowered by Christ's own work. It is "because Christ also suffered" that we are able to follow his example, to "follow in his steps" (1 Pet. 2:21). It is because "he himself bore our sins in his body on the cross" that we are "free from sins" and able to "live for righteousness" (v. 24). Indeed, "by his wounds you have been healed. For you were going astray like sheep, but now you have returned to the shepherd and guardian of your souls" (vv. 24–25). And so the doctrine and practice of Christology leads us, by necessity, to the doctrine and practice of soteriology, the good news of salvation and power, which is ours in the person of Jesus Christ.

---

24. Gaventa and Hays, *Seeking the Identity of Jesus*, 22.

7

The Work of Jesus Christ

Soteriology

Since, therefore, the children share flesh and blood, he himself likewise shared the same things, so that through death he might destroy the one who has the power of death, that is, the devil, and free those who all their lives were held in slavery by the fear of death. For it is clear that he did not come to help angels, but the descendants of Abraham. Therefore he had to become like his brothers and sisters in every respect, so that he might be a merciful and faithful high priest in the service of God, to make a sacrifice of atonement for the sins of the people. Because he himself was tested by what he suffered, he is able to help those who are being tested.

Hebrews 2:14–18

Jesus saves. In the last chapter, we saw how this depends on God's gift in becoming human out of love for us. **Soteriology**, treating matters of salvation, attends to the interconnections between who Jesus is and what he has done, especially in the cross and the resurrection, to bring about salvation. God's salvific work is portrayed in many ways in Scripture, and so Christians talk about salvation using several concepts and categories. Jesus's work as savior is inexhaustible in both breadth and depth, and it is appropriate that

Key Scripture

Now there was a Pharisee named Nicodemus, a leader of the Jews. He came to Jesus by night and said to him, "Rabbi, we know that you are a teacher who has come from God; for no one can do these signs that you do apart from the presence of God." Jesus answered him, "Very truly, I tell you, no one can see the kingdom of God without being born from above." Nicodemus said to him, "How can anyone be born after having grown old? Can one enter a second time into the mother's womb and be born?" Jesus answered, "Very truly, I tell you, no one can enter the kingdom of God without being born of water and Spirit. . . . For God so loved the world that he gave his only Son, so that everyone who believes in him may not perish but may have eternal life. Indeed, God did not send the Son into the world to condemn the world, but in order that the world might be saved through him. Those who believe in him are not condemned; but those who do not believe are condemned already, because they have not believed in the name of the only Son of God. And this is the judgment, that the light has come into the world, and people loved darkness rather than light because their deeds were evil. For all who do evil hate the light and do not come to the light, so that their deeds may not be exposed. But those who do what is true come to the light, so that it may be clearly seen that their deeds have been done in God." (John 3:1–5, 16–21)

soteriology should reflect some of that abundance. The doctrine of salvation is one of the areas of Christian thought where we see wide diversity—including disagreement—among different theological traditions, but this does not mean that there is no recognizable Christian consensus about soteriology.

In this chapter, we will look at the richness of the biblical witness to Christ as savior and some key categories that help us think about salvation. The saving work of Jesus Christ is intrinsically connected to his personal identity. As we become practiced in the doctrine of salvation, we see that Christ's saving work is as rich as Christ Jesus himself. Indeed, the basis of salvation is one of "boundless riches" (Eph. 3:8)—both here and hereafter. As John Wesley preached, "Salvation is not what is frequently understood by that word, the going to heaven, eternal happiness. . . . It is not a blessing which lies on the other side of death, or (as we usually speak) in the other world." Wesley wanted his hearers to recognize the mercy of salvation in the here and now. Salvation, Wesley goes on to say, "is not something at a distance: it is a present thing, a blessing which, through the free mercy of God, ye are now in possession of. . . . The salvation which is here spoken of might be extended to the entire work of God, from the first dawning of grace in the soul till it is consummated in glory."[1]

Richness of Salvation in Scripture

Scripture gives us a dense, layered, and rich account of God's saving work, and our gratitude for salvation can only grow if we make it a practice to attend to this many-layered goodness in soteriology. Two sketches of the biblical witness about salvation will help us get a sense of the doctrine's abundance. The first sketch is from theologian Brenda Colijn, who identifies overlapping New Testament images of salvation. Scripture shows us salvation as an inheritance we receive as God's children, and as citizenship in God's kingdom. These overlapping images carry "an important corrective to a me-centered view of salvation."[2] Scripture shows us salvation as eternal life and salvation as God's work in regenerating us, making us part of the new creation and giving us new birth. Colijn also points to biblical images of salvation as rescue, healing, redemption, ransom, freedom, and forgiveness. Salvation is God's work in past, present, and future, and salvation is about reconciliation, adoption, and peace. Salvation extends beyond human beings to the whole created order. Salvation is about reconciliation between human beings and God; it also reconciles human beings "with other spiritual forces, with one another, and with the rest of creation."[3] Colijn identifies yet more images in Scripture: salvation is God's work in making us righteous, by faith; it is God's election of his beloved people; it transforms us, makes us holy, and calls us to endurance. Colijn summarizes biblical images of salvation.

> Salvation in the New Testament is a vision of God's work for us and in us, through Christ and by the Holy Spirit, a vision that is composed of interdependent and mutually interpreting images. . . . Despite their rich diversity, the New Testament images of salvation tell a single story—the story of God's love for his broken creation, his desire for covenant relationship, and his patient shaping of a people who would reflect his love to one another

---

1. "The Scripture Way of Salvation," in *John Wesley's Sermons: An Anthology*, ed. Albert C. Outler and Richard P. Heitzenrater (Nashville: Abingdon, 1991), 372.
2. Brenda Colijn, *Images of Salvation in the New Testament* (Downers Grove, IL: InterVarsity, 2010), 82.
3. Ibid., 179.

and to the world. In the story's climax, the Creator enters his creation in the person of Jesus of Nazareth, identifying with his creatures in both life and death, and then, through resurrection, opening the way to life eternal. In Jesus Christ, through the power of his indwelling Spirit, God's people now are called to carry on God's redemptive mission. Remembering God's faithfulness, they live and work in anticipation of the conclusion of the story, to be told when Jesus returns. These images reflect a number of common themes. All of them assume a dire predicament that requires divine intervention. . . . While divine grace always has priority, human beings must respond to God's offered grace with faith, expressed as belief, trust and faithfulness.[4]

From Colijn's sketch, we already see an immensely rich picture of salvation. If we set her sketch next to another, the richness only multiplies. Theologian Thomas Weinandy identifies a number of intersecting themes in Scripture, themes that help us to see the breadth of God's salvation.[5] Where Colijn offers images of salvation, Weinandy describes themes in soteriology as he notices the way that salvation is discussed not just at one moment in the biblical story but throughout that story as a whole. He examines themes about salvation in terms of three movements in the biblical narrative: (1) the work of the cross, (2) the resurrection and Pentecost, and (3) the new life in the Holy Spirit. Weinandy names three subthemes in the first category, Jesus's work on the cross: Jesus assumes our condemnation, offers his life as an atoning sacrifice, and puts our sinful humanity to death. Within the movement of resurrection and Pentecost, Weinandy highlights the Father's love for Jesus, the risen Christ's gift to us of the Spirit, and Jesus's resurrection as a "complete man," as fully human in his resurrection as he was in his death. Under Weinandy's third soteriological theme, life in the Spirit, he emphasizes our being made new creations and the life we have in Christ.

Way of Salvation

One approach to comprehending the many-layered biblical witness to Jesus's saving work is to describe salvation in terms of a number of parts or moments. Christian conversation about the "way" of salvation recognizes

4. Ibid., 313–14.
5. Thomas G. Weinandy, *Jesus the Christ* (Huntington, IN: Our Sunday Visitor, 2003).

those moments and reflects on their significance. There are differences among theological traditions and denominations about exactly how to describe the process of salvation, but within those differences there is consensus about the importance of several key concepts. I will describe that consensus in terms of four broadly conceived steps on the path to salvation: beginnings, justification, sanctification, and final redemption. Each of these aspects of salvation is God's work, each a gracious gift from God.

Beginnings of Salvation

God is at work before we come to faith. Salvation does not begin with us, with human actions or decisions or realizations. Salvation begins with God, who works in the world at large, in the church, and in the lives of individual people long before we are aware of what God is doing. Different branches of the Christian tradition have different language for the events that belong to the beginnings of salvation, but the body of Christ, as a whole, recognizes God's work in these beginnings. We may speak of the beginnings of salvation in terms of conscience, contrition, election, and repentance. All of this, even the tiniest first steps that might begin to point us to God, is the work of God's grace. John Wesley speaks of the beginnings of salvation in terms of "all the drawings of 'the Father,' the desires after God, which, if we yield to them, increase more and more . . . all the convictions which his Spirit from time to time works"[6] in every human being. Wesley wants to make it clear that even these beginnings, as much as any other step on the way, are works of God's grace. All that happens, as God leads us on the way to salvation, happens through the goodness and graciousness of God. This is why John Wesley insists that the idea that we often call "natural conscience" is not really natural at all. Instead, even a sense that something might not be right is the work of God's grace. In the beginnings of salvation, we learn that we are sinners, that we have a problem, and that we stand in need of salvation. **Contrition** is that step on the way of salvation when we feel sorry for our sin, when we wish that it could be made right. In **repentance**, we turn away from sin and toward God. The beginnings of the way of salvation also include the means God uses to communicate the gospel of salvation to us. Salvation is for "everyone who calls on the name of the Lord" (Rom. 10:13), and

6. Wesley, "Scripture Way of Salvation," 373.

Paul emphasizes the way that God works in bringing this about through preaching, testimony, and evangelism.

> But how are they to call on one in whom they have not believed? And how are they to believe in one of whom they have never heard? And how are they to hear without someone to proclaim him? And how are they to proclaim him unless they are sent? As it is written, "How beautiful are the feet of those who bring good news!" But not all have obeyed the good news; for Isaiah says, "Lord, who has believed our message?" So faith comes from what is heard, and what is heard comes through the word of Christ. (vv. 14–17)

This means that our witness to Christ's saving work is part of God's work of salvation. God uses us to "bring the good news," and the faith that "comes from what is heard" is central to the next step on the way.

Justification

Justification is God's work in justifying sinners—forgiving our sin and making us right with God. The good news that we are justified by faith, and not by works, is one of the grandest of New Testament themes. Reflection on the doctrine tends to focus on Paul's letters, in which he describes the gift of salvation we receive in Jesus Christ. In Romans 4, Paul recounts the history of Abraham, whose faith was "reckoned to him as righteousness" (v. 22) and whose story is not just about him but also about us. We, like Abraham, may be reckoned righteous. We "who believe in him who raised Jesus our Lord from the dead" (v. 24) receive justification. The "righteousness" (*dikaiosyne*) that is reckoned to Abraham and to us shares a Greek root (*dik-*, what is right) with the "justification" (*dikaiosis*) for which Christ was raised from the dead (v. 25). That justification is at the core of the way of salvation. "Since we are justified by faith," says Paul in Romans 5, "we have peace with God through our Lord Jesus Christ, through whom we have obtained access to this grace in which we stand; and we boast in our hope of sharing the glory of God" (vv. 1–2). Though we were "ungodly" (v. 6) and "still were sinners" (v. 8), Christ died for us, justifying us "by his blood" (v. 9). Sin, death, and condemnation belonged to us in our unity with Adam. In Christ, all that is changed, and we receive righteousness, eternal life, and justification: "Just as one man's trespass led to condemnation for all, so one man's act of righteousness leads to justification and life for all" (v. 18).

Conflict about the doctrine of justification fueled the sixteenth-century debates that would lead to the Protestant Reformation. The story of the divide between Protestantism and Roman Catholicism usually begins with Martin Luther, monk turned reformer, whose understanding of justification is still characteristic of Protestant theologies today. Luther reacted against abuses in the late medieval Catholicism of his time, particularly against the practice of selling indulgences. The Roman Catholic church grants indulgences for "a remission before God of the temporal punishment due to sins whose guilt has already been forgiven."[7] An indulgence is thus understood to cover a punishment for sins, which otherwise would have to be paid by the individual. This punishment is to be covered by the merits of Christ and of saints, which the church holds in treasury. Luther objected to the sale of indulgences (an abuse the Catholic church put a stop to in the Catholic Reformation), but he also railed against the theology behind the practice. "Every true Christian participates in the treasures of the Church, even without letters of indulgence," and "this treasure is the Gospel of the glory and grace of God."[8] These provocative statements were part of Luther's famous "Ninety-five Theses," nailed to the door of the church in Wittenberg in October 1517, which spread like wildfire throughout Germany. Historian Heiko Oberman sums up Luther's theological objection to indulgences: "The profound consequences of sin, namely fear and insufficient love of God and one's neighbors, cannot be removed by indulgences but only by the Gospel."[9]

Justification by grace through faith would form the core message of Luther's theology for the rest of his life, and the Reformation rallying calls—*sola fide, sola gratia, sola Christus*—were all part of this message. Through faith alone, grace alone, Christ alone are we justified, and the *sola*, the only, always implies "and not by our works." *Sola* casts all hope in works aside. Luther wrote about his experience of the concept of justification and his reaction to the biblical testimony to the righteousness of God. "Though I lived as a monk without reproach," he wrote, "I felt that I was a sinner before God with an extremely disturbed conscience."[10]

7. *Catechism of the Catholic Church*, 2nd ed. (New York: Doubleday, 1995), 411, #1471.

8. Quoted in Heiko Oberman, *Luther: Man between God and the Devil* (New York: Doubleday, 1989), 190–91.

9. Ibid., 190.

10. "Preface to the Complete Edition of Luther's Latin Writings, 1545," in *Martin Luther's Basic Theological Writings*, 2nd ed., ed. Timothy F. Lull (Minneapolis: Fortress, 2005), 8–9.

Luther tells how he hated the word "righteousness" and was angry at "the righteous God who punishes sinners," until he came to see that the righteousness that sinners hope in can never be our own righteousness but must always be the righteousness of Christ.

The courtroom is a common metaphor to help us understand the theology of justification. Human beings are like criminals on trial: lawbreakers, guilty of sin, separate from God, bound by chains we cannot break. God is the judge who pronounces the verdict. Though we were guilty—ungodly, still sinners—we are reckoned righteous because of what Christ has done by his blood and resurrection. We receive the verdict Christ deserves—the judgment that we are righteous—and are acquitted of our crimes. At Jesus's trial, Pontius Pilate tells the people that he has found no case against Jesus and then offers to let Jesus go free, saying, "You have a custom that I release someone for you at the Passover. Do you want me to release for you the King of the Jews?" (John 18:39). The people shout in reply, "Not this man, but Barabbas!" (v. 40). The criminal Barabbas goes free, and Jesus goes to the cross. We are all Barabbas, guilty rebels set free while Christ takes our place.

Protestant theology often uses the phrase **imputed righteousness** to refer to the righteousness of Christ that is the basis of our acquittal. God imputes Christ's righteousness to us. "Imputes" is another word for the one translated as "reckons" in Romans 4:22 (referenced above). The righteousness of Christ is imputed, reckoned, or credited to us and becomes the legal basis for our acquittal. New Testament scholar Douglas Moo shows how Paul "preserves . . . the forensic flavor" that the idea of justification carried in the Old Testament context.[11] This legal metaphor is a prominent theme in Scripture, one that is emphasized in Western theology in general and in the Protestant tradition in particular. Martin Luther spoke of the righteousness that God reckons to us as "alien righteousness." This righteousness belongs to Christ and is truly alien to the sinful nature of human beings. Luther's idea of alien righteousness emphasizes a powerful biblical theme: salvation is by grace. Our acquittal is based on a righteousness that is not our own. In fact, righteousness is foreign to who we are as sinners. Luther wanted to exorcise any lingering suspicion that we might be justified by our own righteousness—our own good works—instead of by the righteousness of Christ alone.

11. Douglas J. Moo, *The Epistle to the Romans*, New International Commentary on the New Testament (Grand Rapids: Eerdmans, 1996), 86.

Joint Declaration on the Doctrine of Justification

In 1999, the Lutheran World Federation and the Roman Catholic Church agreed on a shared confessional statement on the doctrine of justification.

> In faith we together hold the conviction that justification is the work of the Triune God. The Father sent his Son into the world to save sinners. The foundation and presupposition of justification is the incarnation, death, and resurrection of Christ. Justification thus means that Christ himself is our righteousness, in which we share through the Holy Spirit in accord with the will of the Father. Together we confess: By grace alone, in faith in Christ's saving work and not because of any merit on our part, we are accepted by God and receive the Holy Spirit, who renews our hearts while equipping and calling us to good works.[a]
>
> The doctrine of justification . . . is more than just one part of Christian doctrine. It stands in an essential relation to all truths of faith, which are to be seen as internally related to each other. It is an indispensable criterion that constantly serves to orient all the teaching and practice of our churches to Christ. When Lutherans emphasize the unique significance of this criterion, they do not deny the interrelation and significance of all truths of faith. When Catholics see themselves as bound by several criteria, they do not deny the special function of the message of justification.[b]

This joint declaration does not erase the differences between Protestant and Catholic soteriologies, but given the enmity between Catholics and Protestants during the Reformation, such a shared vision is a remarkable ecumenical achievement and reason for Christians to rejoice.

a. The Lutheran World Federation and the Roman Catholic Church, *Joint Declaration on the Doctrine of Justification* (Grand Rapids: Eerdmans, 2000), 15.
b. Ibid., 16.

This forensic or legal metaphor for justification offers a powerful explanation of our situation, but the metaphor is also controversial. A critique often leveled against it is that the metaphor suggests that salvation leaves us unchanged. Are justified persons the same sinners they were before God's justifying grace went to work on them? "Should we sin because we are not under law but under grace?" (Rom. 6:15). Paul's answer to that question is a resounding no. Christians who have been justified *are* changed; we are those who, "having been set free from sin, have become slaves of righteousness" (v. 18). This truth—that God transforms the people he justifies—does not, however, undo the power or the purpose of the legal metaphor for justification. In his reading of Romans, Moo argues that "the criticism that a strictly forensic meaning . . . makes the action a 'legal fiction' is wide of the mark: legal it is, but it is no more fiction than is the release from imprisonment

Charles Wesley's "And Can It Be"

And can it be that I should gain
an interest in the Savior's blood!
Died he for me? who caused his pain!
For me? who him to death pursued?
Amazing love! How can it be
that thou, my God, shouldst die for me?
Amazing love! How can it be
that thou, my God, shouldst die for me?

'Tis mystery all: th' Immortal dies!
Who can explore his strange design?
In vain the firstborn seraph tries
to sound the depths of love divine.
'Tis mercy all! Let earth adore;
let angel minds inquire no more.

He left his Father's throne above
(so free, so infinite his grace!),
emptied himself of all but love,
and bled for Adam's helpless race.
'Tis mercy all, immense and free,
for O my God, it found out me!

Long my imprisoned spirit lay,
fast bound in sin and nature's night;
thine eye diffused a quickening ray;
I woke, the dungeon flamed with light;
my chains fell off, my heart was free,
I rose, went forth, and followed thee.

No condemnation now I dread;
Jesus, and all in him, is mine;
alive in him, my living Head,
and clothed in righteousness divine,
bold I approach th' eternal throne,
and claim the crown, through Christ my own.

experienced by the pardoned criminal."[12] Moo's image is much like that in Charles Wesley's hymn of salvation, in which the sinner cries out, "My chains fell off, my heart was free" before leaving the prison of sin. Theologian Bruce McCormack embraces the forensic metaphor for justification while making it clear that God's legal declaration of righteousness can never be fully subject to our metaphors.

In justification, God pronounces a judicial verdict upon the sinner. But God's verdict and the divine word pronounced in it are not at all that of a human judge. The human judge can only describe what he hopes to be the real state of affairs. The human judge's judgment is in no sense effective; it does not create the reality it depicts. . . . God's verdict differs in that it creates the reality it declares. . . . A judicial act for God is never merely judicial; it is itself transformative.[13]

When we look at models for understanding atonement, later in this chapter, we will see some ways the legal metaphor has worked in Christian history.

---

12. Ibid., 86–87.
13. Bruce McCormack, "What's at Stake in Current Debates over Justification? The Crisis of Protestantism in the West," in *Justification: What's at Stake in the Current Debates*, ed. Mark Husbands and Daniel Treier (Downers Grove, IL: InterVarsity, 2004), 107.

We will also see how it is enriched when set alongside other metaphors and biblical themes.

Sanctification

The pardoned criminal is released. Our chains fall off; our hearts are set free. Then what? In Charles Wesley's hymn, the emancipated prisoner, chains clattering to the floor, says, "I rose, went forth, and followed thee." The justified sinner moves into the life of discipleship, following the righteous Christ. We are freed from the tyranny of sin and death and enabled, "as those who have been brought from death to life," to present our bodies "to God as instruments of righteousness" (Rom. 6:13), and "now that you have been freed from sin and enslaved to God, the advantage you get is sanctification. The end is eternal life" (v. 22). Justification passes into sanctification. God forgives us and makes us new. Sanctification is God's work in making us godly, holy, and like Christ, and sanctification—like each step on the way of salvation—is a gift of grace. God *declares* us righteous because of what Christ has done for us, and God *makes* us righteous as we grow in relationship with him. Righteousness, John Wesley would insist, is both imputed and imparted. The righteousness that God imparts to us, that becomes our own, must be understood "in its proper place; not as the *ground* of our acceptance with God, but as the *fruit* of it; not in the place of *imputed* righteousness, but as consequent upon it."[14]

In highlighting the truth that salvation is by grace—and not by works—Protestant descriptions of salvation tend to maintain a "pause"[15] between justification and sanctification, between God's work in forgiving our sin and declaring us righteous and God's work in transforming us into new creatures, making us actually holy. This Protestant pause highlights the gracious truth that justification is *not based on sanctification*. Justification is based on Christ alone, and the conceptual difference between justification and sanctification helps us to keep this straight. A theological pause between justification and sanctification is a safeguard against any tendency to believe that God justifies us because we are holy, because we have performed good work. This pause does important theological work, but no

14. "The Lord Our Righteousness," in *John Wesley's Sermons*, 388.
15. Alister McGrath characterizes this Protestant pause in *Iustitia Dei: A History of the Christian Doctrine of Justification*, 2nd ed. (Cambridge: Cambridge University Press, 1998), 212.

truthful reading of Scripture or honest assessment of the Christian life will allow us to stop there. Salvation does not end with a magic moment, and grace ought never be used as a warrant for sin. John Wesley continues, in the sermon quoted in the previous paragraph, preaching against using the righteousness of Christ as "a cover for" our own unrighteousness.[16]

The doctrine of soteriology must follow the thread of Scripture in rejecting errors on two sides of the truth. The teaching of justification by faith stands against the error of legalism or **works righteousness**, of a doomed Pelagianism in which we attempt to be our own saviors. On the other side, the doctrine of sanctification stands against the error of **antinomianism**, of acting as though God's law has nothing to say to the Christian life, as if it doesn't matter how we live. Justification leads into sanctification. When God forgives us of our sin, God also leads us into the ways of righteousness. All is bathed in grace. There is no necessary interval of time that has to pass between justification and the beginning of sanctification. The theological pause between justification and sanctification is not so much temporal as it is conceptual. Sanctification is a reality because we are in Christ, because we abide in him who said, "I am the vine, you are the branches. Those who abide in me and I in them bear much fruit, because apart from me you can do nothing" (John 15:5). The reality of justification by faith in no way diminishes the reality of abundant fruit. In fact, it produces the only fruit worth having. Martin Luther articulates a classic way of understanding this as he speaks of the tree imagery used by Jesus. Good trees come before good fruits. Sanctification is impossible without justification.

> It is always necessary that the substance or person himself be good before there can be any good works, and that good works follow and proceed from the good person, as Christ also says, "A good tree cannot bear evil fruit, nor can a bad tree bear good fruit." It is clear that the fruits do not bear the tree and that the tree does not grow on the fruits, also that, on the contrary, the trees bear the fruits and the fruits grow on the trees. As it is necessary, therefore, that the trees exist before their fruits and that fruits do not make trees either good or bad, but rather as the trees are, so are the fruits they bear; so a man must first be good or wicked before he does a good or wicked work, and his works do not make him good or wicked.[17]

16. Wesley, "The Lord Our Righteousness," 390.
17. "The Freedom of a Christian," in *Martin Luther's Basic Theological Writings*, 613.

The image of trees and fruits is also helpful in another way. Like fruits that grow and ripen over time, sanctification is an ongoing reality in the Christian life. After justification, we, as God's people, continue to grow in the way of grace and holiness throughout our lives. Although a few branches of the Christian tradition affirm that sanctification can happen in an instant, the vast majority of Christians see sanctification as a process that fills the entire Christian life, and even an insistence that God sometimes gives sudden, dramatic gifts of sanctifying grace is not incompatible with a larger understanding of sanctification as a process. Different branches of the Christian tradition have various understandings of how far the process of sanctification may go in this life. Some parts of the tradition are relatively pessimistic about how much sanctification may be realized in this life and emphasize the continued weight of sin that drags down every Christian. Other traditions are more optimistic about this life, expecting transformation and holiness to happen to a great degree in the here and now. This is a lively debate, but it should not obscure the center.

These branches of the tradition are attached to the same trunk, to Christ, in whom we know that justification and sanctification cannot be split apart. There is wide Christian unity in the truth that, first, we have no power without the righteousness of Christ (2 Cor. 3:5) and, second, faith without works is dead (James 2:26). We are made more and more like Christ as our relationships with him deepen, as we learn to know and love him better, and as we partake in the means of grace that God offers us as tools for our sanctification. These means of grace are legion: reading and studying the Scriptures, prayer, participation in the Lord's Supper, Christian friendship and fellowship, singleness and marriage, caring for the poor and vulnerable, service, fasting, and so many more. God uses such tools to make us holy, to transform us into more faithful disciples of Jesus Christ. We will talk more about the shape of discipleship and holiness in the Christian life in the next chapter.

Final Redemption

The way of salvation does not end with this life. Sanctification passes into everlasting life. While this part of the way is bathed in even more mystery than the other parts, Christians expect God to finish his good salvific work in us and in all of creation. We share Paul's confidence that God, having begun a good work, "will bring it to completion by the day of Jesus Christ"

(Phil. 1:6). At the beginning of this chapter, I quoted John Wesley, who insists that salvation is much more than we usually think of, that it is not just a ticket to heaven. This is as true of the last part of the way of salvation as it is of the first. God's final good intentions for us, the fulfillment of his saving work, are so much more than our going to heaven when we die (a topic we will look at more fully in chap. 10). The whole biblical arc shows a saving God who will finish his work—in individuals, in the body of Christ, and in all of creation—by bringing it to fullness, completeness, and purposeful perfection. Final redemption is God's final victory over sin and death. It is restored and intimate relationship with God. "For now we see in a mirror, dimly," says Paul, "but then we will see face to face. Now I know only in part; then I will know fully, even as I have been fully known" (1 Cor. 13:12).

Dynamics of Grace and Human Freedom

Given that salvation is by grace, given that we are broken sinners in need of rescue, how do we understand the agency of human beings in the process of salvation? Within Protestantism, questions about how God works with us in salvation have been answered in different ways in different segments of the church. This conversation is usually framed as a debate between Calvinist and Arminian schools of theology, though this is an oversimplification of the matters involved (because, for example, John Calvin himself may or may not be best described as a "Calvinist," and because there are more shades and nuances in the conversation than the simple two-sided narrative suggests). Still, we will want to understand the categories as well as what is at stake in the conversation. The **Calvinist** understanding of salvation focuses on the priority and sovereignty of God's grace by emphasizing God as the sole agent of salvation. The **Arminian** understanding focuses on God's loving desire to be in saving relationship with humanity and sees this as connected to God's opening up space for human agency, along with divine grace, in salvation. The two camps often misunderstand each other, but both have emphases worth noting as we practice soteriological reflection.

The Calvinist and Arminian theological views of salvation share a starting place: the Protestant doctrine of justification by grace. Both traditions confess that all of humanity bears the weight of sin, that all human beings are fallen "in Adam," and that we are all incapable of saving ourselves. John Wesley, in the Arminian tradition, preaches "no man loves God by nature. . . . To love God! It is far above, out of our sight. We cannot naturally attain unto it."[18] Wesley's Calvinist friend and colleague, George Whitefield (1714–70), preaches that this "doctrine of original sin is a doctrine written in such legible characters in the Word of God" that it cannot be denied.[19] Both traditions, then, share a diagnosis of the human condition: we are bound by sin and we need to be rescued. We depend on the saving grace of Jesus Christ, not only because we sin as individuals, but also because human nature is fallen. We cannot save ourselves, and we stand in need of grace. We need to know the depth of sin to begin to understand the greatness of grace, and so John Wesley preaches, "By nature ye are wholly corrupted; by grace ye shall be wholly renewed."[20] From this shared understanding, the Calvinist and Arminian traditions emphasize different concerns when addressing soteriology.

Arminianism

Classic Arminian theology takes its name from Dutch theologian Jacobus Arminius (1560–1609), whose disagreement with Calvinism centered on his affirmation that **prevenient grace**—a gift of grace from God that comes before us, preceding anything we do—was for all people, not only the elect. Prevenient grace, for Arminius, is made available through the saving work of Christ and enables sinners to respond to God if we do not resist his grace. Arminian soteriology is summed up in the Remonstrant articles, written in 1610 by a group of like-minded Christians after Arminius's death. Each of the five articles invokes the grace of God in all aspects of salvation.

1. God's will is to elect "those who through His grace believe in Jesus Christ and persevere in faith and obedience."[21]
2. Christ died for all of humanity. The article, along with many Arminians after, quotes John 3:16 here, emphasizing God's love for the whole world.

18. "Original Sin," in *John Wesley's Sermons*, 330.
19. "Marks of a True Conversion," in *Sermons of George Whitefield*, ed. Evelyn Bence (Peabody, MA: Hendrickson, 2009), 72.
20. Wesley, "Scripture Way of Salvation," 334.
21. This and other quotations in this summary of the Remonstrant articles are from A. W. Harrison, *Beginnings of Arminianism to the Synod of Dort* (London: University of London Press, 1926), 150–51, quoted in Roger Olson, *Arminian Theology: Myths and Realities* (Downers Grove, IL: InterVarsity, 2006), 32.

3. We cannot "obtain saving faith" by ourselves, and we stand "in need of God's grace through Christ to be renewed in thought and will." This is an affirmation of the crippling effects of original sin and our need for grace.

4. Grace is "the cause of the beginning, progress and completion" of salvation. The article speaks here of "co-operating" grace, a grace of God that works with human freedom. The article also states that all good works come from the grace of God and that human beings can resist God's grace.

5. In Christ, people receive the strength of the Spirit to "fight against Satan, sin, the world, their own flesh, and get the victory." The article maintains the possibility of apostasy—that someone might turn away from God.

Arminianism may be known popularly as a theology of human free will, but its emphases are more truly on the universal love of a gracious God, who reaches out to all in love, wanting to free and empower bound sinners and be in relationship with them.

Calvinism

The soteriology known as five-point Calvinism was outlined as a response to Arminianism at the Synod of Dort (1618–19). The five points are often indicated by the acronym TULIP, in which the letters stand for the following:

1. *Total depravity*: This point reaffirms the doctrine of original sin. In Adam, all are sinners and unable to choose God. The doctrine of total depravity is sometimes misread as a claim that there is no good in human beings, but this is not the case. The point of the doctrine is to emphasize our complete inability to save ourselves.

2. *Unconditional election*: God chooses—elects—some people "according to the 'good pleasure of his will,' without regard to their foreseen faith."[22] Election is not based on any condition that might be met by human beings. Instead, the basis of election is God's sovereign will. The affirmation that election is unconditional is a response to the first Arminian Remonstrant article, which sees belief and faith

---

22. Translation of the "Canons of Dort," quoted in Peter J. Thuesen, *Predestination: The American Career of a Contentious Doctrine* (New York: Oxford University Press, 2009), 40.

as the reason that God, in foreknowledge, elects some for salvation. The Calvinist fear is that this turns faith into a kind of work.

3. *Limited atonement*: The atoning work of Christ is only effective for the elect. It does not apply to those who will remain in sin.

4. *Irresistible grace*: The electing grace of God will not fail. It cannot be resisted.

5. *Perseverance of the saints*: This fifth point goes along with irresistible grace, affirming that God will finish his saving work in the elect. The elect cannot fall away. The last three points together articulate a vision of God's sovereign grace, always effective and always free.

Calvinism may be known popularly as a theology of deterministic providence, but its emphases are more truly on the magnificent sovereignty of grace, the only hope for bound sinners who cannot free themselves.

While I began this discussion by emphasizing the shared space between Calvinism and Arminianism, there is no doubt that these are two different soteriologies, both of which are grappling with the biblical witness to salvation. Calvinist soteriology is **monergistic**, meaning that God is the only actor in salvation. Arminian soteriology is **synergistic**, meaning that God works together with human beings in the process of salvation. Calvinist soteriology locates the basis for election in God's sovereign will; Arminian soteriology locates that basis in God's foreknowledge of those who will believe in Christ. Calvinists tend to worry that Arminians are underestimating the enormity of sin and returning to the error of works righteousness. Arminians respond that grace empowers every part of salvation, that to claim that grace works *with* human freedom is no insult to grace and, more, is typical of the personal and loving God who wants true relationship with human beings. Arminians tend to worry that Calvinists have created a capricious and unloving picture of God, who would leave some without hope of salvation. Calvinists respond that God needs no defense from us, that whatever God chooses is good because God is God, and, more, it is a loving God who would choose to save anyone when all are justly condemned sinners. Calvinists find comfort in a doctrine of God who elects without imposing conditions, Arminians in a doctrine of God who offers salvation to all, and both Calvinists and Arminians in the God whose magnificent and free grace reaches out to us in our helplessness.

By Grace

While Calvinism and Arminianism both recognize human depravity and while both are theologies of grace, it is the sad case that many of us still live our daily lives in *de facto* Pelagianism, trying and failing to justify ourselves based on our own righteousness. Remember from chapter 5, Pelagius taught that we are capable of turning to God in love. Against Pelagianism, Augustine insisted that we are bound by sin and stand in need of the saving grace of Christ, the only One who is righteous to save. We fall into Pelagian patterns when we fear in secret that we are not saved, because our religious feelings have waned. We try to work up a fervor of feeling that will be worthy of God's attention. Or perhaps we harbor a sense of cold dread because of our repeated failures: failure to read the Bible regularly, failure to give to the poor, failure to love our enemies or even our families, failure upon failure. Our solution is to try harder, to screw up our courage and to hope against hope that, next time, we will get it right.

Our habit of Pelagianism may be part of human nature under sin, but it is also tied to historical realities behind present-day North American faith. One such reality is the influence of the popular preacher Charles Finney (1792–1875), who insisted that turning to God is "the sinner's own act"[23] and who taught that the outcome of revivals is also under human control. Maybe it was Finney's numerical success that cemented his theological error in the consciousness of American evangelicalism, and few of us have been able to shake it entirely. We could speculate that Pelagianism is one of the special temptations of Christians in the American context. Where we value independence and treasure the narrative of the "self-made man," we may need special practice in the doctrine of soteriology to help us unlearn the frantic habit of works righteousness and trust instead in the God of grace.

Both Calvinist and Arminian soteriologies, flowing from the broad Augustinian and more narrow Protestant streams of the Christian faith, teach our *desperate need for grace*. Calvinism does this in viewing grace as irresistible and unconditional, Arminianism in viewing grace as free and universal and in highlighting the category of prevenient grace. Arminian soteriology preserves the gratuity of grace—its character as freely given, without strings

---

23. Charles Finney, "Sinners Bound to Change Their Own Hearts," in *Issues in American Protestantism: A Documentary History from the Puritans to the Present*, ed. Robert L. Ferm (Gloucester, MA: Peter Smith Press, 1983), 158–69.

attached—alongside its belief that salvation is for those who believe and persevere, by insisting that the ability to believe and persevere comes only as a gift, through the regenerating power of prevenient grace offered to all people because of what Christ has done. Both strands of thought contain resources for helping us to unlearn our Pelagianism. We might also benefit from the counsel of evangelist and theologian Phoebe Palmer (1807–74), who reminds us of the sure faithfulness of the God of our salvation: "And now that you believe, hold fast to the profession of your faith, without wavering, for he is faithful that hath promised. You are not required to hold fast to the profession of your *feelings* but the profession of your *faith*. You are all the Lord's, now, and it is your privilege, and also your duty, to believe."[24]

Models of the Atonement

We have now looked at soteriology in terms of biblical themes, moments on the way to salvation, and Calvinist and Arminian traditions. We will now turn to theories about how the work of Christ brings about atonement. The word **atonement** was coined, in English, to describe the way Christ's work undoes the separation between humans and God, opening up the possibility that we may again be reconciled or made one ("at-one-ment") with God. Each model of the atonement has strengths and weaknesses—sometimes the same characteristic is both strength and weakness—as it attempts faithful speech about the work of Christ.

Deification

This first model for understanding atonement emphasizes the connections between the incarnation and the whole of humanity. The idea of deification is summarized by Athanasius in his work on the incarnation; he says that "[Christ], indeed, assumed humanity, that we might become God."[25] This is a startling statement, and Athanasius is well aware of that fact. Athanasius is also aware of the difference between the Creator and creation. Yet he stands in a theological tradition that is willing to speak of human **deification** in strong terms, that sees the work of Christ as draw-

24. *Life and Letters of Mrs. Phoebe Palmer*, ed. Richard Wheatley (repr., New York: Garland, 1984), 543–44.
25. St. Athanasius, *On the Incarnation* (Crestwood, NY: St. Vladimir's Seminary Press, 1993), 93.

ing us into the very life of God. The logic is there in the short statement quoted from Athanasius. Atonement involves a double movement: first, God comes to us, in incarnate unity with us, in order to, second, bring us to God, in unity with the divine life.

Deification is usually identified as the soteriological tradition of Eastern Orthodoxy. Russian Orthodox theologian Andrew Louth writes that deification "has to do with human destiny, a destiny that finds its fulfillment in a face-to-face encounter with God, an encounter in which God takes the initiative by meeting us in the Incarnation."[26] The model's strengths lie in (1) taking the cosmic nature of salvation seriously; (2) dealing with the biblical witness to real transformation as the end of human salvation (for example, Peter's quotation of Leviticus, "For it is written, 'You shall be holy, for I am holy'" [1 Pet. 1:16]); and (3) being based in the person of Jesus, his humanity and his divinity. Critics of a deification model fear that it violates the distinction between Creator and creature. Another drawback of the model is that Christ's work in the cross and resurrection takes a place peripheral to the incarnation itself. Deification, as a model of the atonement, takes a form more like poetry than logic. In Louth's words, "He shared our life, to the point of death, that we might be redeemed from death and come to share the divine life. This notion of an exchange, of what the Latin Fathers call *admirabile commercium* (wonderful exchange), is the place where deification fits; it is not so much a doctrine to be analyzed, as a way of capturing the nature and extent of our response to the Incarnation."[27]

Christus Victor

Gustaf Aulén (1879–1977) made an influential argument that the early church conceptualized atonement in terms of Christ's cosmic victory over sin and death. Aulén describes this **Christus Victor** (Christ the Victor) model of the atonement as "'dramatic.' Its central theme is the idea of the Atonement as a Divine conflict and victory; Christ—Christus Victor—fights against and triumphs over the evil powers of the world, the 'tyrants' under which mankind is in bondage and suffering, and in Him

---

26. Andrew Louth, "The Place of *Theosis* in Eastern Orthodoxy," in *Partakers of the Divine Nature: The History and Development of Deification in the Christian Traditions*, ed. Michael J. Christensen and Jeffery A. Wittung (Grand Rapids: Baker Academic, 2008), 34.
27. Ibid., 32.

God reconciles the world to Himself."[28] The model contains within itself great diversity, and Christ's victory over the powers, imaged in battle metaphors, is the most prominent common theme. The model, as a cosmic view of atonement, sees the work of Christ as extending far beyond the individual into the whole of the world. Many church fathers, in describing Christ's victory, give Satan and evil powers an important role in the drama of redemption: Satan might be envisioned as reigning over creation through death; Satan is then tricked by Jesus's humanity into thinking that Jesus is fair prey, but because Jesus is God, when Satan tries to seize him, the power of death is exploded. A great strength of this model is that it takes death—and not sin alone—seriously as an enemy of God that is defeated in Jesus, and this means the model takes resurrection seriously as well. Different theologians view the role given to Satan as either a strength or a weakness of the model.

Cross-Centered Models: Satisfaction, Forensic, and Substitutionary Atonement

The next category for atonement models is often identified with the explanation offered by Anselm of Canterbury (1033–1109) in his answer to the question, why did God become human? Anselm sees the person of Jesus Christ—two natures in hypostatic unity—as God's uniquely fitting response to sin. He uses a metaphor that fits his context, the debt of honor owed to the feudal Lord. We owe God full honor, and our debt is so large that it is impossible for us to satisfy it. Anselm explains, "All the will of a rational creature ought to be subject to the will of God. . . . Someone who does not render to God this honour due to him is taking away from God what is his. . . . This is what it is to sin. As long as he does not repay what he has taken away, he remains in a state of guilt."[29] We are guilty debtors who cannot pay—or make satisfaction for—what we owe. No human is capable of doing so. Only God has the power to do something so immense. Yet, Anselm argues, justice requires that someone human pay the debt, which belongs to humans. Anselm argues that if God were

28. Gustaf Aulén, *Christus Victor: An Historical Study of the Idea of the Atonement*, trans. A. G. Hebert (New York: MacMillan, 1958), 4.
29. Anselm, "Why God Became Man," in *Anselm of Canterbury: The Major Works*, 283.

to erase the debt without payment, then God would cease to be either just or faithful.

This is the logic behind the gift of the incarnation. Only Jesus, fully God and fully human, is both *able to pay* the debt owed for sin (as God, he is able) and *able to meet justice* by paying the debt as a human (the debt belongs to humans). Other Christian thinkers will emphasize Christ's role here as a **substitute** for us, taking our place to pay the price of sin. Anselm says,

> No member of the human race except Christ ever gave to God, by dying, anything which that person was not at some time going to lose as a matter of necessity. Nor did anyone ever pay a debt to God which he did not owe. But Christ of his own accord gave to his Father what he was never going to lose as a matter of necessity, and he paid, on behalf of sinners, a debt which he did not owe. . . . He was in no way needy on his own account, or subject to compulsion from others, to whom he owed nothing, unless it was punishment that he owed them. Nevertheless, he gave his life, so precious; no, his very self; he gave his person—think of it—in all its greatness, in an act of his own, supremely great, volition.[30]

For Anselm, God's mercy is both great and just. Justice is seen in the fact that God gives to sin the punishment that it demands, mercy in God's willingness to become human in order to pay sin's just price.

Anselm's **satisfaction** theory of the atonement and theories that focus on Jesus's **substitutionary** sacrifice fit into the same conceptual space as their **forensic** cousins (which shift the metaphor from the feudal context to the court of law). Together these form the dominant model of atonement in Western Christianity, both Protestant and Catholic. There is good reason for this, for the model has many strengths. These include (1) being based in the person of Jesus Christ, his humanity and divinity; (2) taking seriously the biblical witness about justification, including the legal or forensic metaphors of Scripture; (3) dealing seriously with the horror of sin, insisting that sin has consequences; (4) emphasizing the justice and faithfulness of God; and (5) dealing with the central place that Christ's substitutionary sacrifice on the cross takes in the biblical narrative.[31] Draw-

30. Ibid., 349.
31. For an account of the centrality of the cross in connection to the many other aspects of the gospel, see Darrell L. Bock, *Recovering the Real Lost Gospel: Reclaiming the Gospel as Good News* (Nashville: B & H Academic, 2010).

Salvation that Matters
to History, Politics, and Spiritual Powers

Ignacio Ellacuria, a priest assassinated in El Salvador in 1989, articulates a soteriology that matters for history.

> They kill Jesus for living a historical life, one that includes a concrete proclamation of the reign of God. Then, that life, taken away, is converted into a life for all human beings in a permanent and transcendent manner that elevates that historical life. Furthermore, this elevation, I believe, should extend to the lives of human beings and the life of society in order to enrich them, because in reality society's life and humanity's life is full of sin. . . . This grace of Jesus, this example of Jesus, this virtue of Jesus, this spirit of Christ continues after the resurrection. It extends to history and really goes on taking away the sins of the world; it attempts to take away the sins of the world; it attempts to convert hearts and convert society.[a]

African theologian Kwame Bediako's soteriology, in conversation with John Mbiti, emphasizes Christ's victory over the powers.

> Jesus is seen above all else as the *Christus Victor* (Christ supreme over every spiritual rule and authority). This understanding of Christ arises from Africans' keen awareness of forces and powers at work in the world which threaten the interests of life and harmony. Jesus is victorious over the spiritual realm and particularly over evil forces and so answers to their need for a powerful protector against these forces and powers.[b]

Roland Chia, from Singapore, writes about the connections between Christ's work on the cross and Christian hope.

> Christian hope is profoundly shaped by the cross of Christ. Through the cross we come to understand that the worst events can be meaningful and that disappointments and tribulations are part of the course of life in the fallen world. But the cross also enables us to see that every disappointment and suffering we now face can be integrated into the story God fashions, which will ultimately serve our welfare. The dialectic of the cross means that hope is both prepared for disappointments here and is sure of eternity in the age to come. The cross and the resurrection of Christ reveal the dialectical nature of hope itself. Hope is dialectical simply because present conditions are antithetical to those for which we hope. We hope for righteousness in the midst of moral degradation, for justice in the midst of injustice and oppression, and for life in the midst of death.[c]

a. Quoted in Michael E. Lee, *Bearing the Weight of Salvation: The Soteriology of Ignacio Ellacuria* (New York: Crossroad, 2008), 84–85.
b. Kwame Bediako, "Jesus in African Culture," in *Evangelical Review of Theology* 17, no. 1 (1993): 56–57.
c. Roland Chia, *Hope for the World: A Christian Vision of the Last Things* (Downers Grove, IL: IVP Academic, 2005), 148–49.

backs include (1) giving relatively less attention to the incarnation, life, and resurrection of Christ (in comparison to the cross); (2) tending to a soteriology focused on individuals, at the expense of the communal and cosmic aspects of salvation; and (3) focusing on justification at the expense of sanctification.

Moral Exemplar

The final category for models of the atonement is linked with its proponent, Peter Abelard (1079–1142). Abelard talks about atonement in terms of the perfect love of Christ, which becomes a **moral example** for us who are witnesses of that love. Abelard suggests that in seeing the love of Christ, especially on the cross, we are moved by love to love in turn. Abelard thus envisions the remedy for sin as a moral transformation. If taken alone, this moral exemplar model of the atonement is the weakest of our models. It shares too much in common with Pelagian heresy and moralism to serve as a true basis for reconciliation between humanity and God. If wed to one of the other atonement models, one that interprets the human situation as standing in need of Jesus, not just as an example but as the savior who gives power, then this emphasis on being transformed by Christ's love can take its place in the practice of soteriology.

Practicing Soteriology

In practice, the doctrine of salvation is richest when we attend to and appreciate the range of treasures in it. The doctrine has coherence, and it has central themes. My sketch of the doctrine in this chapter points, gently, to legal acquittal in justification by grace, Christ's sacrifice on the cross, and God's defeat of death in resurrection as the vital core of soteriology. But to acknowledge a core is not to deny the importance of the rest of the doctrine, and the many soteriological themes that expand on this core will also multiply the richness of the doctrine of salvation for the Christian life.

Take one example: Proclus's (d. c. 446) soteriology dates well before medieval discussion of atonement, though the standard categories would identify him with the *Christus Victor* model. Certainly the theme of Satan's defeat is clear.

Listen to the reason for his coming and glorify the power of the incarnate. Mankind was deep in debt and incapable of paying what is owed. By the hand of Adam we had all signed a bond to sin. The devil held us in slavery. He kept producing our bills, which he wrote on our passible body. There he stood, the wicked forger, threatening us with our debts and demanding satisfaction. One of two things had to happen: either the penalty of death had to be imposed on all, since indeed "all had sinned"; or, else a substitute had to be provided who was fully entitled to plead on our behalf. No man could save us; the debt was his liability. No angel could buy us out; such a ransom was beyond his powers. One who was sinless had to die for those who had sinned; that was the only way left by which to break the bonds of evil.[32]

If Proclus fits the *Christus Victor* model in some sense, he also attends to the wide riches of soteriology. He uses language of ransom and substitution, debt and satisfaction. He connects his model to the person of Christ and to the cosmos, and he draws on many biblical themes. This is all to say that classifying soteriology according to models is useful to help us learn the doctrine, but the practice of soteriology is not about choosing and guarding the one right model. Our attention to the core of the doctrine will be more sensitive if we do not isolate that core from the many biblical themes, steps on the way of salvation, reflections on the goodness of grace, and models for atonement that are part of soteriology.

As we dwell with these riches, we will learn what it means to "work out" our "salvation with fear and trembling" (Phil. 2:12), remembering all the while that "it is God who is at work in you, enabling you both to will and to work for his good pleasure" (v. 13). As redeemed people, we will always stand in awe and fear of God as we practice the Christian life along the way of salvation. Because God is powerful, we will expect our lives to be powerfully transformed. Because the message of salvation is good news for the world, it will be essential to our practice of salvation that we bear testimony to that good news. As slaves who have been set free, we will practice advocacy for others who are still in slavery, working and longing for all to share in the freedom we have in Christ.

---

32. Proclus, "Sermon 1," in *Documents in Early Christian Thought*, ed. Maurice Wiles and Mark Santer (Cambridge: Cambridge University Press, 1975), 63.

8

The Holy Spirit
and the Christian Life

Pneumatology

The practice of doctrine is very much a work of the Holy Spirit, and the doctrine of **pneumatology** (the Greek *pneuma* means "breath" or "spirit") is integral to Christian thought as a whole. Without the active presence and power of God the Spirit, the project of theology could only be a selfish, sinful one, but sometimes we are uncomfortable with talk about the Holy Spirit. Some of this may reflect a proper silence in light of the holiness and transcendence of God, but there are also corrupt reasons for failing to speak of the Spirit, reasons rooted in sin and in fear. In sin, we prefer the selfish life to the life of the Spirit, and in sin, we are wont to turn our backs on the comfort offered by the Spirit of God. In fear, we shrink back from the possibility that the Spirit might do something radically new in our lives, might call us to ministry in places we do not want to go or to love people we do not want to love. Thankfully, the Spirit works against this. The Spirit is one who casts out fear, a Spirit not "of cowardice, but rather a spirit of power and of love and of self-discipline" (2 Tim. 1:7). Mercifully, the same Spirit works new life in us, life in which the power of

Jesus Christ defeats sin, and "the law of the Spirit of life in Christ Jesus" sets us "free from the law of sin and of death" (Rom. 8:2). In short, because of who the Spirit is, we may approach the study of pneumatology with confidence, faith, and joyous anticipation.

The Lord, the Giver of Life

> What then is the charge they bring against us? They accuse us of profanity for entertaining lofty conceptions about the Holy Spirit. . . . We, for instance, confess that the Holy Spirit is of the same rank as the Father and the Son, so that there is no difference between them in anything, to be thought or named, that devotion can ascribe to a Divine nature. . . . But our opponents aver that He is a stranger to any vital communion with the Father and the Son; that by reason of an essential variation He is inferior to, and less than they in every point. . . . He is Divine, and absolutely good, and omnipotent, and wise, and glorious, and eternal; He is everything of this kind that can be named to raise our thoughts to the grandeur of His being. . . . He is Himself Goodness, and Wisdom, and Power, and Sanctification, and Righteousness, and Everlastingness, and Imperishability, and every name that is lofty, and elevating above other names.[1]

Gregory of Nyssa wrote these words against those who denied that the Spirit is truly God. Gregory insisted, to the contrary, that the Spirit is equal to, "of the same rank as," the Father and the Son, and that this is the clear testimony of Scripture. Gregory offers a litany of praise to the Spirit, identifying the attributes of the Spirit with the Spirit's very nature in a way that can belong only to God. The Nicene Creed resonates with Gregory's teaching, confessing that the Holy Spirit is in eternal relationship with the Father and the Son, and that, with them, the Spirit "is worshiped and glorified." These creedal statements form the great affirmations of ecumenical pneumatology. Against detractors who would have demoted the Spirit to sub-divine status, the church recognized that the scriptural story of God's work in the world entails the Spirit's full divinity. Put differently, the story of Scripture makes no sense if the Spirit is not truly and really God. The creedal titles "Lord" and "life giver" are titles that Scripture demands for

---

1. Gregory of Nyssa, "On the Holy Spirit: Against the Followers of Macedonius," in *Nicene and Post-Nicene Fathers,* Second Series, vol. 5, ed. Philip Schaff and Henry Wace, trans. William Moore and Henry Austin (Peabody, MA: Hendrickson, 1994), 315.

the Spirit, titles that can properly belong only to God. No watered-down version of divinity will do.

The title "Lord" respects the Spirit's divinity by placing human beings under the direction and power of the Spirit and by identifying the Spirit with the Father and the Son. The recognition that this Lord is the "giver of life" also respects the Spirit's divinity by acknowledging that the life-giving Spirit, together with the Father and the Son, does the work only God can do. There are many biblical bases for these two affirmations. Both are found together when Paul tells believers we are living letters of recommendation, letters written by the Spirit on human hearts, and he reminds us that we find our competence and confidence, not in ourselves, but in God, clearly identified as the Spirit who "gives life" (2 Cor. 3:6). Later in the same chapter, Paul presses believers to act "with great boldness" as we witness to God's glory, a boldness that is legitimated by the Lord, again clearly identified with the Spirit. "The Lord is the Spirit," Paul preaches, "and where the Spirit of the Lord is, there is freedom" (v. 17). In the freedom of the Spirit of God, we are transformed and enabled to reflect God's image and glory. Again, "this comes from the Lord, the Spirit" (v. 18). Here Paul rejoices in the life-giving power of God the Spirit, power that no mere creature can claim.

> ### Key Scripture
>
> These things God has revealed to us through the Spirit; for the Spirit searches everything, even the depths of God. For what human being knows what is truly human except the human spirit that is within? So also no one comprehends what is truly God's except the Spirit of God. Now we have received not the spirit of the world, but the Spirit that is from God, so that we may understand the gifts bestowed on us by God. And we speak of these things in words not taught by human wisdom but taught by the Spirit, interpreting spiritual things to those who are spiritual. Those who are unspiritual do not receive the gifts of God's Spirit, for they are foolishness to them, and they are unable to understand them because they are spiritually discerned. Those who are spiritual discern all things, and they are themselves subject to no one else's scrutiny. "For who has known the mind of the Lord so as to instruct him?" But we have the mind of Christ. (1 Cor. 2:10–16)

The Spirit's life-giving work begins in the first chapter of Genesis, where Christians have traditionally seen the Spirit at work as God hovers over the waters. That life-giving work continues throughout the story of salvation, and it is seen in special ways in connection to Jesus: it is the Spirit who is

---

Basil's Prepositions

In the midst of church tumult over the Arian controversy, Christians were talking about the proper way to address the Triune God in prayer and worship. The Arians would have demoted not only Jesus but also the Spirit from divine to creaturely status, and Basil the Great (c. 329–379) wrote to defend the divinity of the Spirit. Basil's pneumatology connected doctrine and practice as he jumped into a debate about prepositions and prayer.

Christians were used to praying (note the prepositions)

to the Father, *in* the Son, *through* the Holy Spirit.

This pattern for prayer recognizes the way God works in the world, and Basil thinks that this is fine, but he also points out that we see other relational patterns in Scripture. Basil argues, against the Arians, that it is also appropriate to pray

to the Father, *with* the Son, *with* the Holy Spirit.

This second pattern for prayer emphasizes the shared divinity and coequality of the triune persons. It sets them side by side, so to speak, instead of arranging them in a hierarchy, and so it fits together with the words of Scripture and the practice of Christian baptism.

> They say that it is not suitable to rank the Holy Spirit with the Father and the Son, because He is different in nature and inferior in dignity from them. . . . When the Lord established the baptism of salvation, did He not clearly command His disciple to baptize all nations "in the name of the Father, and of the Son, and of the Holy Spirit"? He did not disdain his fellowship with the Holy Spirit, but these men say that we should not rank Him with the Father and the Son. Are they not openly disregarding God's commandment?[a]

Basil connects worship with theology and theology with worship, and he seeks a doctrine of pneumatology that fits together with Christian practice.

a. Basil the Great, *On the Holy Spirit*, trans. David Anderson (Crestwood, NY: St. Vladimir's Seminary Press, 1980), 10, 24.

---

at work in the life-giving conception of Jesus in Mary's womb, who descends on Jesus at his baptism, and who, at the end of Jesus's life, works in raising Jesus from the dead. The Spirit's giving of life extends to us as well, both by giving us new life in the present and in the future promise of everlasting, resurrected life. "To set the mind on the Spirit is life and peace" (Rom. 8:6), and the new birth that Jesus spoke of to Nicodemus is birth "of water and the Spirit" (John 3:5).

The Personal Spirit

In thinking about the three persons of the Trinity, it seems obvious that the Father and the Son are personal. Father and Son are relational terms. In fact, in the doctrine of the Trinity, these terms make sense only in relationship to each other. The Father is the father of someone: the Son, Jesus Christ. The Son is the son of someone: his eternal Father. This personal, relational language communicates quite a bit about who God is and what kind of relationships human beings can have with God.

When we consider the doctrine of the Holy Spirit, though, we are less certain about personal language and personal relationship. The term "spirit" is not inherently relational like the terms "father" and "son," and so we may be tempted to depersonalize the Spirit. The Nicene Creed recognizes the personal status of the Spirit—and the blessed truth that we can relate personally to the same Spirit—when it describes the Spirit in terms of eternal relationships with the Father and the Son. The Spirit "proceeds" from the Father and the Son, and is worshiped and glorified together with them, indicating personal relationships of the most mutual kind.

What can it mean for the Spirit to "proceed" from the Father and the Son? This is a contested question, and it has threatened the ecumenical status of the creed. The original creedal language stated only that the Spirit "proceeds from the Father," and so it indicated the eternal relationship between Father and Spirit. The phrase "and from the Son"—in Latin, *filioque*—was added to the creed in the Latin-speaking Western church over a period of years.[2] The Greek-speaking East objected—and continues to object—to the West's unilateral addition to an ecumenical creed, made without acknowledgment of or conversation with the East. The Latin addition developed as a way of reaffirming the full divinity of both Spirit and Son in their eternal relationships to one another, and it fits with a

---

2. A. Edward Siecienski, *The Filioque: History of a Doctrinal Controversy* (New York: Oxford University Press, 2010).

tendency to see the three persons of the Trinity in mutuality and coequality. Certainly, the unilateral action of the Western church is no model for doing ecumenical theology, and there is a lesson here about the need for Christians to listen to one another in making doctrinal proclamation.

While the East objects to the Western *filioque*, East and West agree that the Spirit is truly God, that the Spirit exists in eternal relationship with the Father and the Son, and that the Spirit proceeds from the Father. The term "proceeds" is a signpost for the eternal relatedness of Father and Spirit. This relationship is one that has no creaturely parallels. God does not just *have* relationships; God *is* relationship. Our new birth in the Spirit brings us into the relational life of God in a special way. God relates to us as beloved children. New Testament scholar Gordon Fee explores the mystery by which the Spirit brings us into the triune life: "The closest kind of intimate, interior relationship exists between the Father and the Spirit. . . . In our reception of the Spirit, we are on intimate terms with none other than God himself, personally and powerfully present, as the one who . . . reveals God's ways to us."[3] Theologian Kathryn Tanner plays on the same theme as she reflects on the Spirit in relationship with the Father and the Son, a relationship of true unity.

> Reinforcing the unity of being between Father and Son by a unity of love and joyful affirmation, the Holy Spirit is the exuberant, ecstatic carrier of the love of Father and Son to us. Borne by the Holy Spirit, the love of the Father for the Son is returned to the Father by the Son within the Trinity; so the triune God's manifestation in the world is completed in Christ through the work of the Spirit who enables us to return the love of God shown in Christ through a life lived in gratitude and service to God's cause.[4]

God's own life is a life of oneness together with difference. What is more, these features of God's life mark God's loving, personal relationship with us, a relationship in which the Spirit, who is not the Father or the Son, indwells and empowers us, helping us to embody God's love for us. In the Spirit's power, we are truly united with Christ our Lord. Because Jesus has won victory over sin, we are enabled to relate to the Spirit and the Father

---

3. Gordon Fee, *God's Empowering Presence: The Holy Spirit in the Letters of Paul* (Peabody, MA: Hendrickson, 1994), 101.

4. Kathryn Tanner, *Jesus, Humanity and the Trinity: A Brief Systematic Theology* (Minneapolis: Fortress, 2001), 14.

in ways that parallel Jesus's relationships to them during his life on earth. In the Spirit's power, the people of God are also united as one, "even as," again in Tanner's words, "the Holy Spirit encourages the uniqueness of our persons by a diversity of gifts of the Spirit."[5] We see these dynamics in Jesus's words in the Gospel of John.

> If you love me, you will keep my commandments. And I will ask the Father, and he will give you another Advocate, to be with you forever. This is the Spirit of truth, whom the world cannot receive, because it neither sees him nor knows him. You know him, because he abides with you, and he will be in you. I will not leave you orphaned; I am coming to you. In a little while the world will no longer see me, but you will see me; because I live, you also will live. On that day you will know that I am in my Father, and you in me, and I in you. They who have my commandments and keep them are those who love me; and those who love me will be loved by my Father, and I will love them and reveal myself to them. (John 14:15–21)

Notice the mutual relationships between the three divine persons, and notice how Jesus expects the love between Father, Son, and Spirit to be manifested among us. When Jesus ascends to the Father, when we can no longer see Jesus face-to-face, the Father sends the Holy Spirit to us as an Advocate. Like an advocate in court, who speaks for and protects a person on trial, the Spirit as Advocate speaks for us and stands beside us in our times of need. In Jesus, we are made children of the Father, and neither Father nor Son leaves us "orphaned." God the Holy Spirit abides with us and in us, empowering us to love. The Spirit, as the Advocate among us, will point us straight back to the Son. Jesus describes the Spirit's work in the next chapter of John's Gospel: "When the Advocate comes, whom I will send to you from the Father, the Spirit of truth who comes from the Father, he will testify on my behalf" (John 15:26). Notice how the Spirit, sent by the Son from the Father, testifies not on his own behalf but for the Son, with whom he is one.

Gendered Language

God is more than we could ever imagine, and part of what this means is that God is beyond gender. God is neither male nor female. In recent

5. Ibid., 83.

decades, some theologians have argued that using masculine pronouns for God confuses this fact and tempts us to **anthropomorphize** God—form God in our own image instead of remembering it is the other way around. Critics raise the concern that masculine language for God may contribute to the human tendency to fashion false idols, to think of God as a man.

Theologian Janet Soskice responds, "One strategy has been to feminize the Spirit. We can readily uncover a tradition of regarding the Spirit as the maternal aspect of God—brooding, nurturing, bringing new members of the Church to life in baptism."[6] Soskice believes that this strategy tends to fail. Feminizing the Spirit, by implication, further masculinizes the Father and the Son, and so calling the Spirit "she" inadvertently strengthens the idolatrous idea that God is a gendered being, like you and me. A feminized Spirit may also strengthen cultural stereotypes about what it means to be masculine or feminine in the first place. Most problematic, such a strategy introduces division into the Trinity. Soskice rejects any attempt to model human gender roles on God's triune life. "The doctrine of the Trinity tells us nothing about how men and women should relate to one another as males and females. It does not show that all men should be like the 'father' and all women model themselves on a feminized Spirit. In this sense the doctrine tells us nothing about sexual difference. But it does let us glimpse what it is, most truly, to be: 'to be' most fully is 'to-be-related' in difference."[7]

Masculine personal pronouns used for God are not unproblematic. At the same time, when a pronoun is called for, I think that masculine personal pronouns are the *least* problematic route. One explanation for Old Testament use of masculine language for God is to read it as a move against

> ### Prayer to the Spirit
>
> Come Holy Spirit, fill the hearts of your faithful and kindle in them the fire of your love. Send forth your Spirit and they shall be created. And You shall renew the face of the earth. Lord, by the light of the Holy Spirit, you have taught the hearts of your faithful. In the same Spirit, help us relish what is right and always rejoice in your consolation. We ask this through Christ Our Lord, Amen.[a]
>
> a. Quoted in Meredith Gould, *The Catholic Home: Celebrations and Traditions for Holidays, Feast Days, and Every Day* (New York: Doubleday, 2004), 223.

6. Janet Martin Soskice, *The Kindness of God: Metaphor, Gender, and Religious Language* (New York: Oxford University Press, 2007), 112.

7. Ibid., 124.

idolatry. In the Canaanite context, Israel was surrounded by polytheism, by hoards of gods and goddesses. Masculine language for God rejects that context, reiterating the unity of God and the difference between God and idols.[8] In the New Testament, masculine pronouns for God acknowledge the reality of the incarnation and the personal relationship between the Father and his Son. The God of Scripture cannot be depersonalized. We see this in the love shared between the Father, the Son, and the Spirit. To extend the natural masculine pronoun for Father and Son—"he"—to the Spirit as the Third Person of the Trinity is acknowledgment of God's triunity and of the Spirit's personal nature. We see this implicit in the Gospel of John, where the word "Spirit," a neuter noun in Greek, is personalized through a shift to the masculine personal pronoun. Jesus says, "When the Spirit of truth comes, he will guide you into all the truth; for he will not speak on his own, but will speak whatever he hears, and he will declare to you the things that are to come. He will glorify me, because he will take what is mine and declare it to you" (John 16:13–14). The Spirit is personal, in his relationship both to other divine persons and to us, and it will not do to call the Spirit "it."

Spirit and Spirituality

God created humans to be creatures who are both physical and spiritual, creatures for whom the bodily life is the life for which we were made. In chapter 5, we discussed embodiment as central to theological anthropology and to God's good intentions for human beings. As psychosomatic unities, embodied souls or ensouled bodies, we are sometimes surprised to find ourselves in relationship with the God who is so very different from us. The affirmation that God *is* spirit points to the essential difference between God and us. John Wesley, in a sermon on the unity of the divine being, highlights this point. "This God is a spirit; not having such a body, such parts, or passions as men have. It was the opinion both of the ancient Jews and the ancient Christians that he alone is a pure spirit, totally separate from all matter."[9]

8. See Robert Jenson, "The Father, He . . . ," in *Speaking the Christian God: The Holy Trinity and the Challenge of Feminism*, ed. Alvin F. Kimel (Grand Rapids: Eerdmans, 1992), 95–109.

9. "The Unity of the Divine Being," in *John Wesley's Sermons: An Anthology*, ed. Albert C. Outler and Richard P. Heitzenrater (Nashville: Abingdon, 1991), 533.

The word *spirit*, even without the capital letter we use for the Third Person of the Trinity, can be confusing. Various uses of the word *spiritual* only add to the problem. In contemporary life, the language of "spirituality" is employed in incredibly diffuse, obtuse, and generic ways. Some view spirituality as gnostic escape from the body. Others want to be "spiritual but not religious." Eclectic "spiritualities" abound, and these may draw on pagan traditions and "new age" claims or may pillage bits from several religions. All of these trends are problematic for Christian faith. All work against the sweet testimony of the Holy Spirit, both in Scripture and in Christian life, a testimony that is concrete, specific, and matters to us as embodied creatures in distinctly Christian ways. We will look at several ways that the doctrine and practice of spirituality goes wrong in our world, and we will consider correctives that come from pneumatology.

Gnostic pseudospirituality has a long history as a distortion of Christian faith. The doctrine of creation, as we saw in chapter 4, was shaped against the harsh gnostic dualism that saw bodies as antithetical to spirituality. Bodies are not prisons to be escaped or trivialities to be discounted. They are essential to who we are and to the spiritual life. This does not mean that we never have problems with our bodies or with the material world. Bodies are created good, but they, like all of creation, are groaning under the condition of sin. Our problem is not that we have bodies. Our problem is sin. Certainly bodies are fallen, and we face that reality in very tangible ways when we deal with cancer or injury or the consequences of lust. Again, though, our problem is not embodiment; it is that we, body and soul, are sinners in a sinful world. This is not meant to imply that cancer, bodily injury, or even lust is punishment for the personal, individual sin of the one whose body is affected. The fallen state of the world is both individual and communal, and all of us, both when we are blameless and when we are guilty, feel the effects of sin in both body and soul. Bodies are fallen, but the spiritual aspects of human existence are fallen as well. We have hope that God—who made us spiritual creatures able to be in personal relationship with him—will sanctify us, body and soul.

Gnostic spiritualities continue to pop up in the contemporary church, telling the lie that the body is opposed to the spiritual life. They tell the lie that truly spiritual people disdain the bodily life, or the opposite lie that spiritual people may act with complete license when it comes to their bodies. Against this, Scripture testifies that God's redemptive work in human lives is for every aspect of those lives, both spiritual and physical. God works, through the power of the Holy Spirit, to transform us, body and soul, into the loving image of Christ. The spiritual life is the life of body and soul together under the direction of the Holy Spirit. Christian spirituality is physical and spiritual, body and soul, contemplative and active, messy and transformative. Human spirituality embraces the goodness of this life even while recognizing the struggles we face under the condition of sin. Christian spirituality is not about rejecting bodies. It is about the Holy Spirit, who is God, the Lord, the giver of life. Gustavo Gutiérrez puts it beautifully.

> Spirituality, in the strict and profound sense of the word is the dominion of the Spirit. . . . A spirituality is a concrete matter, inspired by the Spirit, of living the Gospel; it is a definite way of living "before the Lord" in solidarity with all human beings, "with the Lord," and before human beings. It arises from an intense spiritual experience, which is later explicated and witnessed to.[10]

Spiritual and Religious

Given that gnosticism is a lie, the claim to be "spiritual but not religious" is a problem. The expression rests on the assumption that spirituality is about the inner person—the heart, the mind, the soul, the emotions, or the intentions—and so it is not concerned with bodily things. Because this version of spirituality is believed to be interior, it is also considered private and not something to be inflicted on the outside world. The same sentiment tends to equate religion with dead forms, meaningless rituals, and unreasonable dogmatic beliefs. This brand of spirituality will not do for Christians, whose spirituality must be about life in the Holy Spirit, who is intimately involved in creation and works with and in the material world.

This is not to say that the critique of "religion" implied in the idea of being "spiritual but not religious" has no merit at all. A religion of dead forms and meaningless rituals *is* a problem for the Christian spiritual life, just as a spirituality made up only of interior feelings is. The Christian spiritual life, following the example of Jesus, is a life in which every aspect of our

10. Gustavo Gutiérrez, *A Theology of Liberation*, 15th anniversary ed. (Maryknoll, NY: Orbis Books, 1988), 117.

being becomes one integrated whole. In that integrity—unity and wholeness of body and soul—we are transformed in holiness and enabled to witness to the love of God. If gnostic spirituality brackets off the exterior from the spiritual life, pushing bodies and action and practices to the side, the dead religiosity, which we can rightly critique, brackets off the interior from the religious life, pushing emotions and commitments and contemplation to the side. Neither kind of bracketing fits with the practice of pneumatology.

In the spiritual life, guided by the Holy Spirit, all is united in an integrated whole: interior and exterior, individual and corporate, soul and body, contemplation and action, commitment and practice, emotion and the day-to-day life of the church. The Christian life must always be spiritual *and* religious in this sense. False spiritualities are revealed as false in the truth of the Holy Spirit, and nominal religiosities are revealed by that same Spirit as the dead things they are. But in no way is it the case that ritual, form, doctrine, corporate worship, sacrament, liturgy, and all the other specificities of religious life in the Christian church must be such dead things. Not at all. The Holy Spirit, the Spirit of life, gives life to these things and to us, offering us a spiritual integrity like that of Christ.

Theologian Eugene Rogers notes that, in Scripture, the Spirit "rests on" bodies. Rogers highlights ways that the Spirit "in classical Christian discourse 'pours out on all flesh,'" and he regrets that "in modern Christian discourse, [the Spirit has] floated free of bodies altogether." Rogers asks a provocative question: "What if the Spirit had grown boring [to modern people] because it no longer had anything to do with the body?"[11] He suggests that neglect of the Spirit may be rooted in this fundamental error, and he insists that the Spirit is "immanent in bodily things."[12] Rogers's thesis agrees with my assessment above. Indeed, the Spirit loves bodies and rests upon them. One of the most marvelous truths of pneumatology is that the Spirit, who is truly God, also chooses to dwell within us. The Spirit rests *on* bodies, and this is no small thing, but the Spirit also lives *in* bodies.

> The body is meant not for fornication but for the Lord, and the Lord for the body. And God raised the Lord and will also raise us by his power. Do you not know that your bodies are members of Christ? Should I therefore take

---

11. Eugene F. Rogers Jr., *After the Spirit: A Constructive Pneumatology from Resources outside the Modern West* (Grand Rapids: Eerdmans, 2005), 1.
12. Ibid., 2.

the members of Christ and make them members of a prostitute? Never! Do you not know that whoever is united to a prostitute becomes one body with her? For it is said, "The two shall be one flesh." But anyone united to the Lord becomes one spirit with him. Shun fornication! Every sin that a person commits is outside the body; but the fornicator sins against the body itself. Or do you not know that your body is a temple of the Holy Spirit within you, which you have from God, and that you are not your own? (1 Cor. 6:13–19)

Bodily matters—in this case, sex—are spiritually important. One cannot split off body from soul, as though what one does with the body is insignificant. Embodied spiritual practices acknowledge this reality. Small group accountability, service to the poor and hungry, meeting for love feasts or potlucks, fasting, kneeling, laying on of hands—all these and many more are practices in which we are gathered by the Spirit, to whom our bodies matter. The body is purposeful, goal oriented. The body is *for* the Lord. What is more, the Holy Spirit indwells us so that our bodies become temples. Here we learn of the miracle that the Spirit—holy and transcendent, utterly different from us—chooses us. The Spirit is with us and loves us and does not disdain us. Poet John Donne relishes just this glorious contradiction.

> Wilt thou love God, as He thee? then digest,
> My soul, this wholesome meditation,
> How God the Spirit, by angels waited on
> In heaven, doth make His Temple in thy breast.[13]

Digest it indeed, this sweet, strange gift. God the holy, other, transcendent, majestic, magnificent, and eternal takes up residence within us. Here is the gift and power of the spiritual life, and—Donne is quite right—here is a testimony of God's love for us that ought to incite us to ardent love for God in return.

Life in the Spirit

Against a popular moralism that offers only generic virtues—bland goodness and vague niceness—the Holy Spirit grows specific fruit in us. Against a moralism that relies on human effort—teeth gritted as we try desperately

13. John Donne, "Holy Sonnet 11 (XV)," in *John Donne's Poetry*, ed. Arthur L. Clements, 2nd ed. (New York: W. W. Norton, 1992), 116.

Sin against the Spirit

The unity of the Father, Son, and Holy Spirit is key to understanding Gospel references to a great sin against the Spirit. In the account in the Gospel of Matthew, Jesus has just had a confrontation with the Pharisees over picking grain and healing on the Sabbath, and he has claimed his mastery over the law: "The Son of Man is lord of the Sabbath" (Matt. 12:8). The Pharisees attribute Jesus's healing power to Satan, charging, "It is only by Beelzebul, the ruler of the demons, that this fellow casts out demons" (v. 24). It is this false charge that prompts Jesus's words about a sin against the Spirit.

> If Satan casts out Satan, he is divided against himself; how then will his kingdom stand? If I cast out demons by Beelzebul, by whom do your own exorcists cast them out? Therefore they will be your judges. But if it is by the Spirit of God that I cast out demons, then the kingdom of God has come to you. . . . Therefore I tell you, people will be forgiven for every sin and blasphemy, but blasphemy against the Spirit will not be forgiven. Whoever speaks a word against the Son of Man will be forgiven, but whoever speaks against the Holy Spirit will not be forgiven, either in this age or in the age to come. (vv. 26–28, 31–32)

Jesus's reference to a sin that will not be forgiven comes in the very clear context of the Pharisees' accusation. To blaspheme against the Spirit is to say that Jesus's power is not from God. It is, finally, to refuse to acknowledge Jesus as "the way, and the truth, and the life" (John 14:6), the one who is "lord of the Sabbath" and full of the Spirit's power. It makes no sense outside the unity of the Father, Son, and Spirit. Christians sometimes worry that they might accidently commit the "unforgivable sin," but what we learn, here and elsewhere in the New Testament, is that we need not fear. To be in Christ and to acknowledge his Lordship is already to be united with the Spirit. To be in Christ is, by grace, to be forgiven of sin. To sin against the Spirit is to refuse God's own self, not some lesser part of God, but the one true God who has opened forgiveness to us through the work of Jesus Christ.

to be good—the Holy Spirit works fruit in us by the power of sanctifying grace. At this most intimate level, God is with us. The Christian spiritual life is possible because of the intimate presence of the Holy Spirit in our lives. Life in the Spirit is a life in which we become the trees who bear the Spirit's good fruit, in which we are given gifts for the building up of the community, and in which we are sanctified, made loving as we are drawn into the love of the Triune God.

When considering the fruit of the Spirit, those fruits that ripen in us as we live the spiritual life, it is helpful to remember that Paul's list of fruit— "love, joy, peace, patience, kindness, generosity [or goodness], faithfulness, gentleness, and self-control" (Gal. 5:22–23)—comes in the context of his letter to the Galatians, a letter that is about the grand themes of the gospel. These fruits, the lush bounty of the spiritual life, are gospel fruits. They grow, not by our own frenetic effort, but from the good trees that God cultivates through the gospel of Jesus Christ. We misunderstand the fruit of the Spirit if we do not recognize that those fruits are gracious gifts, made possible because of what God has done and is doing in our lives. Love, joy, and peace are not about earning God's favor. We are enabled to bear these fruits because God has already forgiven our sin and made us part of his new creation. This fruitful feast is a gift of grace to which we have no access without God.

The word *holiness* has fallen out of our vocabularies, but the truth of God's holiness is central to the biblical witness and to the beauty of the relationship we are called to have with God. To remember that God is holy is to remember that God is set apart, is other, from the world and from us. "There is no Holy One like the LORD, no one besides you" (1 Sam. 2:2). Holiness is shown in divine righteousness, the standard of goodness and justice and truthfulness. Isaiah proclaims, "The LORD of hosts is exalted by justice, and the Holy God shows himself holy by righteousness" (Isa. 5:16). And yet, through the whole story of Scripture, God miraculously calls us into the mystery of holiness, including us in God's own righteousness. The meaning of human holiness is to be like God. "Sanctify yourselves," the Lord tells his people, "and be holy, for I am holy" (Lev. 11:44). If we see holiness as a set of legalistic rules, we are missing the point. Human holiness is seen when we become like God, who is love. Holy human beings, transformed body and soul by the power of the Spirit, receive God's grace by means of practices that involve the body. This may well involve rules, but they will not be bare and senseless ones, and we will be able to be ruled by them as a gift of grace.

There are many biblical motifs that help us to imagine the sanctified life. Sanctification can be seen in terms of the renewal of the image of God (2 Cor. 3), the fullness of the fruits of the Spirit (Gal. 5), the new creation (2 Cor. 5), having the mind of Christ (2 Cor. 2), presenting selves to God as a living sacrifice (Rom. 12), salvation from all sin (Col. 2), and loving the Lord with heart, mind, soul, and strength (Mark 12). These themes overlap, showing us that perfection in love is not a legalistic to-do list but a way of heralding the biblical vision of humans transformed to share a holy life with a holy God. John Wesley indicates this comprehensiveness in a letter in which he explains, "I take religion to be, not the bare saying over of so many prayers . . . but a constant ruling habit of soul, a renewal of our minds in the image of God, a recovery of the divine likeness, a still-increasing conformity of heart and life to the pattern of our most holy Redeemer."[14] The process by which the Spirit works in us and with us is one that continues throughout the Christian life. Sanctification begins with the new birth, and it continues through the days, weeks, and years that follow, as we become more and more like Christ.

Pentecostal Power and Charismatic Gifts

> When the day of Pentecost had come, they were all together in one place. And suddenly from heaven there came a sound like the rush of a violent wind, and it filled the entire house where they were sitting. Divided tongues, as of fire, appeared among them, and a tongue rested on each of them. All of them were filled with the Holy Spirit and began to speak in other languages, as the Spirit gave them ability. (Acts 2:1–4)

Here is the presence of the Spirit, visible to the church and to the world, in terrifying power. Here is the Spirit's work made accessible to the senses. Here the Spirit's work is heard, felt, seen. And here, the Spirit works by providing extraordinary gifts. The church speaks in tongues, and the gathered crowd hears "the native language of each" (v. 6). This power can be embraced with a deep confidence in the Spirit's work, or this power can be rejected and denied. Both kinds of response have existed in every age and may even coexist in an individual Christian's life. In the Acts account, "all were amazed and perplexed, saying to one another, 'What does this mean?' But others sneered and said, 'They were filled with new wine'" (v. 12).

The Spirit is God. Why, then, would we question the powerful gifts of the Spirit in the life of the church? What obstacles stand in the way of our confident embrace of the Spirit's power? There can be both good and bad reasons for hesitation around the powerful work of the Spirit. Some Christians fear talk about spiritual gifts because they have encountered people who misuse the Spirit's name, who justify sin by saying they work under the leading of the Spirit. This kind of hesitation is proper. Embrace of the Spirit's power does not imply that anything goes. Nor does it mean that anything people call "spiritual" is truly of the Spirit. Sometimes, Christians

---

14. Frank Baker, ed., *The Works of John Wesley* (Nashville: Abingdon, 1987), 25:366.

The Spirit's Healing Power

Argentinian pastor and theologian Norberto Saracco writes about a phenomenon that is a reality for an enormous number of Christians around the globe, the experience of the Spirit's healing power. Saracco affirms this power, while also suggesting ways that the church can and does go wrong as we seek healing.

When I speak of the church's mission of healing in the light of the work of the Holy Spirit, I cannot hide the fact that my personal experience affects what I say. At the same time, I do so with the total conviction that the power of the Spirit to heal is today, as always, an undeniable reality. However, we must be careful to avoid acts of magic, the use of power for power's sake and the temptation to indulge in cheap miracle-working, which makes healing a commodity. . . . Illness . . . is more than a physical and individual phenomenon. It has also to do with the mind, emotions, interpersonal relations, i.e., human beings as whole persons. We are not dealing with ill bodies but with people who are ill. . . . Illness is yet another of the results of death, which has come into the world through sin. Illness is a painful anticipation of death. It makes us aware of our fragility and of the fact that, together with all creation, we await the moment of our complete redemption. Similarly, healing is an anticipation of that redemption and serves as a reminder to us that death has been conquered. We are not abandoned to our fate as weak human beings. . . . Healing is part of our Lord's redeeming work.[a]

Saracco goes on to talk about how the Spirit's power must be understood in light of who Jesus is and the mission he gives to us.

Power is subordinate to mission. It is not power for power's sake, nor is its purpose concentration of power upon particular persons or institutions. The gospel in the power of the Spirit cannot, therefore, concentrate on the supernatural and the miraculous, but on the ability of the power of God to bring about change. . . . If a church, in which people are healed, maintains unjust structures, remains silent in the face of corruption or seeks to ally itself with the powers that be, then we cannot say that such a church is under the power of the Spirit. In the perspective of the kingdom, the gospel of power reaffirms the person of the Holy Spirit as such and does not treat the Spirit as a force and no more. It is quite easy for us to be seduced by power and convert the Spirit into a servant to do our bidding or, worse, a power given us to be used as we please for our own benefit.[b]

a. Norberto Saracco, "The Holy Spirit and the Church's Mission of Healing," in *International Review of Mission* 93, no. 370/371 (July–October 2004): 412–13.
b. Ibid., 416–17.

are put off by talk about spiritual gifts because they have encountered churches that insist that people cannot belong to Christ if they do not exhibit specific spiritual gifts, usually the gift of speaking in tongues. Again, I understand this hesitancy. The Spirit is not the leader of some exclusive club, one in which only special Christians can gain membership.

So, there are real reasons to exercise caution around wild claims about the Spirit's power, but there are also bad reasons for such caution, especially when that caution is linked to cowardice and pride. It is very easy to pretend that one has a "good" reason for suspicion about the Spirit when, in truth, that suspicion is rooted in sin. We sometimes shun the Spirit because we are clinging tightly to our illusions of control. We want to be in charge, and we are put off by anything that might reveal our vulnerability. So we turn our backs on the radical things that the Spirit is apt to do in the world, and we may cover that decision with high-sounding excuses. We are also sometimes afraid that embrace of the Spirit's power will open us up to ridicule, or make us look weak in the eyes of the world, or we may fear being identified with people who are not like us. Here, racism, sexism, and classism have, both historically and in the contemporary church, played into temptations for those who are not on the margins to hold themselves aloof from the Spirit's power. If we are suspicious of the Spirit because of our suspicions of "those people" over there, people who are different from us, then we need to pray for the Spirit to work in our lives, to open our hearts to all people, people the Spirit loves.

When thinking about Pentecost and the Spirit's power, the practice of speaking in tongues is a source of confusion. Paul addresses this in 1 Corinthians, and he makes it clear that the Holy Spirit and Jesus Christ can never be in conflict with one another. "No one speaking by the Spirit of God ever says 'Let Jesus be cursed!' and no one can say 'Jesus is Lord' except by the Holy Spirit" (1 Cor. 12:3). Paul goes on to talk about "varieties of gifts" given by the "same Spirit" (v. 4), indicating that a diversity of spiritual gifts is to be found among the people of God and that all these gifts, in the unity of the Spirit, are meant "for the common good" (v. 7). This is the context for Paul's famous illustration of the church as one body in which there are many parts, all needing one another. Tongues are one gift among many possible gifts of the Spirit, but they are not to be demanded of all Christians. Paul advises that those who are eager for spiritual gifts should "strive to excel in them for building up the church" (14:12), and he counsels that spiritual gifts should be directed toward witnessing to outsiders, so that they may learn the good news of Jesus Christ.

Some Christian traditions hold a strong cessationism, the belief that the special gifts of the Spirit ended with the New Testament age. This position is motivated by a desire to curb abuse of charismatic gifts. While this is a good aim, the majority of Christian traditions insist that we must respond to the abuse of gifts not with a denial of those gifts but with discernment. We can discern the right exercise of spiritual gifts when we see that exercise cohering with Scripture. In his sermon "The More Excellent Way," John Wesley begins with a defense of the special gifts of the Spirit. He calls the idea that such gifts ended with the early church "a miserable mistake,"[15] and he attributes any waning of spiritual gifts to watered-down Christianity, connecting it to "that fatal period when the Emperor Constantine called himself a Christian, and from a vain imagination of promoting the Christian cause thereby heaped riches, and power, and honour upon the Christians."[16] Wesley's age, like our own, was one that denied the miraculous.[17] But Wesley points to human sin, greed, lust for power, and collusion between the church and the empire as causes behind the drying up of spiritual gifts; and he calls this a case in which "'the love of many'—almost of all Christians, so called—was 'waxed cold.' . . . This was the real cause why the extraordinary gifts of the Holy Ghost were no longer to be found in the Christian church—because the Christians were turned heathens again, and had only a dead form left."[18]

Gender, Race, Class, and Global Revival

When, in Acts, the Holy Spirit comes on the church in power, we hear a quote from the prophet Joel.

> "In the last days it will be," God declares, "that I will pour out my Spirit upon all flesh, and your sons and your daughters shall prophesy, and your young men shall see visions, and your old men shall dream dreams. Even upon my slaves, both men and women, in those days I will pour out my Spirit; and they shall prophesy." (Acts 2:17–18)

The time of the Holy Spirit is the time of the "last days." This claim is not about prophecies for the end times. Rather, it points to the church, filled with the Holy Spirit, as a kingdom community. The Spirit loves women

15. John Wesley, "The More Excellent Way," in *John Wesley's Sermons*, 512.
16. Ibid.
17. Jeffrey W. Barbeau, "John Wesley and the Early Church: History, Antiquity, and the Spirit of God," in *Evangelicals and the Early Church: Recovery, Reform, Renewal*, ed. George Kalantzis and Andrew Tooley (Eugene, OR: Cascade Books, 2012).
18. Wesley, "More Excellent Way," 512.

and men, poor and rich, young and old, and every shade of black and white and brown. This pneumatological love challenges our practices of sexism, racism, and elitism.

When Christianity is open to the Spirit and takes the work of the Holy Spirit seriously, we recognize that the gospel is about God's love for people who are marginalized in a world of sin. Historian Douglas Jacobsen narrates one example from the twentieth-century Azusa Street Revivals: "If the real sign of the baptism of the Spirit was more love for others, the communal manifestation of that love was the ability to care for and respect each other across the lines of race, class, gender, and age that normally separated people."[19] Another example of the Spirit's work for the marginalized is in black church traditions in the United States, in the history of abolitionism and the civil rights movement. Religion scholar Philip Jenkins says that the "socially liberating effects of evangelical religion should come as no surprise to anyone who has traced the enormous influence of biblically based religion throughout African-American history."[20] A third example can be seen in Latin American Pentecostalism, in which "the prominence of female Pentecostals has affected the machismo culture of the traditional military establishment."[21]

The Spirit's work in breaking down walls between people extends around the globe. The church of the Spirit and the work of the kingdom transcend national, linguistic, and ethnic boundaries. God is the God of all peoples and all nations, and the Spirit loves those peoples and nations, uniting us as one while also loving and preserving our diversity. John Wesley sees this dynamic in his comment on the Pentecost account in Acts: "This family praising God together, with the tongues of all the world was in earnest that the whole world should in due time praise God in their various tongues."[22] The rapid growth of Christianity around the globe is one of the most remarkable religious and sociological trends of our time, and Spirit-centered Christianity is growing exponentially in Asia, Africa, and

19. Douglas Jacobsen, *Thinking in the Spirit: Theologies of the Early Pentecostal Movement* (Bloomington: Indiana University Press, 2003), 79.

20. Philip Jenkins, *The New Faces of Christianity: Believing the Bible in the Global South* (New York: Oxford University Press, 2006), 13.

21. Lamin Sanneh, *Disciples of All Nations: Pillars of World Christianity* (New York: Oxford University Press, 2008), 275–76.

22. John Wesley, *Explanatory Notes upon the New Testament*, vol. 2 (Grand Rapids: Baker, 1981), note on Acts 2:4.

Latin America.[23] Theologian Lamin Sanneh comments on the strength of charismatic Christianity in the growth of world Christianity: "Charismatic Christianity has been the driving engine of the Third Awakening, and it is largely responsible for the dramatic shift [away from Europe and the United States] in the religion's center of gravity."[24]

The Spirit in Salvation History

Many Christians today have a strong sense that we live in the same age as the church in Acts. Like Lydia, Peter, Priscilla, and Paul, we live and work in the time between Jesus's first and second comings. It is in *this* time that we, like the Christians in Acts, relate to God and learn the life of faith. Our location in the biblical chronology is sometimes thought of as the age of the Spirit. In a sense, this designation is just right and can be life giving to the people of God in this very age. In another sense, though, this designation is problematic and, if misunderstood, may be harmful to the life of the church. The key New Testament events follow in chronological order:

1. Jesus of Nazareth is born, lives, and dies. He is conceived by the power of the Spirit, baptized by and filled with the Spirit in his ministry, and goes to the cross in unity with the Spirit's power.
2. Jesus, in the power of the Holy Spirit, is raised from the dead and ascends to the Father.
3. The church receives the Spirit at Pentecost, visibly and powerfully.
4. That same church, created and sustained by the Spirit, lives and works between two realities. On the one hand, we feel Jesus's absence. On the other hand, the Spirit is present with us in power.

What does it mean to live where we live? To work where we work? To long for the visible presence of Christ while also rejoicing in the presence of the Holy Spirit?

To understand the time that we inhabit, we have to understand the events that come before and after it. What does it mean that the resurrected Jesus—truly God and truly human—did not stay here with us but,

---

23. See Allan Anderson, *An Introduction to Pentecostalism* (Cambridge: Cambridge University Press, 2004), and Jenkins, *New Faces of Christianity*, 12.
24. Sanneh, *Disciples of All Nations*, 275.

instead, returned to the Father's side in heaven? Part of what it means is that God's becoming one of us, dying for us, and being raised from the dead still matters. Jesus ascended to the Father in hypostatic unity, divine and human, and so he is still God for us, fully God and fully human. His humanity did not end with the ascension. The ascension means that he has become one of us for keeps, that he represents our humanity, right now, today, to the Father.

The ascension is good indeed, but we do not always feel it that way. The ascension is a signal to us that Jesus is still one of us, still for us, but it is also the beginning of a different kind of life for Jesus's disciples, a life in which we do not see him face-to-face. It is not wrong that we long to do so. It is good and natural that human beings, bodily creatures, should want to see, hear, and touch the One whom we love. Life between the ascension and the second coming of Christ is a life lived with this loss. We, like Thomas, want to touch and see, and being able to do so might well make it easier to confess, as Thomas did, that Jesus is "my Lord and my God" (John 20:28). This loss, though, is not the end of the story. Jesus says to Thomas, "Have you believed because you have seen me? Blessed are those who have not seen and yet have come to believe" (v. 29). It is significant that, only seven verses before this moment in John's Gospel, the resurrected Jesus breathed on his disciples and "said to them, 'Receive the Holy Spirit'" (v. 22). To believe when we have not seen is a great good, a good enabled and empowered by the presence of the Spirit in our lives. Peter tells the truth: "Although you have not seen him, you love him; and even though you do not see him now, you believe in him and rejoice with an indescribable and glorious joy" (1 Pet. 1:8). We learn, in faith, to rejoice in the powerful presence of the Spirit in our lives, a presence that takes its significance partly from Jesus's absence. Jesus describes the goodness of this special time of the Spirit.

> Nevertheless I tell you the truth: it is to your advantage that I go away, for if I do not go away, the Advocate will not come to you; but if I go, I will send him to you. . . . When the Spirit of truth comes, he will guide you into all the truth; for he will not speak on his own, but will speak whatever he hears, and he will declare to you the things that are to come. He will glorify me, because he will take what is mine and declare it to you. All that the Father has is mine. For this reason I said that he will take what is mine and declare it to you. A little while, and you will no longer see me, and again a little while, and you will see me. (John 16:7, 13–16)

Jesus's ascended presence with the Father goes together with this special presence of the Spirit as Advocate among us. The age of the Spirit is an age of God's own advocacy among us, an age in which we come to understand the things of Jesus better, an age in which the Spirit leads us in truth.

We live in a special age of the Spirit, filled with particular gifts and promises, but it would be a mistake, one that has been made too often, to limit the Spirit's work to the present age. The Spirit, coeternal with the Father and the Son, is the God of every age because God is the God of every age. All the work of the Triune God, from creation through final redemption, is the work of the Holy Spirit together with the Father and the Son. These affirmations work against the heresy of modalism, which would suppose that the Spirit is not truly God but is only a way God acts sometimes. Such a mistake is a sad diminishment of who the Spirit is and what the Spirit does among us. The Spirit works in the Old Testament and the New, during the earthly life of Christ and after the ascension, in biblical times and today. The Spirit is not absent before Pentecost or after it.

What, then, is the special quality of the Spirit's work in Acts and in our own age? What does it mean that the Spirit comes in a special way in the events of Pentecost? In his book *Classic Christianity*, theologian Thomas Oden titles the section on Pentecost "The Spirit No Longer a Transient Visitor," language he draws from Augustine.[25] Oden describes the Spirit's descent on the church at Pentecost as a move in which the "one Holy Spirit who before had sporadically called, anointed, and visited chosen vessels, at last came to dwell in and with the faithful community, and in the form of hope with the whole of humanity."[26] Notice that Oden's language acknowledges that the Spirit has always worked among us, while also paying attention to the special presence of the Spirit in the church. Calling the Spirit before Pentecost a "transient visitor" would not be my first choice of phrase if transience implies a fickle or flighty Spirit, but I do think this phrase from Augustine points to something of the depth and richness of the Spirit's presence in the time of Acts and in our own time. I like the words Augustine contrasts with transience, naming the Spirit in the church "a perpetual Comforter" and "eternal inhabitant."[27]

25. Thomas C. Oden, *Classic Christianity: A Systematic Theology* (New York: HarperCollins, 2009), 546.
26. Ibid. Oden references Heb. 8:10 and John 14:15–19 here.
27. Ibid.

We might also describe the Spirit's work in our age as, in a special way, internal, ecclesial, global, and powerful. While the Spirit of God has always been with God's people, it is only after the ascension that the Spirit indwells us. While the Spirit of God has always worked among God's people, the Spirit after Pentecost creates and dwells with the church in a special way. While the Spirit of God has always been at work to draw in the nations, it is only in the age of Acts and our own age that the gospel is preached to all the world and the gentiles are fully included among God's people. While the Spirit has always been a Spirit of power, the signs and wonders of the present age, which began with Pentecost, have special significance and visibility as they help us to witness to the gospel of Christ. This last point raises one more. Part of the special quality of the Spirit's work in the present age is that, in Acts and now, the Spirit works to bring glory to the historical work of Jesus Christ. The Spirit in the church helps us to testify to who Jesus is and what he has done.

Practicing Pneumatology

As we become practiced in pneumatology, we learn that we have ways to distinguish truth from falsehood. We have grounds for the hope that, through the power of the Spirit, we may move past delusion and into holiness. We must take care, lest we claim stupid, selfish, and sinful things in the name of the Spirit, but we have been given ways to take that care, means to discern the truth of the Spirit. Discernment is a key pneumatological category, and the Christian life is one in which we grow in the ability to discern wisdom and to recognize truth. A passage from the book of 1 John, often turned to by Christians who seek discernment, links together this warning and this hope, and it links them through a trinitarian theology of the Holy Spirit.

> Beloved, do not believe every spirit, but test the spirits to see whether they are from God; for many false prophets have gone out into the world. By this you know the Spirit of God: every spirit that confesses that Jesus Christ has come in the flesh is from God, and every spirit that does not confess Jesus is not from God. And this is the spirit of the antichrist, of which you have heard that it is coming; and now it is already in the world. (1 John 4:1–3)

We need discernment. We need sound ways to distinguish between "every spirit" and the "Spirit of God." John's community needs discernment in light of heresy that would have seen Jesus as less than fleshly and human, and so the community can "test the spirits" by weighing them in light of the Word of God made flesh. Prophecy, spiritual gifts, personal experiences, communal practices, and claims to new revelation can all be tested by the criterion of faithfulness to God's Word. John's pneumatological test, here, is christological. The normative apostolic witness to Jesus teaches us that truth is found where Christ is confessed as the One who came in the flesh. John sounds a loud warning: "Many deceivers have gone out into the world" (2 John 1:7). But John also trusts that Christians, empowered by the Holy Spirit, "have knowledge" (1 John 2:20), and he addresses a people who know the truth.

We can pray that the Spirit would nurture in us power of wise discernment, and we can open ourselves to that discernment by seeking more and more familiarity with the Scriptures. We learn certain habits in the doctrine of the Spirit. We learn the habit of confidence in the Spirit's presence and power, a habit that allows us to live in the world with strength, courage, purpose, and hope. We learn to adopt postures of trust and interdependence as we grow used to working with the Spirit. Instead of relying on our own power, we learn to trust the power of the Spirit who dwells within us. We learn to open our hands to the church and the world, asking the Spirit to direct the gifts he gives us toward the church community and toward a world in need of the good news. We do not practice pneumatology alone. We do so in the Spirit's power, as people filled by the Spirit, people being made holy under the direction of the Spirit who is God.

9

Church in a Diverse World

Ecclesiology

The grace of God displayed at the Council of Jerusalem, recorded in Acts 15, goes right to the heart of what it means to be the church of Jesus Christ. In the time following Jesus's resurrection and ascension, God surprised the church by working the conversion of the gentiles, a matter of "great joy to all the believers" (Acts 15:3). God was grafting in the nations to become one with the people of God. Most Christians today are gentiles; we are those who "have been cut from what is by nature a wild olive tree and grafted, contrary to nature, into a cultivated olive tree" (Rom. 11:24). The church cannot forget the graciousness of the God who takes "strangers and aliens" and makes us "citizens with the saints and also members of the household of God" (Eph. 2:19).

What were the people of God to do with all these gentile believers? Circumcision was—and is—no small thing. It marks Israel as the people of God, those whose *identity as God's people* is witnessed to visibly, on the body, through the covenant of circumcision. It is also a difficult—and painful—thing to ask an adult to do. Did gentile believers need to be circumcised? Paul and Barnabas went "up to Jerusalem to discuss this question with the apostles and the elders" (Acts 15:2), and the first ecumenical church

Key Scripture

For just as the body is one and has many members, and all the members of the body, though many, are one body, so it is with Christ. For in the one Spirit we were all baptized into one body—Jews or Greeks, slaves or free—and we were all made to drink of one Spirit.

Indeed, the body does not consist of one member but of many. If the foot would say, "Because I am not a hand, I do not belong to the body," that would not make it any less a part of the body. And if the ear would say, "Because I am not an eye, I do not belong to the body," that would not make it any less a part of the body. If the whole body were an eye, where would the hearing be? If the whole body were hearing, where would the sense of smell be? But as it is, God arranged the members in the body, each one of them, as he chose. If all were a single member, where would the body be? As it is, there are many members, yet one body. The eye cannot say to the hand, "I have no need of you," nor again the head to the feet, "I have no need of you." On the contrary, the members of the body that seem to be weaker are indispensable, and those members of the body that we think less honorable we clothe with greater honor, and our less respectable members are treated with greater respect; whereas our more respectable members do not need this. But God has so arranged the body, giving the greater honor to the inferior member, that there may be no dissension within the body, but the members may have the same care for one another. If one member suffers, all suffer together with it; if one member is honored, all rejoice together with it.

Now you are the body of Christ and individually members of it. And God has appointed in the church first apostles, second prophets, third teachers; then deeds of power, then gifts of healing, forms of assistance, forms of leadership, various kinds of tongues. Are all apostles? Are all prophets? Are all teachers? Do all work miracles? Do all possess gifts of healing? Do all speak in tongues? Do all interpret? But strive for the greater gifts. And I will show you a still more excellent way. (1 Cor. 12:12–31)

council was under way. Some believers "stood up and said, 'It is necessary for them to be circumcised and ordered to keep the law of Moses'" (v. 5). Perhaps there was a time when Peter would have agreed with this stance, but the Peter who stands to speak at the Jerusalem council is the Peter who has seen a vision from God that changed his understanding of the law. In that vision, Peter saw all kinds of animals—creatures the law forbids God's people to eat—and heard a voice saying, "What God has made clean, you must not call profane" (10:15). The Peter who had seen this vision would not speak for those demanding that gentiles follow the law. Instead, he proclaims a message of salvation through grace.

God, who knows the human heart, testified to [Gentiles] by giving them the Holy Spirit, just as he did to us; and in cleansing their hearts by faith he has made no distinction between them and us. Now therefore why are you putting God to the test by placing on the neck of the disciples a yoke that neither our ancestors nor we have been able to bear? On the contrary, we believe that we will be saved through the grace of the Lord Jesus, just as they will. (15:8–11)

At this, the assembly is silent and listens as Barnabas and Paul add their testimony to Peter's, telling about "all the signs and wonders that God had done through them among the Gentiles" (v. 12). The church makes a *decision that will define its identity*, the decision "that we should not trouble those Gentiles who are turning to God" (v. 19).

It matters that this decision is made, not against what God has done in Israel, but in *continuity* with God's work in Israel as testified to in Scripture. The new church agrees "with the words of the prophets" (v. 15) and with things God has been making "known from long ago" (v. 18). To free gentile converts from the requirement of circumcision is not to ignore the holiness of God's law, but it is to recognize the heart of the law. Gentile converts will avoid the knife, but they will still be holy witnesses to the identity of the church as the people of God. The council sent out representatives to spread the word to the gentiles: "It has seemed good to the Holy Spirit and to us to impose on you no further burden than these essentials: that you abstain from what has been sacrificed to idols and from blood and from what is strangled and from fornication. If you keep yourselves from these, you will do well. Farewell" (vv. 28–29). How did the church respond to the council's decision? "They rejoiced" (v. 31).

The church of Jesus Christ is *this* joyous community: the community that rejoices in God's gracious salvation. The church is the community that opens up, through that grace, to proclaim Christ's peace to those "who were far off" and to "those who were near" (Eph. 2:17). This is the community that makes room for the gentiles to be grafted in, not by sacrificing its identity, but by clarifying that identity: the church is the people of God, called out to bear visible witness, in the body and as a body, to the free and transformative gift of grace we have received in the death and resurrection of Jesus Christ. As we practice **ecclesiology**, the doctrine of the church, we learn what it means to be the people who were once "called 'the uncircumcision'" (Eph. 2:11) because we were estranged from God, a people of aliens made citizens, strangers made children, those "who once were far off" and have "been brought near by the blood of Christ" (Eph. 2:13).

Body and Bride

A number of the global theologians featured in this book have expressed ways that Christianity in communal cultures challenges the individualistic and gnostic tendencies of European and North American Christianities. Scripture brings these challenges too, not least in the very communal and very material reality of the church. Where those of us who breathe the air of individualistic cultures tend to speak in the singular, "I," biblical language speaks often in the plural. Our bodies (plural), which Paul appeals to us to lay on the altar, become not many sacrifices, but one (singular) "living sacrifice, holy and acceptable to God" (Rom. 12:1). Two biblical images of the church—the church as body and the church as bride—help us to see what it means for many bodies to become one sacrifice, what it means to be the people of Acts 15, visible witnesses to God's grace. Both are corporate images, challenging a purely individualistic faith. Both images point to the church's relationship with Jesus Christ, who is the bridegroom and the head of the body.

Christ is "the head over all things for the church, which is his body, the fullness of him who fills all in all" (Eph. 1:22–23). The image of church as the body of Christ is one of organic community. "Just as the body is one and has many members, and all the members of the body, though many, are one body, so it is with Christ" (1 Cor. 12:12). This image disallows an individualistic faith, one that is self-centered and reads the whole of Christian doctrine and life through the lens of the "I." In the body, "the eye cannot say to the hand, 'I have no need of you,' nor again the head to the feet, 'I have no need of you'" (v. 21). The body parts are interdependent, and all are joined in Christ the head. The inherent corporate nature of the image does not reject the existence or the importance of diversity in the body. The differences between members are for the good of the body, and we learn that the weakest members deserve special respect and protection. All the members of the body exist in relationship to one another and to Christ, and the image of the body is one of strong unity. If severed from the head, the hand's lot is far worse than isolation. The severed hand loses power and purpose. The severed hand dies. Paul pushes his image to delicious absurdity: "If the whole body were an eye, where would the hearing be? If the whole body were hearing, where would the sense of smell be?" (v. 17). The difference that exists within the body's unity, the "varieties of gifts" (v. 4) given by the same Spirit, is essential to the body's life. The image of church as body points to the church's real unity with Christ. We are, in both physical and communal senses, identified with him.

The image of church as the bride of Christ is also one of materiality and of unity, both in the life lived among believers and in the material unity between Christ and the church. In the new heavens and new earth of Revelation, the church is the "holy city, the new Jerusalem, coming down out of heaven from God, prepared as a bride adorned for her husband" (Rev. 21:2). The bride image is even stronger than that of the body in what it implies about the corporate nature and the unity of the church. Put bluntly: Christ has one bride, not many. Bridal imagery also highlights the love between Christ and the church. Christian husbands are to imitate Christ by loving "their wives as they do their own bodies" (Eph. 5:28). This kind of love is intimate, personal, and immediate. "He who loves his wife loves himself. For no one ever hates his own body, but he nourishes and tenderly cares for it, just as Christ does for the church, because we are members of his body" (vv. 28–30). Here, the image shifts to emphasize the unity between spouses, a unity that is so strong and so physical that it is spoken of as a "one-flesh" union in Genesis, by Jesus, and here in the letter to the Ephesians. This unity is strong and real, and it extends to physicality. Married unity does not, however, dissolve the difference between the spouses. The bride remains the bride, the groom the groom. The reality of unity between Christ and the church does not mean that the church *is* Christ, and this is especially important to remember under the condition of sin. Christ is faithful, but his bride, like the prophet Hosea's, "commits great whoredom by forsaking the LORD" (Hos. 1:2).

Marks of the Church

So far, we have recognized the church as the body and bride of Christ, corporate and physical in nature. We have also seen that this body and bride, the people of God, is meant to bear visible witness to the grace of Jesus Christ. If we set all of that alongside the sad facts of the church's faithlessness under the condition of sin, we find ourselves wading in a deep swamp of contradictions. How does the church as body and bride make sense alongside our individualism and gnosticism? How can we claim that the church is the community of witness to grace when the church is mired in frank evil? As we sort through the doctrine of the church, we will have to grapple with these contradictions if we hope to put the doctrine into practice. We cannot pretend that the church is what we ought to be. Nor can we throw out the doctrine, acting as though we can practice the Christian faith outside the church. And it would be a terrible loss to give up the communal, material witness that God wants from the church. We need to proceed with ecclesiology in a way that tells the truth about sin but also tells the greater truth about Jesus, whose body and bride we are.

Traditional language about the **marks of the church** gives us some descriptive clarity. Like the mark of circumcision for the people of Israel, the church is to be the people who bear, visibly and in the body, four marks confessed in the Nicene Creed: the church is "one holy catholic and apostolic." When the church is faithful, we embody these marks as a witness to the grace of Christ. We also have to acknowledge the ways in which the church fails to be the church, when we hide or deface these realities meant to mark us. The church bears these four marks, but we do so in tension. These marks are the truth about the church, and some of the time we are faithful to that truth. Until the kingdom of God is present in its fullness, the church bears its marks partially and brokenly, in anticipation of the day when God will complete his good work in making us into the church he intends.

We will consider the four marks of the church in turn—what they ought to be and how the church fails to make them visible in the world. In each case, when the mark is embodied faithfully, that mark is a witness to the goodness and the grace of Jesus Christ.

Unity

The church is one. Given the fragmented state of the church, this ecclesiological truth may be even harder to understand than the oneness of the three persons of the Trinity. The church's unity, very often, is more a matter of faith than of sight, but this does not undo the truth of that unity. In John 17, Jesus prays to the Father for the sanctification of the church, that we "may all be one" (v. 21). Several features mark this text's call for church unity.

The Communion of the Saints

This 1864 hymn by William W. How expresses the belief of the communion of the saints: the whole church, living and dead, is in fellowship in the unity of Christ. The saints, here, are not rare Christians but all of us who are in Christ.

For all the saints who from their labors rest,
Who Thee by faith before the world confessed,
Thy name, O Jesus, be forever blest.
Alleluia! Alleluia!

Thou wast their rock, their fortress, and their might,
Thou, Lord, their captain in the well-fought fight;
Thou, in the darkness drear, their one true light.

Oh, may Thy soldiers, faithful, true, and bold,
Fight as the saints who nobly fought of old
And win with them the victor's crown of gold!

Oh, blest communion, fellowship divine,
We feebly struggle, they in glory shine;
Yet all are one in Thee, for all are Thine.

And when the fight is fierce, the warfare long,
Steals on the ear the distant triumph song,
And hearts are brave again, and arms are strong.

The golden evening brightens in the west;
Soon, soon, to faithful warriors cometh rest.
Sweet is the calm of paradise the blest.

But lo, there breaks a yet more glorious day;
The saints triumphant rise in bright array;
The King of glory passes on His way.

From earth's wide bounds, from ocean's farthest coast,
Through gates of pearl streams in the countless host,
Singing to Father, Son, and Holy Ghost:
Alleluia! Alleluia![a]

a. *Lutheran Service Book* (St. Louis, MO: Concordia Publishing House, 2006), no. 677.

First, Jesus compares the Father's sending him into the world to his sending us into the world (v. 18). The church is to be in the world, like Jesus. If this extraordinary comparison were not enough, Jesus then makes one that is even more daunting, praying that church unity would be like the unity he shares with the Father. Trinitarian unity is the truest and realest unity, and Jesus wants the church to be a reflection of that. Next, Jesus names the basis on which the church may hope to be one: the glory of the Father given to us by Jesus (v. 22). Unity, no less than any other aspect of sanctification, is not a work we can perform under our own power. Unity is something that must come by the grace of Christ. Finally, Jesus names a reason for his prayer for unity: unity is for mission. The oneness of the church is "so that the world may know" about God's love for the world in the Father's sending of the Son (v. 23). Unity is part of the church's visible witness to the grace of Jesus Christ.

Holiness

When the grace of Jesus goes to work, we become "members of the household of God" (Eph. 2:19); the church is God's holy household, "built upon the foundation of the apostles and prophets, with Christ Jesus himself as the cornerstone. In him the whole structure is joined together and grows into a holy temple in the Lord; in whom you also are built together spiritually into a dwelling place for God" (vv. 20–22). The holiness of the church is not always any more evident than its unity is, but it is just as important to what we are called to be. For as Paul says,

> Christ loved the church and gave himself up for her, in order to make her holy by cleansing her with the washing of water by the word, so as to present the church to himself in splendor, without a spot or wrinkle or anything of the kind—yes, so that she may be holy and without blemish. (5:25–27)

Holiness, like unity, is not ours by will or work. It is a gift of the grace of Christ, a gift the church receives by the power of his sacrifice. Peter also makes the connection between holiness and grace as he exhorts the church to "set all your hope on the grace that Jesus Christ will bring you when he is revealed. . . . As he who called you is holy, be holy yourselves in all your conduct" (1 Pet. 1:13, 15). Ours is a "holy calling, not according to our works but according to his own purpose and grace" (2 Tim. 1:9). This truth, that holiness is not about works but about grace, is not intuitive. The church must learn it as we practice being God's people together, as we try, and fail, to achieve holiness in our own right, and as we open ourselves to the power of the Spirit.

The church Jesus loves is the community created by the Holy Spirit, the sanctifier who shares his holiness with us. Full of the Spirit, God's people are to "worship the LORD in holy splendor; tremble before him, all the earth" (Ps. 96:9). Reference to "holy splendor" points to the majestic quality of holiness, that sense that there is something terrible in the wonder of God's love. It also points to the magnetic beauty of holiness. To look on it, though it burns, is to wish never to look away. God's holiness is such that the psalmist sings, "There is none like you . . . nor are there any works like yours. All the nations you have made shall come and bow down before you, O LORD, and shall glorify your name. For you are great and do wondrous things; you alone are God" (86:8–10). God is the only standard for holiness, and for the church to be holy is for the community to be like God. When the church is holy, we bear visible and material witness to God's love for the world.

Catholicity

The word **catholic** (lowercase *c*, distinguished from the uppercase C used for Roman Catholicism) implies both universality and wholeness. The church universal is the church of the whole world and of all time, and in this sense catholicity is closely related to ecumenicity. The church catholic, as we saw in the decision of the Jerusalem council, graciously makes room for all peoples, nations, races, and cultures. The wholeness of the church includes all this and more. The church is whole in the sense of completeness. It is not missing anything that the people of God need. The catholicity of the church is not just a matter of distribution; it is also a matter of the church's wholeness, health, and faithfulness. The church catholic holds and shares the many gifts of God, gifts that nourish us to be a visible, material witness in the world. Those gifts, essential to the wholeness and health of the church, include so many riches: preaching, teaching, doctrine, worship, communion, baptism, leadership, service, evangelism, and much more. The church is catholic in all these senses.

The church catholic is the whole and healthy church of Acts.

They devoted themselves to the apostles' teaching and fellowship, to the breaking of bread and the prayers. Awe came upon everyone, because many wonders and signs were being done by the apostles. All who believed were together and had all things in common; they would sell their possessions and

---

Apostolic Authority in
Protestant and Catholic Perspective

Protestant and Catholic ecclesiologies offer different accounts of the church's apostolicity. Protestants locate apostolic authority primarily in the Scriptures. Catholics locate that authority both in the Scriptures and in the church's faithful transmission of apostolic tradition through the centuries. Apostolic authority is connected to **apostolic succession**, the line of church leaders who trace their authority directly back to Peter and to Jesus. The Roman Catholic doctrine of the **papacy** centralizes apostolic authority in the pope, who as bishop of Rome is Peter's successor in the church. When Peter confesses that Jesus is "the Messiah, the Son of the living God" (Matt. 16:16), Jesus answers: "Blessed are you, Simon son of Jonah! For flesh and blood has not revealed this to you, but my Father in heaven. And I tell you, you are Peter, and on this rock I will build my church, and the gates of Hades will not prevail against it" (Matt. 16:17–18). Protestant and Catholic Christians interpret this passage in different ways. Catholic readings identify the rock on which the church will be built as the man Peter (whose name means "rock"), the first pope. Protestant readings identify the rock as Peter's confession of the identity and Lordship of Christ, a summary of the apostolic teaching that will become the message of the New Testament.

---

goods and distribute the proceeds to all, as any had need. Day by day, as they spent much time together in the temple, they broke bread at home and ate their food with glad and generous hearts, praising God and having the goodwill of all the people. And day by day the Lord added to their number those who were being saved. (Acts 2:42–47)

And the church catholic is the ecumenical church of Revelation.

There was a great multitude that no one could count, from every nation, from all tribes and peoples and languages, standing before the throne and before the Lamb, robed in white, with palm branches in their hands. They cried out in a loud voice, saying, "Salvation belongs to our God who is seated on the throne, and to the Lamb!" (Rev. 7:9–10)

Catholicity, like the other marks of the church, is a gift of grace, and when the church bears its catholicity faithfully, it contributes to our visible, material witness to God's grace in the world. The church is such a witness because it will advertise the catholic nature of salvation by grace and because it will offer, to those who see and hear that good news, the good gifts of the church in its rich wholeness.

Apostolicity

We have already seen the final mark of the church in the discussion of the relationship between Scripture and tradition and of the nature of Scripture in chapter 2. The **apostolic** church is the same church as that of the apostles. Apostolicity is about authority and truth, and the authority of the apostles is in their eyewitness testimony to Jesus (2 Pet. 1:16). The church teaches the apostolic faith, sound doctrine that is true to the gospel of Jesus Christ. Apostolicity is a gift of grace, and truth is something we receive from God. When the church is faithful in apostolicity, the church can be a true witness to the grace of Christ.

God's Faithfulness in Our Brokenness

The marks of the church—oneness, holiness, catholicity, and apostolicity—are the truth about the church in much the same way that the image of God is the truth about human beings. It is God's good intention for the church to be the community that embodies this kind of visible witness in a variety of ways.

1. In a world of dissension, the oneness of the church is a witness testifying to the Father's loving action in sending the Son into the world. By living in profound unity, the body of Christ should mirror the Son's unity with the Father.
2. In a broken world, the holy church is a witness that displays to that world the alternative to brokenness: the beauty and goodness of God's holiness.
3. In a world of racism, elitism, classism, and nationalism, the catholic church is a witness that embodies a reality wherein "all tribes and peoples and languages" (Rev. 7:9) are truly welcome as members of the household of God, welcome in the unity of a church that will treasure particularity and difference.
4. In a world full of emptiness and unmet longing, the catholic church lays a family table where people are fed with the good things of God.

5. In a world of lies, the apostolic church is a witness that tells the truth about God, proclaiming the good news of the grace of Jesus Christ.

We have seen the church distort these marks, with grave results. Too often, the church becomes a sad caricature of the witness it ought to be. Oneness is twisted into power grabbing or devolves into endless discord. Holiness is warped into self-righteousness, and catholicity into provincialism or imperialism. Where apostolicity ought to witness to the truth, we witness instead to our own sinful, selfish deceits. We know all too well what it is to replace unity with division, holiness with sin, catholicity with brokenness and insularity, and apostolicity with unfaithfulness and untruth. We also know that this can devastate the witness of the church, making the community that ought to be as compelling as the love of Christ itself into something repugnant.

But the church is not defined by sin, because the church is not ours. The church exists only by grace, and in that grace, faithfulness happens. On this side of the new heavens and the new earth, that witness is partial and broken. Sometimes we glimpse it only to see it flit away. But that witness is nonetheless real, a foretaste of what the church will finally be, at the marriage feast of the lamb. God uses the church, even in its brokenness, to witness to the healing that is in Christ. We are called to love the church, to be the church, even in the midst of difficulty, even when its proper marks are very hard to see, because God has chosen to work in the world through the broken and holy reality of the church.

As we practice being the church in the world, in love, we can rest in the knowledge that the goodness God works through the church is God's goodness, and so our human brokenness cannot erase it. Augustine learned this lesson in the midst of the **Donatist controversy**. The Donatists wanted a pure church and demanded holiness from their leaders. They objected to the possibility that people who had betrayed the church might be able to repent and be reinstated. The Donatists thus formed a separatist church. For Augustine, bishop of the North African city of Hippo Regis, this was schism, an attack on the unity of the body of Christ. Augustine saw the importance of the church's visible and material witness, a witness that requires a visible and material church, but he was faced with pastoral questions that would require some flexibility from his ecclesiology. If a Donatist were to see the error of schism and come to Augustine for membership in his church, what would he make of the work of the Donatist church in this new penitent's past?

The ecclesiological question turned on the practice of baptism. Would Augustine accept the validity of a schismatic baptism? Would someone who had been baptized by the Donatists need to be baptized again? Augustine's answer, which flowed from his theology of grace, would shape ecclesiology ever after: "We act rightly who do not dare to repudiate God's sacraments, even when administered in schism."[1] Notice who Augustine names as the agent in these schismatic sacraments: God. Because the work of the church is *God's work*, it cannot be overthrown by human error. Because the good things of the church are grace, our unrighteousness cannot cancel them out. If Augustine were to deny the genuineness of the separatist baptism, he would share in the Donatist error, the belief that the church's value rests on what human beings do instead of what God does. Augustine's is an ecclesiology of grace. Though he is appalled by schism, he trusts in the grace of God. He denies that we can create a pure church by human fiat, and teaches instead that the church, this side of heaven, is always a **mixed body**, full of both the wheat and the tares of Jesus's parable. Though the enemy has sowed tares among the master's good seed, the servants are not to pull the weeds lest they "uproot the wheat along with them" (Matt. 13:29). Instead, we are to "let both of them grow together until the harvest" (v. 30). The work of separating righteousness from unrighteousness is God's, not ours.

Witness through Brokenness

As we practice ecclesiology, we learn to live faithfully in the light of two competing realities. First, the visible church matters, and second, in a world of sin, there is no pristine church. The first reality is doctrinal. Given that bodies and materiality are good things made and loved by God, we cannot advance a gnostic ecclesiology, one that would confine the church to the realm of the invisible and the spiritual. The church *is* invisible and spiritual, but it is, at one and the same time, visible and material. God uses this for witness in the visibility and

---

1. Augustine, "On Baptism, against the Donatists," in *Nicene and Post-Nicene Fathers*, vol. 4, ed. Philip Schaff (Grand Rapids: Eerdmans, 1996), 1.1.2.

The Church and Reconciliation

Emmanuel Katongole and Chris Rice, a Ugandan theologian and an American working against racism, look at ecclesiology from the context of the evils and brokenness of racial division in the Rwandan genocide and the legacy of slavery in the United States. Together, Katongole and Rice write about reconciliation and ecclesiology.

The problem with individualistic Christianity is what we call "reconciliation without memory," an approach that ignores the wounds of the world and proclaims peace where there is no peace (see Jer. 8:11). This shallow kind of Christianity does not take local places and their history of trauma, division, and oppression seriously. It abandons the past too quickly and confidently in search of a new future. Reconciliation as evacuation detaches the gospel from social realities and leaves that messy world to social agencies and governments. The result is a dualistic theology and superficial discipleship that separates individual salvation from social transformation.[a]

The scene of a divided church on its knees, washing one another's feet, pointed to a communion beyond race, tribe, nation, and denomination. The primary task of the church in reconciliation is not to mediate but to point beyond the conflict. New creation directs us beyond radical divisions to an alternative way of living together. This is the very nature and essence of the church: to exist as a sign of a reality beyond itself. It is not that the church is the new reality. The church's mission is to gesture to this reality beyond us.[b]

a. Emmanuel Katongole and Chris Rice, *Reconciling All Things: A Christian Vision for Justice, Peace and Healing* (Downers Grove, IL: InterVarsity, 2008), 28.
b. Ibid., 111–12.

materiality of creation. How can the church make the grace of God known if that church cannot be seen and touched? Given the very definition of church as a people, imaged as body and bride, the practice of the visible church is to challenge autonomous individualism. Individualistic understandings of the faith are linked with gnostic understandings, for individualism can be used as one more way to keep matters of faith safely in the realm of the unseen: the individual's heart. A church that lives in hearts is far less threatening than a visible, embodied church. It is also a much less effective witness. God uses the communal nature of the church for witness among people whom he made to be in relationships. We cannot, even in the midst of brokenness, give up on the visible church.

The path forward, though, is not to deny the church's brokenness. Some narrations of ecclesiology would tell the story of a pristine church. Once upon a time, the story goes, the church was what it is supposed to be; sadly, this pure church was lost, and the only way forward is to return to that purity (whether that of the biblical church, the early church, the Roman Catholic Church, or the separatist church). This is a powerful story because it provides a solution to our ecclesiological difficulty: join up with the right church. Many Christians are convinced this is the only ecclesiology that is able to account for the importance of the visible church. I disagree for three reasons. First, purity-ecclesiology discounts the brokenness of the church, glossing over ways that brokenness is apparent throughout church history. Second, God is powerful enough to create visible unity in the church, even in the midst of brokenness. Finally, the brokenness of the church is crucial to the beauty of its witness. Without honesty about that brokenness, our witness to grace is impossible.

There is no pristine church for us to go back to, because the whole history of the church has been lived in the space between Jesus's first and his second coming, a space in which we are always still dealing with the effects of sin. From the church's very beginning, we were already bearing the marks of the church in tension. Already, God was making us one, holy, catholic, and apostolic, and already, we were smudging those marks. Feel the pain behind Paul's words to the church at Corinth:

> I feel a divine jealousy for you, for I promised you in marriage to one husband, to present you as a chaste virgin to Christ. But I am afraid that as the serpent deceived Eve by its cunning, your thoughts will be led astray from a sincere and pure devotion to Christ. For if someone comes and proclaims another Jesus than the one we proclaimed, or if you receive a different spirit from the one you received, or a different gospel from the one you accepted, you submit to it readily enough. (2 Cor. 11:2–4)

All the church's marks are at stake in Paul's speech here. The bride, already, is subject to dissension, corruption, loss of the wholeness of the church, and rejection of the apostolic teaching. The New Testament accounts of the earliest church are full of such examples.

Postbiblical church history is not one of purity and perfect unity either. I will name a few examples, but we could point to many more. The emperor Constantine's legalization of Christianity (313) carried dramatic implications for church membership. Before, joining the body of Christ might well have brought a martyr's death. After Constantine, the church could be an avenue leading to state power. The label **Constantinianism** is used to point to the church's collusion with and corruption by the state, to the bride's trading Christ's love for worldly power and wealth. Some churches did not accept the Council of Chalcedon (451), leading to a split between Chalcedonian (today's Eastern Orthodox and Roman Catholic) and non-Chalcedonian (Coptic, Syrian, Armenian, and Ethiopian) churches. Given the ambiguities of Chalcedon, ecumenical conversation today suggests this split may be one founded more in misunderstanding than substantive doctrinal disagreement, but it is a real breach of unity nonetheless. The Great Schism (1054) separated East (Orthodoxy, capital O) from West (Catholicism, capital C). In the Western Schism (ended 1417), Catholicism saw a pope seated in Avignon and another in Rome, as competing claimants to the papacy divided the church. The separation between Protestantism and Catholicism in the Reformation was preceded by plenty of dissent and division as well as abuses in the church and attempts at reform. The history of political and doctrinal division is a tiny pill to swallow compared to the massive and bitter history of abuse in the church: power grabbing; backstabbing; adultery and murder; Christians burning Christians at the stake; crusade and inquisition and colonialism; emotional, spiritual, and sexual abuse. To ignore all this is injustice and untruth, and these are only some of the biggest moments in a church history that was never pristine. We acknowledge this, not to be pessimistic or to dismiss the church, but to attempt to speak truth in the practice of ecclesiology.

Our horrible brokenness as the church is not enough to destroy the work of God. As we practice being the church together, we learn that God is powerful enough to work unity even in brokenness. Our ecclesiological practice needs to absorb the lesson Augustine learned in the Donatist controversy. The church is God's and not ours. The church is grace and not works. Even in our brokenness, perhaps especially in that brokenness, God still creates and recreates the visible church in the world. There are two primary models for conceiving church unity in the midst of brokenness. The first locates that unity in the body's shared connection to a common root, which is Jesus's death and resurrection; the second finds unity in faithful practice. When we take both of these models together, we have a powerful alternative to purity-ecclesiology. Together, our shared embodied and historical connection to Jesus along with our shared faithful practice gives us an ecclesiology for a visible church, unified and tangible, to witness faithfully to grace in the midst of brokenness.

The body's unity is found in Christ. We can narrate our unity in terms of shared historic connection to our head. The word *historic* here does not mean "in the distant past." The historic unity of the church in Jesus is a unity that connects past with present as the church lives as the body of Christ in the world. That body takes specific, concrete, historic form, and it is no wonder that this involves diversity. As the parts of the body stretch out into the entire world, they will be fitted for their locations. We cannot read the fact that the church looks different in different times, cultures, and places only as brokenness. It also must be read as healthy and appropriate adaption to the diversity of a world God loves. If we picture the church as one large tree, every branch of that tree organically connected to its root in Christ, we can see the different branches of that church in their unity and diversity.[2] This model for ecclesiology is stronger when joined to a model that finds unity in faithful practice, for faithful practice makes visible the church's living connection to Christ.

When ecclesiology centers on church practice, we see the body's unity in our faithful life together as the people of God. For Luther, the church happens when we faithfully preach the Word and administer the sacraments. "Wherever you hear or see this word preached, believed, professed, and lived," Luther writes, "do not doubt that the true *ecclesia sancta catholica*, 'a Christian holy people' must be there."[3] Church happens when the gospel is proclaimed, when new Christians are "buried with" Christ (Rom. 6:4) in baptism, and when the family of God is fed at the communion table. This is visible, material unity: hear the Word preached. Feel the water running down your face. "Taste and see" (Ps. 34:8) the goodness of the Lord.

This kind of visible, unified practice strengthens and nurtures the body for a second kind of practice, one identified by many contemporary

2. "Branch theory" is often invoked in the Anglican Church; see William Palmer, *A Treatise on the Church of Christ: Designed Chiefly for the Use of Students in Theology* (London: Rivington, 1838). I am using the branch image much more loosely than Palmer.

3. "On the Councils and the Church," in *Martin Luther's Basic Theological Writings*, ed. Timothy F. Lull (Minneapolis: Fortress, 1989), 547.

ecclesiologists who see that church happens when we are faithful in mission. Christian faith is a missionary faith, and the Christian church is a missionary church. The risen Lord sends his people on a mission, to "go into all the world and proclaim the good news to the whole creation" (Mark 16:15). After Jesus eats a piece of fish (Luke 24:43), a physical reminder of his bodily victory over death, he reminds his disciples of the story of his suffering, death, and resurrection, of the gospel of "repentance and forgiveness of sins" (v. 47). This, says Jesus, is to be proclaimed "to all nations, beginning from Jerusalem. You are witnesses to these things" (vv. 47–48). The church is this witness and must embody this witness. This happens by the Spirit's power, which makes us "witnesses in Jerusalem, in all Judea and Samaria, and to the ends of the earth" (Acts 1:8). Faithful practice of mission, like faithful practice of Word and sacrament, is visible and tangible in the world. When the church's branches bear this good fruit, we have evidence of their unity with Christ. When we have fruit on our branches, the church is a faithful witness, one that can be seen and touched, one that can nourish a hungry world. The fruits we bear are gifts of grace, and the holiness of the church flows from grace. The unity of the church is the work of the Triune God, active among broken sinners, transforming us into a beautiful witness.

Unity + Diversity in a Global Church

Our witness is a global reality. Theologian Samuel Escobar celebrates the ways that the gospel becomes concrete and particular in different cultural contexts. "Men and women everywhere," writes Escobar, feel that Jesus "is 'theirs,'" and artists in the past and present have proved the point by representing Jesus in their own cultural terms. At this point in history the global church stands closer than ever to the vision of the seer in Revelation."[4] That glorious vision is of "a great multitude that no one could count, from every nation, from all tribes and peoples and languages, standing before the throne and before the Lamb, robed in white, with palm branches in their hands" (Rev. 7:9). The church's oneness, holiness, catholicity, and apostolicity—worked by God amid our brokenness—is

---

4. Samuel Escobar, *The New Global Mission: The Gospel from Everywhere to Everyone* (Downers Grove, IL: InterVarsity, 2003), 12.

also a global reality. This means that we will have to practice ecclesiology in a way that appreciates that, in God's kingdom, diversity fits together with unity.

The church around the world is seeing astonishing growth, and most of that growth is happening outside of Europe and North America. Philip Jenkins writes about this trend, which he describes as "a powerful south-ward shift." Jenkins expects there will be six countries by 2050 with 100 million or more Christians, and "only one represents what is presently the advanced industrial world, namely the United States." The church is flourishing in sub-Saharan Africa, which is fast becoming what Jenkins calls the "chief Christian heartland."[5] Churches in the "old" Christian heartlands cannot ignore the global church. To do so would be to violate unity, holiness, catholicity, and apostolicity and to work against our very nature as witnesses to the grace of Christ. "A truly vibrant theology," writes Timothy Tennent, "cannot exist in some hermetically sealed vacuum, blissfully ignorant of the real and difficult cultural and contextual challenges of our world."[6] Tennent sees the global church in mutual service, as we bring theological questions and practical issues from each context to the common table of the whole church, listening to others and seeking faithfulness together.

Particularity and context are inherent to the beauty and the unity of the body of Christ. For a church to be contextual does not mean that it has failed. We fail when we try to impose contingent aspects of one con-text—things that are not part of the church's shared apostolic and catholic heritage—on all contexts. All churches are—blessedly—contextual, and all contexts have particular strengths and gifts as well as characteristic temptations and weaknesses. In the church's diversity, we turn to one another for mutual correction. To see what is contextual about faith in another culture is often to have our eyes opened to what is contextual about faith in our own culture. To learn from other parts of the body can bring new insight into some part of our own context, helping us see whether that part is good and beautiful or whether it is contrary to the gospel. The church seeks this faithfulness together, as a people who have

5. Philip Jenkins, *The Next Christendom: The Coming of Global Christianity* (New York: Oxford University Press, 2007), 89–90.
6. Timothy Tennent, *Theology in the Context of World Christianity* (Grand Rapids: Zondervan, 2007), 193.

been "born of water and Spirit" (John 3:5) and are nurtured in the church as the household of God.

A Church That Bears and Feeds

This birth and nurture happens as we receive the gifts God has placed in the church's life. Special among these gifts are those called sacraments. A **sacrament** is a visible sign of spiritual grace. In the sacraments, there is a connection between visible, material creation and the grace of the Spirit. The visible sign, when we come to the Lord's Table, is the bread and the cup. In baptism, the visible sign is the water. The church is a church of human beings, psychosomatic creatures who learn through seeing, tasting, touching, hearing, and smelling. God is a gracious God who meets humans where we are, using the stuff of creation—stuff like bread and water—for spiritual purposes.

Sacraments share three features: (1) they are tangible, (2) they are communal, and (3) God has made gracious promises about them. Baptism has all of these characteristics. We can touch the water. Baptism is a corporate, public practice of the church. God has promised to work in baptism, and as God is faithful to that promise, we receive grace. Sometimes Christians, excited about the idea of God using creation for holy purposes, start to talk as if every material thing were a sacrament. While there may be a sense in which many things are **sacramental** or sacrament-like, this kind of all-inclusive talk about creation as sacrament misses something very important: the community and the promise aspects of sacraments. The church is a communal reality, and it matters that the most important gifts in church life have meaning, not just to one person or a few individuals, but to the whole body of Christ. It also matters that those gifts are available to that whole body. Finally, it matters that God's Word contains promises about the sacraments, promises that are not attached to every material thing.

There are differences, among the branches of the church, in which practices are recognized as sacraments. The Roman Catholic Church identifies seven sacraments: (1) baptism, (2) communion (also called **eucharist**, from the Greek word for giving thanks), (3) penance and reconciliation, (4) confirmation, (5) marriage, (6) holy orders or ordination, and (7) anointing of the sick (the sacrament that used to be called last rites or extreme unction).

The Eastern Orthodox Church recognizes these same seven sacraments without limiting the list of sacraments to seven in number. Protestant churches, during and after the Reformation, moved to recognize only two sacraments: baptism and communion.

There are several reasons for this Protestant move. First, abuses in the life of late medieval Roman Catholicism moved the Protestant Reformers to consider the theology of sacraments. The second reason flows from the Protestant principle of *sola scriptura*. Protestants participate in many of the practices defined by Catholics as sacraments, but Protestants reserve the special concept of sacrament to baptism and communion because Jesus commands these two for the church. At the end of the Gospel of Matthew, Jesus tells the disciples to go "and make disciples of all nations, baptizing them in the name of the Father and of the Son and of the Holy Spirit" (Matt. 28:19). Before his crucifixion, Jesus breaks bread and tells his disciples to do the same "in remembrance of me" (Luke 22:19). Protestant theology also emphasizes the **priesthood of all believers** (1 Pet. 2:9) and so limits sacraments to church practices that truly belong to all Christians. Protestants get married and may well see marriage as somehow sacramental, but Protestants do not consider marriage a sacrament, because it is not available to all Christians everywhere and because Christ does not command it for the church.

Baptism is the sacrament of new birth, and communion is the sacrament of the Christian life. The waters of baptism remind us of the waters of birth. Those waters also evoke a watery grave, in which we are "united with" Jesus "in a death like his," as the prelude to our new life in Christ, one of union "with him in a resurrection like his" (Rom. 6:5). Baptism is tied, as the sign of new birth, to repentance and the forgiveness of sin. Once we have been born, we need to be fed on an ongoing basis, and the bread and the cup of the communion table are the sign of that feeding. As we practice communion, we are connected to Christ's words in John 6.

Very truly, I tell you, unless you eat the flesh of the Son of Man and drink his blood, you have no life in you. Those who eat my flesh and drink my blood have eternal life, and I will raise them up on the last day; for my flesh is true food and my blood is true drink. Those who eat my flesh and drink my blood abide in me, and I in them. Just as the living Father sent me, and I live because of the Father, so whoever eats me will live because of me. This is the bread that came down from heaven, not like that which your ancestors ate, and they died. But the one who eats this bread will live forever. (John 6:53–58)

Christians have visible and spiritual unity in these good gifts of God, and in the new birth and growth in the faith that are attached to these gifts. There is "one Lord, one faith, one baptism, one God and Father of all, who is above all and through all and in all" (Eph. 4:5–6). God's grace is the grace in which, "because there is one bread, we who are many are one body, for we all partake of the one bread" (1 Cor. 10:17). The fact that we do not share a common understanding of how God works in the sacraments does not undo the graciousness by which we share in the bread and the water. Within Protestant theology, there is a range of understandings of the sacraments. On one end of the spectrum is Martin Luther, who had many criticisms of the Catholic practice of communion, but the belief that Christ is truly present in the bread and cup was not one of those complaints. Luther, and many Protestant traditions following him, affirms the real, physical presence of God in the stuff of the sacrament. For Luther, Christ is truly present in and with the bread, an understanding called **consubstantiation** because it affirms that God is with (con-) the substance of the bread. On this view, God's real presence is a further affirmation of the teaching of justification by grace. Luther does not want the meaning of the sacrament to depend on human works or feelings. He insists that God is the agent of the sacrament and that grace is present there regardless of how we feel or what we do.

Other Protestants have a very different understanding of the sacraments, but this understanding is also rooted in the affirmation that salvation comes through grace. While Luther saw "real presence" as real grace, the Swiss reformer Huldrich Zwingli (1484–1531) feared that real presence theology would turn sacraments into works. His pastoral experience had made him wary of any sacramental practice that looked like magic. Fearing idolatry, Zwingli reminded his congregation that worship is for God, never for created things, and he taught that the Lord's Supper is an act of remembrance. On this view, the bread is a symbol of Christ. Protestants in Zwingli's line often prefer the term **ordinances** to the language of sacraments. An ordinance is something done in obedience, and Zwingli sees our participation in baptism and the supper as obedient responses to grace that has already been given, not as means of grace in and of themselves. John Calvin tried to offer a mediating position between Luther's realism and Zwingli's symbolism by talking about the "real spiritual presence" of Christ in the supper. These differences in sacramental theology remain part of Protestant church life today. Despite differences, all these theologies are committed to witness to God's unmerited grace as we practice baptism and come to the table.

The sacramental life of the church is central to the goodness of our holy—sacred—life together. In sacrament, we learn that the church's sacred life is a life in which body and soul, material and spiritual, are united. It is a life perfectly fitted for the material and spiritual human beings who are the people of God. In the church, we are born of water and the Spirit, and we are fed, body and soul, at the family table. In commanding them for the church's life, God has attached promises of grace to the special sacraments of baptism and communion. The church's broader life, full of many, many gifts that God uses as means of grace, is initiated by baptism and nurtured at the Lord's table. And so that sacramental life—service, relationships, small-group accountability, tending the sick, visiting the imprisoned, preaching and testifying, marriage and singleness, healing, many "styles" of worship that draw on the good gifts of many particular contexts, discipline, potlucks, Sunday school, evangelism, and on, and on, and on—is an extension, into diversity, of the unity God grants in baptism and the supper.

Practicing Being the Church

The burden of this chapter is to encourage the hopeful practice of the church in a world in which many, even among those who profess Christ, have given up on or grown cynical about that practice. The church today, like in Acts, has hope and can rejoice in what God had made us to be, a community of grace, which embodies that grace in witness to the world. We can rejoice that we are "no longer strangers and aliens, but . . . citizens with the saints and also members of the household of God" (Eph. 2:19). We can rejoice that we are "built upon the foundation of the apostles and prophets, with Christ Jesus himself as the cornerstone" (v. 20), and we can trust in the fact that "in him the whole structure is joined together and grows into a holy temple in the Lord" (v. 21). Ours is the trust and the rejoicing of people with eyes wide open, aware of the brokenness of the body but grateful for God's work in that brokenness.

To be a Christian is to know the failures of the church. The practice of ecclesiology is to pray for the grace to love and to live in the life of that church without denying what we know. The practice of ecclesiology is one of openness to the ways that God will use the rejoicing, broken church as a witness to his grace. It is the practice of the early church, which "brought forward stunning examples of bravery, as women and men stepped forward to bear witness to their faith. Crowds of pagans watched as Christians went to their death cheerfully, singing psalms and glorifying in an expected victory in the afterlife."[7] It is the practice of the church through the ages, whose witness God has used again and again. It is the practice of the church today around the world as countless people are baptized, are empowered to live in faithfulness to the Word of God, and go out into that world: many bodies, one witness to the gospel. Finally, it is the practice of the church as it will be, the church that will "rejoice and exult and give him the glory" when the time comes for the "marriage of the Lamb" (Rev. 19:7). It is the church to whom it will be "granted to be clothed with fine linen, bright and pure" (v. 8), as our unified, holy, catholic, and true testimony is finally made whole and beautiful. This is the church of the future, but God's future reaches back into the here and now. Already, God begins to transform us into what is to come. Already, we are allowed to be, together as God's people, visible witnesses to the marriage supper of the lamb. Already, we see glimpses of the vision of Samuel Escobar: "When the church is faithful to the Lord and to the gospel in its nature and life, the global and the local meet in the new creation."[8]

7. Joyce E. Salisbury, "Witness, Women's Bodies, and the Body of Christ," in *Witness of the Body: The Past, Present, and Future of Christian Martyrdom*, ed. Michael L. Budde and Karen Scott (Grand Rapids: Eerdmans, 2011), 63.
    8. Escobar, *New Global Mission*, 62–63.

10

Resurrection Hope

Eschatology

The last chapter ended with the hope that the church, in the present, might begin to embody the church of the future. That future belongs to God, and Christians look to it in hope, trusting that God's good purposes are being worked out in creation and that the day will come when those purposes will be made clear and visible. "All things" were made by God for a purpose, were created both "through" and "for" Jesus Christ (Col. 1:16), and the Christian life is lived in *this* hope. "The Christian life is all about trust," says Richard Mouw, "in the promises of a personal God, a sovereign Ruler who assures us of the ultimate victory over all that oppresses us."[1] All things are "for" Jesus, and in him that victory is sure.

This is true in the present, and its fullness will be seen and known and touched at the last day, when "every knee" will bend at the "name of Jesus" (Phil. 2:10), and "every tongue" will "confess that Jesus Christ is Lord, to the glory of God the Father" (v. 11). **Eschatology** (*eschaton* means "last") is Christian teaching about the last things: heaven, hell, death, judgment, the second coming of Christ, and the kingdom of God. Last things are

1. Richard J. Mouw, "Where Are We Going? Eschatology," in *Essentials of Christian Theology*, ed. William C. Placher (Louisville: Westminster John Knox, 2003), 338.

about God's ends for creation, ends both in terms of time and in terms of goals—God's good and final purposes for creation. Those last things are already becoming present realities. God's purposes for creation are not restricted to the end. Those purposes, even now, are the meaning and direction and substance of all God has made. This means that the practice of Christian doctrine is always purposeful eschatological practice, practice worked out in the dawning light of the new heaven and the new earth (Rev. 21).

Eschatological Tension

Christian eschatology is about the future, but it is also about the present. The practice of eschatology is not only something removed from us, far away in time. The kingdom of God is a future that we long for, but it is also already breaking into the world. This double aspect of eschatology is widely recognized by biblical scholars and theologians, who sometimes talk about it as an **eschatological tension** between the **already** and the **not-yet**. The "already" of eschatology is the present-tense reality that began with the life, death, and resurrection of Jesus Christ and continues right up to the present moment. The "not-yet"

> ### Key Scripture
>
> Now if Christ is proclaimed as raised from the dead, how can some of you say there is no resurrection of the dead? If there is no resurrection of the dead, then Christ has not been raised; and if Christ has not been raised, then our proclamation has been in vain and your faith has been in vain. We are even found to be misrepresenting God, because we testified of God that he raised Christ—whom he did not raise if it is true that the dead are not raised. For if the dead are not raised, then Christ has not been raised. If Christ has not been raised, your faith is futile and you are still in your sins. Then those also who have died in Christ have perished. If for this life only we have hoped in Christ, we are of all people most to be pitied. But in fact Christ has been raised from the dead, the first fruits of those who have died. For since death came through a human being, the resurrection of the dead has also come through a human being; for as all die in Adam, so all will be made alive in Christ. But each in his own order: Christ the first fruits, then at his coming those who belong to Christ. Then comes the end, when he hands over the kingdom to God the Father, after he has destroyed every ruler and every authority and power. For he must reign until he has put all his enemies under his feet. The last enemy to be destroyed is death. (1 Cor. 15:12–26)

of eschatology is the future-tense reality of the kingdom come in fullness, visibility, and power. The whole of Christian life and doctrine is practiced in this tension, between the already and the not-yet of the kingdom. In that tension, we have the present-tense mission of proclaiming the "good news of the kingdom," making Christ known "throughout the world," as we look forward to the day when "the end will come" (Matt. 24:14). We live and work between the first and second comings of Christ, between the manger in Bethlehem and the marriage feast of the New Jerusalem.

Already

The alreadiness of the kingdom is as real as Jesus. The kingdom has already come among us in Jesus's incarnation, life, death, and resurrection, and "we have seen his glory" (John 1:14). Already, the kingdom is here in Jesus's proclamation that "the time is fulfilled, and the kingdom of God has come near; repent, and believe in the good news" (Mark 1:15). The reality of the kingdom has already been accomplished, "once for all" (1 Pet. 3:18) in Christ's "single sacrifice for sins" (Heb. 10:12) and in his victory over sin and death when he was "declared to be Son of God with power according to the spirit of holiness by resurrection from the dead" (Rom. 1:4). The alreadiness of the resurrection is in Jesus who is "the resurrection and the life" (John 11:25), in whom we "have confidence to enter the sanctuary" (Heb. 10:19) because he has, already, "opened for us through the curtain (that is, through his flesh)" the way to salvation (v. 20).

After Jesus's resurrection and ascension, the alreadiness of the kingdom continues into the life of the church, as the members of Christ's body join as "co-workers for the kingdom of God" (Col. 4:11). The kingdom is as real as salvation. It has already come among us in our relationships with Jesus and in our being indwelt by the Spirit. If the kingdom were not already real, it would be impossible for the church to take Paul at his word when he advises us to "keep alert, stand firm in your faith, be courageous, be strong. Let all that you do be done in love" (1 Cor. 16:13–14). The kingdom is real as we serve and love, as the church gathers around the Lord's table, as we receive power to share the good news in a world in need. It is real because "our old self was crucified with him" (Rom. 6:6) and "if we have died with Christ, we believe that we will also live with him" (v. 8). The present reality of the kingdom is as real as the risen Lord, in whom we have "the victory" (1 Cor. 15:57).

Karl Marx (1818–83) dismissed religion as an "opiate," a drug meant to keep people too sleepy to protest against evil. Marx can only have had

Eschatology Matters for Community and History

Emmanuel Katongole, whose work with Chris Rice we met in the last chapter, writes about how eschatology matters for Christian practice.

It is unfortunate that eschatology has not been made interesting. For the doctrine of Christian eschatology is not meant to be merely information about the future. It is meant to be a lively conversation about the "end of things"—the end, that is, toward which all our present life is lived. Eschatology is about the *telos* to which all economics and politics—indeed, all our plans and activities—are directed. Eschatology is not a "belief" or set of beliefs about the future. It is a posture with which we live our lives now. . . .

An African perspective might help to recover this sense of Christian eschatology as a determinative posture in the present. Moreover, recovering this deep sense of Christian living as deeply eschatological not only makes the subject of eschatology far more interesting, it also helps to recover a more biblically grounded view of the subject.[a]

Katongole goes on to suggest corrections to individualistic and dualistic eschatologies.

As with time, the sense of community moves backward and extends beyond those currently living to the ancestors who are not really dead but are the living dead. This means that one's life now is a participation in the living and the living dead. It is this deep sense of participation that sustains life and meaning beyond the individual, and that sustains the dynamic interaction between past, present and future, individual and community, spiritual and material. Accordingly, gaining an African perspective might help to overcome the overly individualistic and docetic accounts of eschatology dominant within a Western preoccupation with individual survival. What is more, the increased sense of participation might lead to a renewed appreciation of the church as an eschatological community that brings together the living and the dead, the present, future and past. It is in this sense of deep communion across time that one can rightly say that the church does not *have* an eschatology (as if it were a set of beliefs distinct from its own existence); the church *is* eschatology.[b]

a broken eschatology—one that ignores the present—in mind. Sometimes, though, we do underemphasize the present-tense reality of God's eschatological goodness. When Christian hope is bracketed off from the present by focusing *only* on life-after-death at the expense of life-right-now, Marx's claim gains ground. When we grow unresponsive to the reality of the kingdom among us, the church stands in danger. We may be tempted by quiet resignation, tempted to give up on this life and this world, to act as though hope cannot touch life in the here and now. We may treat sin as intractable, living as though the reign of sin—in our individual lives, in the life of the church, and in the world—is inevitable or natural.

Eschatology Matters for Community and History *(cont.)*

Roland Chia, whose work we met in chapter 7, writes about eschatology and history as a correction to world-denying religious traditions.

> In Asia, the idea of world denial and separation embodied in either Buddhist or Hindu mysticism is common, especially in countries like Thailand and India, where the ubiquitous monumental monasteries and holy men serve as constant reminders. Christian hope, however, betokens a very different form of spirituality. Originating as it does from the ancient Hebrews, Christian hope, profoundly rooted in history, believes that God is the sovereign creator of space and time. The same observation may be made when Christian hope and the vision of the Greeks are compared. The Greeks see the world as mere reflections of some eternal order. Jews and Christians see the heavens as "the new heavens and new earth," a new creation in which the evils of this present age, the "night" and the "sea," are eradicated. . . . Because it is so rooted in history, Christian hope envisages the story of humankind, not just our personal stories, as part of God's story, a story fashioned by the sovereign and merciful God.[c]

a. Emmanuel Katongole, "Eschatology (within an African Perspective)," in *Global Dictionary of Theology*, ed. William A. Dyrness et al. (Downers Grove, IL: IVP Academic, 2008), 283.
b. Ibid., 284.
c. Roland Chia, *Hope for the World: A Christian Vision of the Last Things* (Downers Grove, IL: IVP Academic, 2005), 148–49.

To practice eschatology without awareness of God's already-present kingdom is to deny the kingdom reality of God's transforming grace. When we do so, we deny the efficacy of Christ's work on the cross and the "power of his resurrection" (Phil. 3:10). We become liars as we fail to tell the truth about the horror of sin and God's victory over that horror. We are in danger of becoming complacent about sin. When we lose sight of the alreadiness of the kingdom, the church—all too easily—becomes guilty of collusion with evil, of facilitating injustice, of failure to protect the weak and the vulnerable, and of despair. Eschatology practiced as though the kingdom were only a distant thing strips us of abundant life. Such an eschatology would suck the meaning out of life in the here and now. It is a crippled and crippling eschatology that fails to see and to act within the present reality of the kingdom.

Not-Yet

The present character of the kingdom, though, is not the whole of Christian eschatology, and it is as disastrous to lose faith in the future as it is to give up on the present. The biblical witness opens our eyes to the already of the kingdom, but it also teaches us to look to the future in hope, remembering that the fullness of the kingdom is not yet here. A characteristic posture of Scripture is to long for God's future, trusting that the day is coming when God's good purposes for creation will be fulfilled. When, in the practice of eschatology, we act as though those purposes have, in fact, been fully realized in the present, we make the mistake of an overly **realized eschatology**, one that forfeits future hope, discounting the fullness of the kingdom which has not yet been revealed. An early instance of this mistake is referenced in 2 Timothy, where we hear of the error of those "who have swerved from the truth by claiming that the resurrection has already taken place," a teaching that was "upsetting the faith of some" (2 Tim. 2:18). And well might it upset faith, for to claim that the present—with all of its pain—is all that God has in store for us is to drain life of meaning and hope. It is to believe that this broken life is all there is, to believe that sin and death will have the final word. An overly realized eschatology (all already, no not-yet) is just as deadly to the abundant life as one that forgets God's work in the present. Indeed, Paul's metaphor is one of rot, of death: this sort of error spreads "like gangrene" (v. 17).

Millennial Expectation

Theologies of the millennium offer different interpretations of Revelation read in light of other eschatological passages in Scripture. The "millennium" in question is a reference to Revelation 20:6, in which "those who share in the first resurrection . . . will be priests of God and of Christ, and they will reign with him a thousand years."

Premillennialism expects Christ to return before (pre-) the thousand years referenced in Revelation 20. Premillennial theologies expect life to grow worse and worse as we get near to the coming of Christ.

Postmillennialism looks for Christ's second coming after (post-) the millennium, which is understood as a time when Christ will reign from heaven through the power of the gospel. Postmillennial theology looks on the world with optimism, expecting things to grow better as we approach the millennium.

Amillennialism does not see the millennium in Revelation as a future thousand years. The millennium is read as a symbolic reference to the kingdom reign of Christ, a reign which is both already and not-yet.

Paul knows the cure is resurrection. Our healing is of one piece with our future hope in Christ, the hope that "if we have been united with him in a death like his, we will certainly be united with him in a resurrection like his" (Rom. 6:5). Christ's resurrection, in the past, is the power of our sanctification in the present and the certainty behind our hope for the future. "Now that you have been freed from sin and enslaved to God," something that has already happened, "the advantage you get is sanctification" (v. 22). The fruit of what Christ has done is sanctification in the here and now, and the future "end is eternal life" (v. 22).

When eschatology neglects that future, we are opened to the danger of equating the church with the kingdom and to the pitfalls of hubris, overconfidence, and confusing human achievement, pride, and power with holiness. When eschatology loses sight of the future, we are vulnerable to one more version of works righteousness, succumbing to the false belief that it is our job to make the kingdom happen. We may be deceived into trading the kingdom of grace for the kingdoms of this world, or we may end in despair when our human efforts at kingdom building fall short. Paul, knowing that the fullness of hope is yet to come, thus practices an **eschatological reservation**, acting in the knowledge that something is always reserved for the not-yet. The eschatological reservation trains us in a posture of present humility, humility required by our confidence in the future. Now "we know only in part, and we prophesy only in part" (1 Cor. 13:9), but the day is coming when nothing will be held back, for "when the complete comes, the partial will come to an end" (v. 10). Though we now know in part, we look forward to what is not yet, the day when we "will know fully, even as [we] have been fully known" (v. 12).

Eager Expectation of Christ's Coming

The eschatological practice of the body of Christ must be lived in the tension between all that God has already done and all that is yet to come. Life between God's already and God's not-yet is life full of meaning. In the present, it is a life that matters because it belongs to the kingdom. It is a life full of good work and good rest. It is a life with present purpose, a life that is already for Christ. Looking to the future, it is a life that matters because God has more in store for it. It is a life lived in both humility and confidence, a life moving toward its final purpose, a life that will be

Isaac Watts Looks toward the Kingdom

This hymn by Isaac Watts, from 1707, compares Christian hope to the hope of Moses, who glimpsed the land of Canaan before his death (Deut. 34).

> There is a land of pure delight,
> where saints immortal reign,
> infinite day excludes the night,
> and pleasures banish pain.
>
> There everlasting spring abides,
> and never-withering flowers:
> death, like a narrow sea, divides
> this heavenly land from ours.
>
> Sweet fields beyond the swelling flood
> stand dressed in living green:
> so to the Jews old Canaan stood,
> while Jordan rolled between.
>
> But timorous mortals start and shrink
> to cross this narrow sea;
> and linger, shivering on the brink,
> and fear to launch away.
>
> O could we make our doubts remove,
> those gloomy thoughts that rise,
> and see the Canaan that we love
> with unbeclouded eyes!
>
> Could we but climb where Moses stood,
> and view the landscape o'er,
> not Jordan's stream, nor death's cold flood,
> should fright us from the shore.

fulfilled in Christ. Eschatology is practiced between Christ's coming in the incarnation and his second coming in glory. To practice eschatology is to take a stance of eager expectation of the *parousia*, the second coming of Christ. Sometimes, we think that expectation means standing around, watching and waiting, but we should heed the question spoken to those who had just witnessed Christ's ascension: "Why do you stand looking up toward heaven? This Jesus, who has been taken up from you into heaven, will come in the same way as you saw him go into heaven" (Acts 1:11). A stance of eager expectation is not to watch the heavens; it is to live on earth, doing the work of the kingdom. The eschatological life is the active life. It is lived in mission and service, in love and in worship. None of this activity diminishes our longing, as we join with the "Spirit and the bride" to say "Come." The eschatological life is the thirsty life, and "anyone who wishes" will receive "the water of life as a gift" (Rev. 22:17). The active, thirsty church continues the prayer of the end of Scripture: "Come, Lord Jesus!" (v. 20).

The Day and the Hour

Living in eschatological expectation, we may be tempted to try to pin down our hope, to pretend to grasp all the specifics about God's ends in history. Such attempts have, again and again, fallen flat as predicted dates for the eschaton come and go. Some readings of Revelation see the book as predictive prophecy about future events, but there are other ways of reading the book. Some read Revelation as witness to historical events that are now in the past, events centered on the persecution of the early church. Other readings place the events of Revelation partly in the past and partly in the future, and still others read the book as theological, pointing to truth about God's triumph over evil but not corresponding to precise historical events. There is little space here to do justice to these readings. All have something to recommend them, and it is possible to read the book with a combination of these interpretative lenses.

Certainly, if we are to read the book of Revelation well, we will read it together with the whole of Scripture. In the Gospel of Matthew, Jesus speaks of the eschaton, and he attaches several warnings to that speech. When thinking about the end, Jesus warns us to "beware that no one leads you astray" (Matt. 24:4). Jesus speaks peace into the panic that comes when we "hear of wars and rumors of wars." "See that you are not alarmed," says Jesus, "for this must take place, but the end is not yet" (v. 6). Jesus likens terrible events in a world under sin to "birthpangs" (v. 8), and he prepares his followers to suffer because of his name. The centerpiece of Jesus's speech is a warning against grasping for certainty. When "neither the angels of heaven, nor the Son" knows about "that day and hour" (v. 36), it seems good counsel to surrender our own attempts at knowing. Indeed, the point of Jesus's speech is that we do not and will not know, that life will go on as usual, with "eating and drinking, marrying and giving in marriage" (v. 38). Jesus wants us to stop trying to figure out the "day and hour" of his coming.

When we stop doing so, though, we do not go back to business as usual. Instead, we live in trembling expectation. The practice of eschatology is to "keep awake" (Matt. 24:42) and to "be ready, for the Son of Man is coming at an unexpected hour" (v. 44). Such practice fits squarely with the active and thirsty practice proposed above. We are to live in the expectation of children on Christmas Eve, our sleep unsettled by the excitement of what is coming. Ours is the joyous expectation of a nesting mother preparing for the birth of a new baby, busy and active in preparation for what is to come. Ours is also the expectation of a people whose hope gives us power, allowing us to speak truth in a world of lies and to embody love in a world of hate. Richard Hays reads Revelation theologically, as a book meant to shape the imagination and the practice of an eschatological people. His is a reading of a church empowered by the future, a church that "refuses to acknowledge the legitimacy and authority of earthly rulers and looks defiantly to the future, when all things will be subjected to the authority of God."[2]

Meaty, Meaningful Hope

As we live in expectation, active and thirsty, our lives are shaped by the character of God's promises and the kind of future for which we hope. Our hope is defined by the distinctive Christian belief in the **resurrection**. Resurrection is not reanimation or resuscitation. When we meet the resurrected Jesus, we meet someone who has been transformed. He has not just been brought back to life. He has been raised to a new kind of life. Resurrection is also not about souls going to heaven. Instead, resurrection is for whole people, body and soul together. The church has sometimes highlighted this truth—that resurrection is about hope for bodies—by confessing belief in the resurrection of the "flesh." Flesh is a strong word, one that works against any tendency to cut our hope off from muscles and marrow. In the resurrection, we have meaty hope, hope that extends into every part of creation and every aspect of human being. Wrapped up in

2. Richard B. Hays, *The Moral Vision of the New Testament: A Contemporary Introduction to New Testament Ethics* (New York: HarperCollins, 1996), 170.

the resurrection of Jesus on that first-century Easter day, we find hope for the **general resurrection**, in which we, like Jesus, will be raised from the dead to new life in new creation.

Where other kinds of hope might be escapist—looking to get out of this world and away from its problems—resurrection hope is redemptive. Where other kinds of hope might look for meaning in some other life, resurrection hope reveals the meaning of this life. In resurrection hope, we expect God to save and transform *this* world and free us from sin and death, bringing his good purposes for all things to completion in Christ. Moment by moment, the life and work of the body of Christ should be shaped by the promise of resurrection. Our hope is not for heaven alone but for the new heavens and new earth to be united in the kingdom (Rev. 21). Our hope is not for souls alone but for transformation, body and soul, in embodied love (1 Cor. 15). Our hope is not for the world's destruction but for the world to meet the God who is "like a refiner's fire" (Mal. 3:2) and to reemerge transformed, all that is straw burnt away while all that is "gold, silver, precious stones" (1 Cor. 3:12) discloses God's goodness.

Easter

Jesus died, and Jesus was raised from the dead. The New Testament accounts emphasize the physical and spiritual reality of both his death and resurrection. As he truly died, he was truly raised to new life. When his friends went to visit his tomb, they were not expecting resurrection. They expected to tend to their loved one's corpse, which is why they brought spices to "anoint him" (Mark 16:1). But God shatters expectations, and the women saw the stone covering the entrance to the tomb rolled away. In Luke an angel asks, "Why do you look for the living among the dead? He is not here, but has risen" (Luke 24:5). And in Matthew the angel says, "Come, see the place where he lay. Then go quickly and tell his disciples" (Matt. 28:5–7). The response of Mary and Mary is to be our response as well, to go "quickly with fear and great joy" (v. 8) to spread the good news of resurrection.

In the Gospel accounts of Jesus's resurrection, we learn a lot about resurrection hope. First, it is physical, embodied hope. The resurrected Jesus is the same Jesus who died on the cross. We see this continuity in his body and his actions. Like he did at the Last Supper, he breaks and blesses bread

(Luke 24:30), and as he has always done, he opens the Scriptures to those who listen (vv. 32, 45). He eats fish (v. 42), and he bears the marks of the crucifixion, visible in his flesh. He says, "Look at my hands and my feet, see that it is I myself. Touch me and see; for a ghost does not have flesh and bones as you see that I have" (v. 39). He shows them that he is, in the flesh, the same Jesus who was crucified (v. 40; John 20:20), and he abolishes doubts with his scars. "Put your finger here," Jesus says to Thomas, "and see my hands. Reach out your hand and put it in my side. Do not doubt but believe" (John 20:27).

An Easter poem by John Updike emphasizes this resurrection fleshiness. "If the cells' dissolution did not reverse," writes Updike, "the molecules reknit, the amino acids rekindle, the Church will fall."[3] The poem, attaching meaning to the physicality of the resurrection, points to an important truth, but there is also another side to resurrection power. Resurrection hope is hope for transformation. There are differences between Jesus's body hanging on the cross and Jesus's resurrected body, differences that testify to his victory over sin and death. The way his friends recognize him changes. Sometimes they know him, but sometimes they do not until he reveals himself by action or by calling out a name (Luke 24:16, 30–31; John 20:14, 16). His relationship with the stuff of material creation also is transformed, as he passes through doors that had been "locked for fear" (John 20:19). Most important, we see in Jesus's ascension to heaven (Luke 24:51) that resurrected life is human life made fit to dwell in the presence of God. The Easter Jesus is resurrected in the flesh, inescapably physical and miraculously transformed. New Testament scholar N. T. Wright connects this physicality and transformation to our hope in the world. "Precisely because the resurrection has happened as an event within our own world, its implications and effects are to be felt within our own world, here and now."[4]

The General Resurrection

Hope for the general resurrection is born of Jesus's resurrection. "Christ the first fruits, then at his coming those who belong to Christ" (1 Cor. 15:23). Because Christ is the "first fruits" of our resurrection, we have good

3. John Updike, "Seven Stanzas at Easter," in *Telephone Poles and Other Poems* (New York: Knopf, 1964), 72–73.
4. N. T. Wright, *Surprised by Hope: Rethinking Heaven, the Resurrection, and the Mission of the Church* (New York: HarperOne, 2008), 191.

reason for hope that ours will mirror his. We hope for continuity and transformation as we have seen them embodied in Christ, for identity between bodies now and bodies as God will raise them up, and for transformation such that we may be fitted for life in the presence of God.

Poet John Donne (1572–1631) calls on death to "be not proud" because "one short sleep past, we wake eternally / And death shall be no more; Death, thou shalt die."[5] Singers chorus the words of G. F. Handel's *Messiah* (1742), "For as in Adam all die, even so in Christ shall all be made alive." In J. K. Rowling's novel, Harry Potter finds engraved on his parents' headstone, "The last enemy that shall be destroyed is death."[6] All of these are allusions to Paul's great riff on resurrection in 1 Corinthians 15. This chapter has always been a central text for reflection on the doctrine of the resurrection. It is a long chapter in Scripture and a rich one. Paul relates a summary of the gospel, reminding the church of Christ's death for our sins, his burial, and his resurrection. Then Paul lingers over Jesus's resurrection appearances, recalling all the people who witnessed the resurrection: "more than five hundred . . . at one time, most of whom are still alive" (v. 6), as well as James and the apostles (v. 7), and last "as to one untimely born," Paul (v. 8). Paul does not want his audience to forget these witnesses to the risen Lord. Having brought Jesus's resurrection to mind, Paul asserts an inseparable connection between that resurrection and the general resurrection. The whole faith hangs on this link between Jesus and us, for "if there is no resurrection of the dead, then Christ has not been raised; and if Christ has not been raised, then our proclamation has been in vain and your faith has been in vain" (vv. 13–14). Without the resurrection, life is futile, sin-bound, perishable, and pitiable (vv. 17–19). Rejecting this hopelessness, Paul turns us to hope, for "in fact Christ has been raised from the dead, the first fruits of those who have died. For since death came through a human being, the resurrection of the dead has also come through a human being; for as all die in Adam, so all will be made alive in Christ" (vv. 20–22).

The second half of the chapter is a revelation of the general resurrection. Paul's metaphor, like so many of Jesus's, is botanical. Resurrection

5. John Donne, "Holy Sonnet 6 [Death, be not proud]," in *John Donne: The Major Works Including Songs and Sonnets and Sermons*, ed. John Carey (New York: Oxford University Press, 1990), 175.
6. J. K. Rowling, *Harry Potter and the Deathly Hallows* (New York: Scholastic, 2007), 328.

Imagining Resurrection

While imaginings of the general resurrection are always speculative, they can also be rooted in Scripture. When we look forward to the resurrection, thinking about the qualities of resurrected life, we may find fuel for the present life, lived in anticipation of the resurrection.

Augustine, in *City of God*, imagines resurrected bodies as visible witnesses to God's goodness, suggesting that resurrected humans incite one another to praise of God.

> When the body is made incorruptible, all the members and inward parts which we now see assigned to their various necessary offices will join together in praising God; for there will then be no necessity, but only full, certain, secure and everlasting felicity. For all those elements of the body's harmony of which I have already spoken, those harmonies which are now hidden, will be hidden no longer. Distributed through the whole body, within and without, and combined with the other great and wondrous things that will then be revealed, the delight which their rational beauty gives us will kindle our rational minds to the praise of so great an Artist.[a]

John Wesley, in a sermon on new creation, imagines the glorious change God will work in human life.

> Hence will arise an unmixed state of holiness and happiness far superior to that which Adam enjoyed in paradise. . . . As there will be no more death, and no more pain or sickness preparatory thereto; as there will be no more grieving for or parting with friends; so there will be no more sorrow or crying. Nay, but there will be a greater deliverance than all this; for there will be no more sin. And to crown all, there will be a deep, an intimate, and uninterrupted union with God; a constant communion with the Father and his Son Jesus Christ, through the Spirit; a continual enjoyment of the Three-One God, and of all the creatures in him![b]

bodies are like plants that grow from bare seeds, and "what you sow does not come to life unless it dies" (v. 36). This seed-plant metaphor implies material identity between bodies now and resurrection bodies. Seeds are continuous with seedlings. The metaphor also implies change, as plants are transformed far beyond the seeds from which they grow. Both material identity and transformation are features of Jesus's resurrection and the general resurrection, and both are good news.

The body now, the seed, is a *soma psychikon* ("physical body"), and the body that is to come a *soma pneumatikon* ("spiritual body") (v. 44). It is important to notice that, in both cases, we are talking about an actual, material body (*soma*), and here we see that the general resurrection is consistent with what we have seen in Jesus's resurrection. Our hope is

---

Imagining Resurrection *(cont.)*

N. T. Wright, thinking about the materiality of resurrection, likes C. S. Lewis's idea of substantial bodies.

> I pay homage again to one of the few modern writers who has tried to help us with the task of imagining what the risen body might be like: C. S. Lewis . . . manages to envision bodies that are more solid, more real, more substantial than our present ones. That is the task that 2 Corinthians in particular invites us to. These will be bodies of which the phrase "the weight of glory" taken from that letter (4:17), will be seen, felt, and known to be appropriate.[c]

Wright also envisions resurrected life as life with the purpose "to rule wisely over God's new world."[d]

> Forget those images about lounging around playing harps. There will be work to do and we shall relish doing it. All the skills and talents we have put to God's service in this life—and perhaps too the interests and likings we gave up because they conflicted with our vocation—will be enhanced and ennobled and given back to us to be exercised in glory.[e]

Perhaps these images from Augustine, Wesley, and Wright can help us to practice resurrection in the here and now: to be people who embody our witness to God's love and spur one another to praise the Creator, people who are holy and happy, who are not controlled by fear of death and who trust in God's grace as remedy for sin, people who live in intimacy with God, and people who exercise dominion by working well and with delight, offering up our lives to the One whose love works in new creation.

a. *City of God*, ed. and trans. R. W. Dyson (Cambridge: Cambridge University Press, 1998), 22.30.1178.
b. "The New Creation," in *John Wesley's Sermons: An Anthology*, ed. Albert C. Outler and Richard P. Heitzenrater (Nashville: Abingdon, 1991), 500.
c. Wright, *Surprised by Hope*, 159.
d. Ibid., 161.
e. Ibid.

---

material hope. Our hope is to see continuity between what God is doing in our lives in the present and what God will do in our lives in the future resurrection. In present and future, God is working with the same *soma*. The identity between the body now and the resurrection body is good news for a people who long for this life to mean something. If the final eschatological meaning of the body is continuous with the body in the here and now, then our bodies now matter. The truth of 1 Corinthians 6:20 is both a present and future reality: "You were bought with a price; therefore glorify God in your body." Bodies are not disposable or pointless or problematic. They are the very stuff of redemption.

It is good news that our bodies now matter, but the transformation of resurrection is also inherent to the good news of the doctrine. Right now, the embodied life is good and beloved and purposeful, but it is also life pressed down by the weight of sin. Embodied life now is vulnerable and mortal. We stand in need of change, and we long for transformation, to be freed from the effects of sin and the domination of death. The doctrine of resurrection helps us to understand this hope rightly. The difference between present and future is *not* a difference between materiality and spirituality. The difference is between bodies ruled by sin and death and bodies freed from the power of sin and death through the Holy Spirit.

That transformation, as we saw above, is from *soma psychikon* to *soma pneumatikon*. The *soma psychikon* is the body dominated by the human soul (the Greek *psychikon* is from *psyche* or soul), and this means that, under the condition of sin, the *soma psychikon* is always self-interested. Because the "wages of sin is death" (Rom. 6:23), the *soma psychikon* also stands under death's dominion. The transformed *soma pneumatikon* is the body led by the Holy Spirit (the Greek *pneumatikon* is from *pneuma* or spirit). The NRSV calls the two kinds of bodies "physical" and "spiritual." This is very misleading, implying that physicality is erased in the resurrection. Other English translations use "natural" and "spiritual," but it might be more to the point to talk about "selfish bodies" and "Holy Spirited bodies." In the general resurrection, we, like Jesus, "will all be changed" (1 Cor. 15:51). God will free us from the sinful orientation of the fallen, selfish body and from bondage to death. God will free us to work with and in the power of the Holy Spirit, giving us holiness and everlasting life. In 1 Corinthians 15, Paul draws a series of contrasts between the present and the future.

	The body sown	The body raised
v. 42	perishable	imperishable
v. 43	dishonor	glory
	weakness	power
v. 44	selfish	Holy Spirited
v. 53	mortal	immortal

The resurrection body is God's victory over sin and death (vv. 55–57), God's transformation of selfishness and mortality into everlasting witness to the

Spirit's holiness. The selfish body bears "the image of the man of dust," but the Holy Spirited body will "bear the image of the man of heaven" (v. 49). God's promised redemption is that in which Jesus Christ "will transform the body of our humiliation that it may be conformed to the body of his glory, by the power that also enables him to make all things subject to himself" (Phil. 3:21).

Death as Conquered Enemy

In the hope of resurrection, we begin to see death in the light of Christ. We learn, in the words of N. T. Wright, that "death is a great enemy, but it has been conquered and will at the last be conquered fully."[7] The practice of eschatology is to know death for what it is: an enemy, a consequence of sin, outside of God's good, creative intentions for us. The practice of eschatology, more importantly, is to live in God's resurrection triumph over that enemy. To face death as a conquered enemy is a peculiarly Christian way of being in the world. Theologian Alexander Schmemann (1921–83) believes that every other religion or philosophy tries to deal with mortality by accepting it, trying to see death as natural. Schmemann says, "Only Christianity proclaims it to be abnormal and, therefore, truly horrible."[8] The sinful condition of the world, Schmemann continues, "can be truly revealed only by Christ, because only in Christ is the fullness of life revealed to us, and death, therefore, becomes 'awful,' the very fall from life, the enemy."[9]

We can see death as Jesus sees it: as loss, as pain, as God's enemy. Schmemann would have us stand with Jesus outside Lazarus's tomb and watch the tears fall down his face. "It is when Life weeps at the grave of the friend, when it contemplates the horror of death, that the victory over death begins."[10] The practice of eschatology is to tell the truth about death, not to sugarcoat it with platitudes. Death is horrible, and God is with us as we face that horror. Paul encourages Christians to claim the hope of the resurrection, not so that we will not grieve, but so that ours will not be the hopeless grief of those who do not know resurrection power (1 Thess. 4:13). The practice of Christian eschatology is to grieve and to hope, knowing death will be followed by resurrection.

7. Ibid., 15.
8. Alexander Schmemann, *O Death, Where Is Thy Sting?*, trans. Alexis Vinogradov (Crestwood, NY: St. Vladimir's Seminary Press, 2003), 100.
9. Ibid., 101.
10. Ibid.

Waiting in Hope of Resurrection

Contrary to some popular mythology, we do not become angels when we die. Human beings and angels are two different types of creatures. Humans are physical and spiritual, and angels are spiritual. If our hope is resurrection hope, what happens in the interval between death and the general resurrection? Most of the Christian tradition reads the biblical texts as pointing to a conscious **intermediate state**, a life for the soul in the time between an individual's death and the day of resurrection. On this reading, death is a tearing apart of human psychosomatic unity, a temporary split between body and soul that will be healed in resurrection.[11]

This is not hierarchical dualism, for separation of soul from body is not salvation. Instead, it is the wages of sin, and it is contrary to God's intentions in creating human beings as psychosomatic creatures. The human being will be made whole again, as God reunites body and soul in resurrection. A conscious intermediate state, in which the soul enjoys the presence of God and waits in hope for resurrection, makes sense in light of the communion of the saints, the belief that the whole church, living and dead, is in fellowship. It also makes sense of important biblical texts, the most central being that in which the dying Jesus tells the thief on the cross, "Today you will be with me in Paradise" (Luke 23:43). Since on that day the thief's body, like Jesus's, would be a corpse, it makes sense to believe that his soul would be in a conscious intermediate state.

A minority of Christians in the tradition read the biblical texts as pointing to **soul sleep** in the interval between death and resurrection. This reading understands the dead to be like sleepers, not conscious until the resurrection day. Some Christians worry that belief in a conscious intermediate state undermines the importance of physical resurrection, and they often see soul sleep as honoring the biblical testimony to the resurrection. Christians trust that the dead are safe in the hands of God, and we know that our final and best hope is not for the interval between death and resurrection but for resurrection itself. We practice eschatology as a people who look forward to the hour "when all who are in their graves will hear his voice" (John 5:28).

11. John W. Cooper, *Body, Soul and Life Everlasting: Biblical Anthropology and the Monism-Dualism Debate* (Grand Rapids: Eerdmans, 1989).

New Creation Fit for Resurrection

Resurrection hope is the centerpiece of eschatology, and so our teachings about the future of the world need to make sense in light of that hope. When we imagine, with the writers of Scripture, the future reality of the new heaven and new earth, we must imagine creation fitted for resurrected life. God's redemptive power is not just for human beings. It is for all creation. As we practice eschatology, we learn to envision the new heaven and new earth in parallel to the resurrection. As with resurrection, we hope that God's good eschatological purposes for creation include both material continuity and transformation, and we live in and steward creation now, in awareness of its future in the kingdom.

New creation is continuous with God's original work of creation. In new creation, God redeems all that was polluted by the fall. God is the God who is "making all things new" (Rev. 21:5). In the new creation, heaven and earth come together, and God's world is transformed into a world for resurrection life, one in which the body of Christ, risen from the grave, may live in holiness, worship, and freedom from death. The vision of Revelation is of a new creation in which "the holy city, the new Jerusalem" comes "down out of heaven from God, prepared as a bride adorned for her husband" (v. 2). The new creation is that in which God will "dwell" with humanity (v. 3). We will be "his peoples," and the God who is with us in the incarnation will be with us in new ways (v. 3). Hope for new creation is that in which God "will wipe every tear" (v. 4) from the eyes of his people, and "death will be no more; mourning and crying and pain will be no more" (v. 4).

As we anticipate the new creation, we begin to see its reality. In light of resurrection, biblical language about new creation coming through cataclysm must be read not as creation's destruction but as creation's transformation. Resurrection bodies are the stuff of new creation, and Jesus's empty tomb shows us that they are also the stuff of creation now. Peter's vision in which "the elements will be dissolved with fire" is the same vision in which "the earth and everything that is done on it will be disclosed" (2 Pet. 3:10). The eschaton is not the annihilation of creation but its transformation as God reveals his glory in it. God's eschatological power is redemptive, bringing creation through the catastrophic effects of sin to reveal the good intentions of the Creator. The eschaton does not annihilate. It discloses. The day of the Lord reveals sin for what it is and gives sin its due. That day also reveals creation for what it is and purifies it for its purpose in Christ. Peter expects continuity between creation now and new creation when he calls on God's people to life that fits with new creation. "Lives of holiness and godliness" (v. 11) are based on God's new creation power. We live holy lives as "we wait for new heavens and a new earth, where righteousness is at home" (v. 13).

Righteous Judgment

When God, in the eschaton, discloses the truth about sin, that sin will meet the righteous judgment of God. The coming Lord is Christ the judge, who will "set the world right once and for all."[12] N. T. Wright challenges negative connotations often attached to judgment, reminding us that "throughout the Bible . . . God's coming judgment is a good thing, something to be celebrated, longed for, yearned over."[13] Judgment is God's true and final word against evil. Given the horror of evil, "a world in rebellion, a world full of exploitation and wickedness, a good God must be a God of judgment."[14]

God's righteous judgment is part and parcel with God's promise of eschatological holiness and goodness, and "all of us must appear before the judgment seat of Christ" (2 Cor. 5:10). Hell, too, fits together with God's goodness, for hell is justice in the face of recalcitrant refusal of God's loving offer of salvation. To claim that there is no one who will make such a refusal is to ignore the depth and horror of evil. God's grace is goodness and love, and the Lord "is patient . . . not wanting any to perish, but all to come to repentance" (2 Pet. 3:9). God's patient love is not divided from his righteous justice, in which there is the "fearful prospect of judgment" (Heb. 10:27) if "we willfully persist in sin after having received the knowledge of the truth" (v. 26).

The salvation that is ours, in grace, is salvation from sin and for holiness. Without that holiness, "no one will see the Lord" (12:14). Protestant theology generally teaches that God will give us the gift of perfect holiness in the moment of death, fitting us to come into God's presence. The Catholic doctrine of **purgatory** posits a postmortem process in which God purges all that remains of sin, often over a period of time, for those who have died in

12. Wright, *Surprised by Hope*, 137.
13. Ibid.
14. Ibid.

Christ but are not yet holy. Purgatory is an interpretation of Paul's words about "the work of each builder" being "revealed with fire" (1 Cor. 3:13). Popular ideas about purgatory have been prone to extreme mythological excess, imagining all kinds of horrors on the path of purgation. Even without such excess, Protestants still object to purgatory as extrabiblical and as a version of salvation by works. There is, in recent Roman Catholic theology, much that suggests commonality with the Protestant tradition of holiness as an immediate gift of grace. Pope Benedict XVI offers reflection on God's purgative love, one that looks quite different from medieval visions of purgatory. While impurity will not "suddenly cease to matter," he writes,

> some recent theologians are of the opinion that the fire which both burns and saves is Christ himself, the Judge and Saviour. The encounter with him is the decisive act of judgment. Before his gaze all falsehood melts away. This encounter with him, as it burns us, transforms and frees us, allowing us to become truly ourselves. All that we build during our lives can prove to be mere straw, pure bluster, and it collapses. . . . Indeed, [defilement] has already been burned away through Christ's Passion. At the moment of judgment we experience and we absorb the overwhelming power of his love over all the evil in the world and in ourselves. The pain of love becomes our salvation and our joy. It is clear that we cannot calculate the "duration" of this transforming burning in terms of the chronological measurements of this world.[15]

While Protestant Christians will not talk about God's purifying holiness as purgatory, we can join with Roman Catholic Christians in anticipating the purifying grace of God, in which the kingdom of holiness will be made perfect.

Practicing Resurrection

We have considered the theology of resurrection in 1 Corinthian 15, but the account above is missing the chapter's last verse: "Therefore, my beloved, be steadfast, immovable, always excelling in the work of the Lord, because you know that in the Lord your labor is not in vain" (v. 58). Paul's "therefore" is a word that stands on resurrection hope. Because hope is in Christ and his resurrection, because we look forward to the general

15. Benedict XVI, *Spe Salvi*, 46, 47.

resurrection, we have reason and power for practice. Because of resurrection, we can "be steadfast . . . always excelling in the work of the Lord." Because resurrection means our "labor is not in vain," we have power to live life for Christ. Resurrection means that this life matters. Resurrection is power for the practice of discipleship. Resurrection hope "does not," writes theologian Donald Bloesch, "leave us imprisoned in ourselves but takes us out of ourselves into the trials and dreams of others."[16] That hope "is not an escape from the problems of the world but the assurance that we can deal with these problems in the light of God's grace."[17]

Paul's "therefore" at the end of 1 Corinthians 15 fits with the consistent, sweet pattern of the New Testament, a pattern in which hope for future resurrection is immediately connected to meaning and work and hope in the present. In Hebrews 10, we learn to "consider how to provoke one another to love and good deeds" (v. 24), meeting together and giving each other courage "all the more" as we "see the Day approaching" (v. 25). The coming Day spurs us to Christian practice. With 2 Corinthians 4, we hope to carry "in the body the death of Jesus, so that the life of Jesus may also be made visible in our bodies" (2 Cor. 4:10). We learn that this practice—visible and tangible witness to the goodness of God—is possible "because we know that the one who raised the Lord Jesus will raise us also with Jesus" (v. 14). Resurrection hope means embodied practice. In Colossians 3, this connection is drawn even further into the present: "If you have been raised with Christ, seek the things that are above" (Col. 3:1). The Christian "life is hidden with Christ in God" (v. 3), and we look to the future: "When Christ who is your life is revealed, then you also will be revealed with him in glory" (v. 4). Benedict XVI identifies the risen Christ as "our certainty that history can be lived in a positive way, and that our finite and feeble rational activity has a meaning."[18] In the resurrected Jesus, we see—in history, in the flesh—the promise of our own practice of resurrection, also historical and fleshly, both now and in the kingdom come.

---

16. Donald G. Bloesch, *The Last Things: Resurrection, Judgment, Glory* (Downers Grove, IL: InterVarsity, 2004), 246.

17. Ibid., 248.

18. Joseph Ratzinger, *Eschatology: Death and Eternal Life*, ed. Aidan Nichols, OP, trans. Michael Waldstein, 2nd ed. (Washington, DC: Catholic University Press of America, 2007), 214.

Benediction

A Prayer for the Practice of Christian Doctrine

Holy God: Father, Son, and Holy Spirit,

Be with your people as we seek your face. As it pleases you, Lord, use doctrine as a teacher for your people, opening our eyes to whatever is good, true, and beautiful. Take our lives and make us witnesses to your goodness, truth, and beauty so that the world may see your love and mercy.

Lord, empower the discipline of theology. Wrench us out of ivory towers, and lead us into your world. Shape us for the faithful practice of doctrine, and give us power for that practice.

Illumine the darkness of our ignorance. Shape us in trusting confidence in the truth of your revelation. Make us grateful for the sweetness of your Word, and drive us to the Scriptures again and again. Free us from doubt and unbelief and from the hopelessness that would give up on knowing you.

Shatter our idols, Lord, and lead us to worship you. Let us know your triune goodness, and help us to give praise to you, Father, Son, and Holy Spirit, in all that we do.

Break us of our habits of disdain for your creation. Shape us, Lord, as people who delight in your world. Make us faithful stewards, helping us to exercise the servant dominion we have learned from Christ.

Make us truly human, God. When we try to find our identity in other people, in careers, or success, or power, free us for confident identity in Christ. Restore your image in us so that we may be faithful witnesses to your grace.

Come to us in our loneliness, when we feel that you are far away, and let us know that you are the God who is with us and for us in the most mundane realities of human life. Let us grow in intimacy with Jesus, and draw us from distance to discipleship.

We need you, God, to set us free from the tyranny of self-righteousness. Rescue us from the clutches of sin and death, and let us know, instead, the salvation that is ours through the death and resurrection of Jesus Christ.

Free us from our bonds to sin, from doing what we hate. Through the sanctifying presence and power of your Spirit, we pray that you would make us holy like yourself.

Challenge our selfish individualism and divisiveness, O God, and knit us together in the body of Christ. Make us one body, and let us be a visible witness in the world.

Lord God, release us from meaninglessness, and let us find meaning and purpose in you, trusting in the power of the resurrection, the truth that our lives matter now and will matter in the kingdom that is to come. Put us to kingdom work, Lord, and make us thirsty for you.

In the name of the Father, the Son, and the Holy Spirit. Amen.

Subject Index

Scripture Index